Bottom Line's

BEST-EVER
HOME
SECRETS

Joan Wilen and Lydia Wilen

Over 1,000 Closely Guarded
Magical and Money-Saving Secrets Hidden In Your Home

Bottom Line
Books
www.BottomLineSecrets.com

Table of Contents

Chapter 1 • Floor-to-Ceiling Magic

Floors 1
    Caring for Hardwood Floors..........................1
    Managing Creaky/Squeaky Floors..................3
    Caring for Vinyl and/or Linoleum Floors........3
    Removing Scuff Marks (and Crayon) 4
    Caring for Tile Floors 4

Carpets & Rugs...4
    Cleaning Carpets 4
    Cleaning Fringe...5
    Cleaning Stains 5
    Removing an Existing Stain 6
    Removing Candle Wax 6
    Removing Pet Urine 6
    Removing Chewing Gum.................................6
    Removing Coffee or Tea..................................7
    Removing Crayon Marks 7
    Removing Fresh Fruit 7
    Removing Grease/Oil.....................................7
    Removing Latex Paint 7
    Removing Mud 8
    Removing Red Wine 8
    Getting Rid of Insects 8
    Raising a Matted Nap 8
    Removing Loose Threads................................8
    Dealing with Static Electricity.......................9
    Anchoring Throw Rugs.................................9
    Vacuuming 9

Walls 11
    Cleaning Painted Walls...............................11
    Cleaning Textured Plaster Walls 12
    Cleaning a Smoky Wall...............................12
    Removing Wall Stains..................................12

Wallpaper 13

Removing Old Wallpaper...............................13
Preparing the Walls 13
Applying Wallpaper Paste..............................14
Creating a Wallpaper Patch 14
Using Leftover Wallpaper 15
Cleaning Washable Wallpaper........................15
Cleaning Wallpaper Stains 15
Cleaning Other Types of Wall Coverings 16

Painting (Indoors) 16
    Preparing the Painter...................................16
    Preparing the Room 18
    Preparing the Tools......................................18
    Preparing to Paint.......................................18
    Painting Doors 20
    Painting Stairs 20
    Painting Closets 20
    Painting Radiators.......................................20
    Painting Baseboards.....................................20
    Easy Drip Catchers 20
    Dealing with Paint Problems........................21
    Saving Leftover Paint 21
    Cleaning Up After Painting 22

Painting (Outdoors)..................................22
    Painting a Deck 23
    Prepping Metal Surfaces 23
    Painting Wrought-Iron Furniture................23
    Painting Odd-Shaped Things.......................23

Products 23

Chapter 2 • Fantastic Furniture

Wood Furniture 24
    Flanigan's Furniture Philosophy 24
    The Best Way to Protect Furniture...............25

Remove Polish and Dirt 25
Remove a Water Mark/White Ring 25
Removing Scratches 26

Upholstered Furniture 26
Cleaning Upholstery (By Code) 26
Removing Candle Wax 27
Cleaner for Leather Upholstery 27
Cleaning Vinyl Upholstery 27

Wicker (Cane) Furniture 28
Preventing Yellowing 28
Fixing a Sagging Seat 28

Dusting 28
Shake That Dust Mop 28
Dusting High-Ups, Unders and Behinds 28

Metals 29
Cleaning Metal Objects 29
Removing Tarnish 29
Silver 29
Mixed Metals 32
Cleaning Brass and Unlacquered Copper 32
Removing Bronze Patina 33
Cleaning Aluminum 33
Cleaning Stainless Steel 33
Caring for Stainless Steel Sinks 33
Cleaning Chrome 34
Cleaning Pewter 34

Ivory & Bone 35
Piano and Organ Keyboards 35

Marble 35
Caring for Marble 35

Mirrors 36
Cleaning a Mirror 36
Creating Fog-Free Mirrors 36
Removing Hairspray 37

Fish Tanks 37
Cleaning a Fish Tank 37

Products 37

Chapter 3 • Loads of Laundry Care

Washing Machines 38
Maintaining a Washer 38

Laundry Sorting & Prepping 39
Sort Socks in the Hamper 39
Know Your Colors 39
Delicates vs. Indelicates 39
Lint Producers 39
Going to the Laundromat 40

Colorfast Garments 40

Hard Water 41
Hard-Water Remedy 41

Detergent 41
Use the Right Stuff 41
Avoid Overload 41
Get a Brightness Boost 41
Detergent Extender 42
Detergent Substitute 42
Bleach Substitute 42

Washing Instructions 42
Dry-Clean Only...or Not 42
Permanent-Press Clothes 42
Silk and Other Fine Washables 43
Wool 43
Whites 44
Colors 45
Jeans 45
Other Fabrics 46
Plastics 46

Dryers & Drying 47
Lint Catcher 47
Wash-and-Wear 47
Drying Delicates 47
Drying Wet Sweaters 47
Speedy Sweater Drying 48
Revive Stored Woolens 48
Try to Be Static-Free 48
Down-Filled Drying 48
Unwrinkle Your Sheets 48
Slipcovers 48

Fabric Softener & Starch 49
Suffering Sneezes? 49
Less Cents and Less Scents........................... 49
Starch 49

Smells 50
Steam Out Cigarette Smoke 50
Booze for Cigarettes 50
Just Like New..50
Hinder Hamper Smells 50
Scentsational Gym Bag 50
Managing Mothballs 51
Tablecloths, Mats, Curtains (Plastic) 51

Cleaning Non-Clothing Items 51
Artificial and Dried Flowers 51
Children's Toys..51

Stains A to Z 52
The Simple Solution for UFOs 52

Ironing 60
    Prepping Your Clothes................................ 60
    Supercharge Your Iron 60
    All the Right Moves 61
    Shine Prevention 61
    Velvet and Velveteen 61
    Ironing Sleeves 61
    Pucker Prevention 61
    Unsticking the Iron 61
    Scorch Prevention 61
    Pleats 61
    Buttons...62

No-Iron Needed **62**
    Pants 62
    Vinyl Tablecloths, Shower Curtains,
        Shelf Paper..63
    Sheer Curtains..63
    Ribbons..63
    Sheets...63
    Pantyhose 63

Shoes & Boots..**64**
    Shining Shoes and Boots........................... 64
    Mold and Mildew 64
    Scuff Marks 65
    Dark Leather 65
    White Shoes (including Leather).................65
    Black Shoes...65
    Gold or Silver Shoes 66
    Suede Shoes 66
    Salt and Grease Stains on
        Leather and Suede 66
    Salt Stains 66
    Wet Shoes and Boots 66
    Once-Wet-Now-Dried-and-Stiff Shoes..........66
    Buffing Shoes...66
    Waterproofing Shoes...Sort Of 66
    Patent Leather 67
    Shoe Polish Reviver..................................67
    Keeping Tall Boots in Shape 67
    Safer Shoes 67
    Squeaky Shoes..67
    Deodorizing Smelly Shoes 67
    Loosen a Tight Spot 67
    Shopping for Shoes 68
    Cleaning Sneakers....................................68
    Shoelace Maintenance.............................. 68

Leather Accessories **69**
    Liven Up Leather Luggage 69
    Remove Scuff Marks on Luggage................69
    Stains on Leather Gloves 69
    Dirt on White Kid Gloves 69

Hats **69**
    Clean and Brighten 69
    Revitalizing Your Hat's Nap.....................70
    Drying a Beret 70
    Wash Your Caps 70

Sewing..**70**
    Needles and Pins 70
    Thread 70
    Hems..71
    Sewing Machines 71
    Buttons...72
    Zippers...73
    Patches...73
    Pockets...73

Products **73**

Chapter 4 • Better Bath Basics

Toilet **74**
    Cleaning the Bowl....................................74
    Toilet Seat 75
    Toilet Tank 75
    Overflow Prevention 76
    Clogged Toilet 76

Bathtub..**76**
    Cleaning the Tub......................................76
    Cleaning Bathtub Mats 77
    Removing Nonslip Bathtub Appliqués 77
    Cleaning Whirlpool Tubs 78

Sink **78**
    Cleaning the Sink.....................................78
    Fixing a Faucet Drip 78

Shower...**78**
    Cleaning the Showerhead 78
    Cleaning Glass Shower Doors 79
    Cleaning Shower Door Tracks 79
    Cleaning a Plastic Shower Curtain............79

Tile & Grout **80**
    Cleaning Solutions 80
    Mold and Mildew 80
    Preventing a Steamy Bathroom....................81
    Cleaning Chrome Fixtures 81

Drains..**81**
    Clean and Deodorize 81
    Fixing Clogged Drains..............................81

Soap **82**
    Preventing Messes 82
    Soap Slivers 82

Freshen Up 83
   Safe and Natural Room Deodorizer..............83
   Fresher Clothes Hamper....................................83
   When Company Is Coming 83
   Extra Towels..83
   Bathtub Toys...83
   Guest Amenities 83

Products 84

Chapter 5 • All-Around-the-House Hints

Inside the Home 85

Home Office 86
   Pens and Pencils.. 86
   Paper Shredder 86
   Correction Fluid Extender............................ 86
   Dry-Erase Board Cleaner 86
   Packing and Shipping Hints 87

Lighting Know-How 87
   Halogen Bulbs 88

Getting Organized..............................88
   Storing Manuals, Guarantees
      And Warranties 88
   Storing Take-out Menus 89
   Storing Posters..89

Books..89
   Preventing Mustiness, Mildew and
      Silverfish.. 90
   Removing Mustiness 90
   Removing Mold or Mildew 90

Home Electronics 90
   Cleaning a Telephone 91
   Caring for a Computer 91
   Caring for Batteries 92
   Caring for CDs, DVDs and Other Media.......93
   Cleaning a Camera 94
   Cleaning Photos 94
   Unsticking Stuck Photos 94

Air Conditioners & Humidifiers 94
   Cooling a Room Efficiently.......................... 94
   Unclogging a Humidifier 94

Windows 95
   Preparing to Clean Windows 95
   Window Cleaner and Primer........................95
   Cleaning High Windows................................96
   Preventing Window Frost.............................96
   Windowsill Cleaner 96
   Cleaning Window Screens.............................96
   Cleaning Venetian Blinds..............................96

Ceiling Fans 96
   Dusting..97

Fireplace 97
   Read All About Substitute Firewood 97
   Feeding the Fire Efficiently 97
   Make a Scented Fire......................................97
   Managing Soot 98
   Cleaning Glass Fireplace Doors 98
   Cleaning the Hearth.......................................98

Even More Hints...................................98
   Cabinet Magnets...98
   On the Level…or Not.....................................99
   The Return of Your Stuff................................99

Closets..99
   Making Hangers Glide 99
   Extra Hanging Space....................................100
   Hanging Accessories....................................100
   Shelves Made Easy 100
   Entryway Closet Convenience....................100
   Removing Moisture and Musty Smells........100
   Protecting Clothes.......................................100
   Storing Blankets 100

Do-It-Yourself Secrets........................ 101
   Cleaning Rusty Tools 102
   Removing Nuts, Bolts and Screws 102
   Tightening Loose Screws 102
   Keeping Screws, Nails, Nuts and
      Bolts Together......................................103
   Dealing with Drywall 103
   Hammering Made Painless 103
   Using a Screwdriver 103
   Fixing Squeaky Hinges 103
   Making Drawers Glide 104
   Fixing a Sticky Door 104
   Hiding the Dark Marks 104

Pest Control 104
   Repelling Flying Insects 104
   Battling Fruit Flies 105
   Fighting Silverfish 105
   Removing Bugs from Grains and Beans......105
   Dealing with Ants 106
   Rousting Out Roaches 106

Outside the Home 107
   De-Icing the Sidewalk, Steps,
      Driveway, Patio 107
   Safer Concrete Steps 108
   Snow Shoveling Made Easier 108
   Removing Moss 108
   Removing Stains on Concrete......................108
   Removing Storm Windows and Doors 108
   Unlocking Door Locks 108

Unsticking Outdoor Bulbs 108
Cleaning a Plastic Kiddie Pool 109
Cleaning a Swimming Pool 109
Cleaning Plastic Patio Furniture 109
Using an Outdoor Grill..........109
Handling a Garbage Can 110
Dealing with Outdoor Pests..........110

Products **113**

Chapter 6 • Great Greenery Solutions

Tools..........**114**
Organizing Tools..........115
Caring for Rusty Tools 115
Sanitizing Tools..........116
Caring for Hoses 116

Gloveless Gardening **116**
Ensuring Clean Nails..........116
Blister Prevention 117
Infection Prevention..........117
Garden Lime Neutralizer 117

Soil **117**
Testing Your Soil's pH 118
Supplementing Your Soil..........118

Seeds **118**
Dump the Clump 118
Storing Leftover Seeds 119
Caring for Seedlings..........119

Watering..........**119**
Watering Your Lawn and/or Garden 119

Fertilizing..........**120**
Using Natural Fertilizers 120

Lawns..........**120**
Mowing the Grass 120

Weeds **121**
Eliminating Garden Weeds..........121
Eliminating Patio or Sidewalk Weeds 122

Plant & Garden Pests A to Z **123**

Plant & Garden Friends **127**
Beneficial Bugs 128
Butterflies 128

Popular Garden Plants A to Z..........**128**

Trees..........**136**
Planting Trees..........136
Apple Trees..........136
Other Fruit Trees 137

Houseplants..........**137**
New Plants 138
Cuttings 138
Live-Long-and-Prosper Plants 138
Sun-Loving Plants 138
Shade Plants 138
Potting 138
Pot Liners 139
Enhancing the Sun 139
Misting 139
Watering Houseplants 140
Enriching Elixirs 140
Flowering Plants 141
Luminous Leaves 141
Hanging Plants 141

First Aid for Plants..........**142**
"Planti-Aging" Cure 142
Infections 142
Mealybugs 142

While You're Away...........**142**

Cut Flowers **143**
Cutting Live Flowers 143
Life Extenders (General)..........143
Life Extenders (for Specific Cut Flowers) 144
Daily Care 145
Flower Arranging 145

Products **145**

Chapter 7 • Car & Travel Smarts

Car Safety **146**
Baby on Board 146
Buckle Up *Everyone*..........147
Steering..........147
Driving in Fog..........147

Cold Weather Cures..........**147**
Stuck in Snow..........148
Frosty Windshield Prevention..........148
Defrosting the Windshield 148
Frozen Door-Lock Prevention 149
Opening Frozen Door Locks 149

Fuel Economy..........**149**
Keep Windows and Sunroof Closed..........149
Keep Tires Properly Inflated..........149
Penny for Your Tires 149
Less Is More Cost-Efficient..........150
Cruising Speed..........150
Cheapest Gas Prices..........150
Car Battery 150
Caring for a Fan Belt..........151

Car Comfort 151
 Shade Against a Hot Seat 152
 Smoother Antenna 152
 Sun Visor Trapper Keeper 152

Car Cleaning 152
 Bugs Off 152
 Cleaning Windshields 152
 Cleaning Wipers 153
 Fixing Nicks, Chips and Scratches 153
 Cleaning Tree Sap 153
 Cleaning Bird Droppings 153
 Howzabout Those Headlights? 153
 Bye-Bye Tar 154
 Grease Away 154
 Removing Decals and Bumper Stickers 154
 Cleaning Vinyl or Cloth Upholstery 154

Garage Floor & Driveway Cleanup 155
 Wiping Out Oil or Grease Stains 155
 Stain Prevention 155

Garage Parking 155
 X Marks the Perfect Spot 155
 Prevent Dings 156
 Finding Your Car 156

Car Smells 156
 Cigarette Smoke 156
 Bad-Smell Neutralizer 156
 Sweeten the Air 156

Checklist of Car Should-Haves 157

Car Travel 157
 Packing Clothes 158
 Pillowcase Smarts 158
 Directions on Tape 158
 Traveling with Pets 158

Travel Fun & Games 158
 Create a Trip Travelogue 158
 Geography—A Classic Game 159
 A Game of Questions 159
 Essence—A Game of Perception 159
 Watch What You Say—
  A Gotcha! Game 159
 Story Time—A Game of Imagination 160

General Travel 160
 Travel Planning 160
 Before the Trip 160
 During the Trip 164

Travel Safety 165
 Money Smarts 165
 Prevent Hotel Break-ins 165
 Let There Be Light 166
 Common Sense 166

Airline Travel 166
 Luggage Allowances 166
 Better Packing 167
 Luggage Identification 167
 More Comfortable Airplane Travel 167
 Water on Airplanes 168

Foreign Travel 168
 International Travel Warnings 169
 US Representatives 169
 Electrical Appliances 169
 Money 169
 Water and Food Precautions 170
 Pack Washcloths 170
 Contact Lens Caution 170

Home Again! 170

Products 171

Chapter 8 • Care For Your Fuzzy Friends

Pet Safety 173
 No "Strings" Attached 173
 Electrical Cords 173
 Toxic Plants 174
 Accidental Falls 174
 Fire 174
 Pools/Water 174
 The Kitchen 175
 The Bathroom 175
 Every Room in the House 175
 The Garage and Driveway 175

Medicine for Cats & Dogs 176
 Giving Your Cat Medicine 176
 Giving Your Dog Medicine 176

Weather 177
 Cold-Weather Insulation 177
 Dogs Walking in Snow 177
 Dog Days of Summer 178

Food & Drink 178
 Chocolate? Never! 178
 Grapes, Currants and Raisins? Never! 179
 Onions? Bad! 179
 Yogurt for Gas Prevention 179
 Dry Food vs. Canned Food 179
 Cat's Bowl 180
 Place Mat 180
 Making Cat's Food Appetizing 180
 Garden Water Dish 180
 Hydrate Outdoors 180

Fleas 181
 Check for Fleas 181

Lemon Chaser 181
Fleas Hate Vinegar 181
B-1 Without Fleas...........................181
Cat Coat Shiner and Flea Repellent 182
Flea Collar 182
Flea-Repellent Pillow 182
Getting Fleas Where They Live 182
Old-Fashioned Soap and Water 182
Salt Them Away...............................182
Let Fleas Take a Powder...................183

Cleaning & Grooming **183**
Dog Hair–Catcher 183
Eye and Ear Protection 183
Soft and Shiny Coat.........................183
Stop the Water Shake 183
Dry Shampoo 184
De-Skunking 184
Shedding......................................184
Removing Burrs, Tree Sap, Gum 185
Nail Care 185

Calming Influences.....................**185**
Respect Your Pet's Hangouts.............185
Nervous Reaction to Strangers 185
When Company Comes 186
Petting the Pet..............................186

For Dogs Only **186**
Stop the Barking............................186
Stop Hole Digging 186
Stop Furniture and Paw Chewing 186
Leaving Dogs Home Alone 187
Doghouse Wood 187
Giving Away Puppies 187
Adopting a Puppy.........................188

For Cats Only **188**
Pick-Me-Up..................................188
Cat Litter 188

Cat-alog **189**
Marking *Your* Territory.................189
Bringing in a New Cat 189
Fur-Ball Prevention 189
Repel with Cat's Sense of Smell........189
Stop Furniture Scratching 189

Puppy & Kitten Overpopulation **190**
Benefits of Spaying Female Pets 190
Benefits of Neutering Male Pets............190
When to Spay or Neuter..................190
Low-Cost Programs 190

Products **191**

Index **192**

CHAPTER 1

Floor-to-Ceiling Magic

Let's start with the basics. Every room in every house —no matter how grand or how humble—will have a floor, a ceiling and walls that need your care and attention.

Take a look around the room you're in now. There are 3 givens…floor, walls and a ceiling. The ceiling is generally out of reach and requires the least amount of care. The walls are an excellent showcase for your inner interior decorator as well as for various do-it-yourself painting or wallpapering projects. (Lots more on that later in this chapter.)

The floor you walk on, however, needs attention on a regular basis. *So let's start with caring for everything underfoot…*

FLOORS

Floors. We all have them. Some common types are vinyl or linoleum in the kitchen… tile in the bathroom or entryway…and hardwood floors in the rest of the rooms. It may surprise you to know that *hardwood* does not refer to the hardness of the wood. It's a classification of broad-leaved flowering trees including oak, maple, ash and elm. Aspen is a hardwood tree whose wood is soft. Needle-leaved trees—pine, fir or evergreen—are softwood trees. Mahogany is from a softwood evergreen. Go figure! Well, don't be floored. *Consider these suggestions…*

Caring for Hardwood Floors

◆ To revive your finished hardwood's shine, mix equal parts of distilled white vinegar and vegetable oil, and put the mixture in a spray bottle. Work small sections of the floor at a time. Start by spritzing the mixture and rubbing it in with a clean cotton cloth. With another clean cotton cloth, buff that section until it's as shiny as can be. Then start on the next section of floor. And so on and so on and so on.

> **(** **FYI: Are You Protected?**
> Most newly installed floors have a urethane finish. You can tell simply by looking at the floor. If it looks glossy and as if it has a layer of clear plastic on top of the wood, chances are it is a urethane finish. This kind of finish is a shield, protecting the wood from scratches, water damage and other boo-boos.

◆ To remove any scuff marks, get out an old, clean toothbrush, apply some non-gel toothpaste and scrub off the scuff mark. Then wipe the area clean with a damp cloth or sponge.

◆ Depending on the size of the scuff mark, put a little petroleum jelly or baby oil on a cloth and work it into the floor to remove the mark. Once it's gone, go over the area with dry paper towels, making sure there's not a trace of the slippery jelly or oil.

◆ If a clump of grease dripped on the floor, cover it with 1 or 2 ice cubes. As soon as the grease hardens, carefully scrape it off with the dull side of a knife, an expired credit card or a spatula.

 Brew Up Beautiful Floors

Boil 1 quart of water, then throw in 2 bags of black tea (such as Pekoe). Let it steep for about 20 minutes, then dampen a cloth or mop with the tea and wash your wood floor with it. The tea's tannic acid should cut through grease and grime. Then buff the wood with a clean, soft cloth—or not. If your floor looks fine, forget the buffing (unless you want the exercise).

Cleaning a Waxed Hardwood Floor

Waxing a hardwood floor is not a popular idea, due to the amount of upkeep necessary. If you insist on it, wax should be applied in light, even coats. Stop when the floor has the sheen and protection level you desire.

◆ If you want the dirt to come off, but the wax to stay on your floor, use a sponge mop that's been dipped in a mixture of ¼ cup of distilled white vinegar and 1 gallon of water. Wring out the mop so that it's damp (not sopping wet) before it touches the floor.

◆ Between waxings, put a piece of waxed paper—waxy side down, of course—over the mop head and give the floor the once over.

 CAUTION: Never wax a urethane floor. Wax and urethane are not compatible.

Sweeping a Hardwood Floor

◆ Try a Japanese cleaning method—sprinkle damp tea leaves on the floor. Don't think of it as adding to the dirt...the tea helps to weigh down the dust, making it easier to sweep up.

◆ If there's a little mound of dirt that can't be swept into the dustpan, wet a paper towel and blot it all up.

 Make Your Own Dustpan

If you don't have a dustpan and don't want to buy one, cut a paper or plastic plate in half. POOF! A dustpan.

Covering Up a Hardwood Scratch

Hardware stores have wax crayons that match most shades of hardwood. Or look in that old box of crayons for a color that matches your floor. This works best for very long and/or deep scratches—take the paper off the crayon, then put it in a small glass container and melt it in your microwave. Start by setting it for 10 seconds. (You may end up needing to give it another 10 seconds to melt, depending on the power of your microwave.)

Carefully pour the melted wax into the scratch. Before it completely hardens, use a piece of plastic—such as an expired credit card or a section of a yogurt container lid—and glide it over the treated area, removing the extra wax, making the filled-in scratch level with the rest of the floor. (Take care not to scratch the floor again with the plastic.)

Microwave Alternative

If you don't want to zap a crayon in your microwave, grate the crayon carefully with a knife or your cheese grater (wash it thoroughly afterward). Then line a section of a muffin tin with aluminum foil, and put the grated crayon in it. Put the muffin tin in a preheated 350°F oven. It should take about 2 or 3 minutes for the crayon to melt. And the foil prevents a messy cleanup.

If you don't want to work with the melted crayon, grate a piece of crayon and press the little pieces into the scratch. Next, use a blow-dryer set on *low* to help harden the wax, then level it off with a piece of plastic.

When the melted crayon cools and completely hardens, buff the area with a soft, clean cloth. (If you're into waxing the floor, this would be the time to do it.)

 Put a Sock on It!

◆ *Temporary solution:* If you are rearranging furniture or moving furniture to clean, put old socks—the heavier the better—on the furniture legs. Or rip off pieces from a cardboard box, or cut off the bottom half from a milk or juice carton. Once the carton is washed and dried, it makes a great coaster for furniture legs. You can also use plastic containers that are completely flat on the bottom.

Socks, cartons and containers will protect the floor from scratches, and they make the furniture a lot easier to move around.

◆ *Permanent solution:* Stick clear adhesive tape or strips of weather-stripping on the bottom of furniture legs so that the wood floor will not be scratched when the furniture is moved.

You can also glue pieces of felt or carpet—pile side down—to the bottom of furniture legs. Self-stick bunion pads and moleskin patches will also serve the same purpose.

Managing Creaky/Squeaky Floors

Start by sweeping cornstarch or talcum powder between the noisy floorboards. Once the spaces are completely filled in with the powder, the creaking should be gone.

If the creaking continues, the nails in the floorboard may be loose and need to be hammered back into place. In that case, lay a piece of thin wood or thick cardboard over the part of the floor that seems to creak. This will protect the bare floor or the floor covering (linoleum or carpet) when you pound-pound-pound it with the hammer. But once you hammer down the nails that were loose, there should be no more creaking.

Caring for Vinyl and/or Linoleum Floors

◆ If you want to clean and shine your floor between waxings, mix ½ cup of liquid fabric softener in 1 gallon of water, then mop the floor with the solution. Your floor will get clean and keep its shine.

◆ If your floor has any wax buildup, take club soda and pour it on a small section of the vinyl flooring. Scrub it in with a brush, and give it a few minutes as you start the process on the next small section, then go back to the first section and wipe it off.

◆ If you don't want to wax your floor, but it needs to be mopped clean, you can mix 1 cup of distilled white vinegar into 1 gallon of water and rinse the floor. The linoleum will become clean and shiny. Why bother waxing?

◆ To remove old grease stains from your floor, pour cola on the stain and let it stay there for 1 hour. Then wipe it off—both the soda and the stain. (Legend has it that Coca-Cola works best due to its acidic content, so you might want to try it first.)

Removing Scuff Marks (And Crayon)

◆ Try scrubbing the mark with non-gel tooth-paste on a toothbrush or on a dry cloth. Then wipe it clean with a damp sponge or cloth.

◆ Pour a little bit of baking soda on a damp cloth and rub the scuff mark, then wipe it with a clean cloth.

◆ Take a gum or pencil eraser and use it to erase the heel mark.

◆ When a skid mark is not responding to the toothpaste, baking soda or eraser, rub the mark with nail polish remover. Dab and rub, then quickly wipe it clean with a damp cloth.

CAUTION: Before you use nail polish re-mover to take off a scuff mark, test a small area of the floor to make sure that it's safe to use. If it is, and you do use the remover to clean the skid mark, wipe it clean with a damp cloth afterward.

FYI: Preventing Picasso
These solutions should also clean off mas-terpieces made by young budding artists whose medium is "Crayon on Household Floor and/or Wall."

★ **High-Heel Horrors**
Do not wear high, thin heels on linoleum and some wood floors. The heels will make dents in the flooring.

Caring for Tile Floors

◆ A simple cleaning formula is to mix ½ cup of distilled white vinegar in 1 gallon of water. Dampen a mop or—if you're a down-on-your-knees kind of cleaner—dampen a sponge and clean the tile floor. Depending on the ventilation in the tile-floored room, the vinegar smell will disappear in a short amount of time.

◆ If the floor hasn't been cleaned in awhile… and you can see the grime…and you suspect that the floor needs to be disinfected, it's probably time to mix up some heavy-duty tile tonic.

In a large spray bottle, combine 1 cup of distilled white vinegar, 1 cup of rubbing alcohol, 1 cup of water and 3 drops of liquid dish detergent. Spray, mop and rinse the tile with plain water.

CARPETS & RUGS

Carpets and rugs often add warmth to a room. To keep your floor coverings look-ing their best, you have to take care of them. Do not let your carpet bathe in prolonged peri-ods of direct sunlight—not unless you want it to fade or discolor. Protect it by covering your windows with drapes, blinds or shades.

We hate to have to tell you this, but experts agree that carpets and rugs should be vacuumed at least once a week to stay in good shape, and to keep dirt from getting embedded in the fibers.

To prevent dirt from being tracked into the house, place walk-off mats at each entrance. The mats will absorb and help trap dirt, sand and grit from outside.

Do not forget to clean these mats regu-larly—either hose them down or vacuum them—so that they don't become the *cause* of the dirt that's being tracked into the house.

Here are more suggestions to help you care for your fibrous floor coverings…

Cleaning Carpets

◆ Dry-clean your carpet by sprinkling it liber-ally with baking soda. Use a flour sifter to help distribute it evenly. If you can leave the baking soda on your carpet overnight, do it. If not, let it stay for at least 1 hour.

Meanwhile, sprinkle 1 tablespoon of your favorite fragrant herb—such as lavender, cinnamon or potpourri*—on the floor. After a few minutes, vacuum up the baking soda and whichever herb you used. The unpleasant carpet odors—cigarette smoke, mustiness, wet dog, cat urine—should be gone, and the fragrant aroma of the herb should be in the air.

◆ In a spray bottle, mix 1 part liquid fabric softener (any scent you prefer) to 6 parts water. Spray the carpet with the solution, then vacuum. The carpet should be more dust-resistant, generate less static electricity and smell fresh, too.

*Optional

Cleaning Fringe

Fringe on area rugs looks nice but collects dust and dirt and is difficult to vacuum. Save yourself the trouble by whisking out the dirt instead. With a dry scrub brush, use down-and-away strokes. Then brush the dirt away from the fringe and vacuum it up off the floor.

 Keep Your Carpet Clippings!
When you get new carpeting, be sure to keep several swatches of it. They will come in handy when you're decorating and want to coordinate or match draperies or upholstery fabric or paint. You may also want to use the swatches to test cleaners and stain removers, or if your carpet needs fiber replacements.

Cleaning Stains

You may want to consider treating your carpet with a commercial stain guard, especially if you have children and/or pets or if you do a lot of entertaining.

But if you haven't stain-guarded your floor covering, stock your pantry with a case of distilled white vinegar and club soda, then read on.

 CAUTION: Be sure to test any solution you use as a stain remover on a carpet swatch or on a small, inconspicuous spot of your carpet or rug. Not all colors or fabrics will react the same way.

If something is dropped on your carpet and there are pieces involved (for example, a bowl of chili, cornflakes and milk, or chicken noodle soup), pick up all the pieces of food first. Then get paper towels and blot up as much of the liquid mess as possible, as quickly as possible. You may want to step on the towels to help the blotting process.

Once you're finished picking and blotting, you're ready to use 1 of the following stain solutions…

 Be Stain Savvy
Try not to rub the stain. Rubbing can spread it, embed it deeper and cause damage to the carpet fibers.

◆ Put club soda or seltzer water on a fresh stain and let the carbonation loosen it. After a couple of minutes, blot it up with paper towels, a clean cloth or a sponge.

◆ Work a heaping tablespoon of foam shaving cream into the stain. Wait for it to dry, then rinse with cold water. (The glycerin in shaving cream is the compound that helps dissolve stains.)

◆ Put some vodka on a washcloth and work it into the stain. Wait a minute, then blot it with a paper towel.

◆ If you're sure your carpet or rug is colorfast, work some 3% hydrogen peroxide into the stain, then blot it with a paper towel.

◆ Use a fresh baby wipe to lift the stain off the carpet or rug.

Removing an Existing Stain

If you're wondering how old a stain is—a week, a month, a year or more—we can't tell you. What we do know is that this remedy is worth trying. It should work, but even if it doesn't, it will not make the stain worse.

Combine 1 tablespoon of liquid laundry detergent, 1½ tablespoons of distilled white vinegar and 2 cups of water. Gently work the mixture into the stain, then blot it dry.

Removing Candle Wax

◆ Place a few ice cubes in a plastic bag and put it against the wax that dripped on the carpet. The ice will make the wax brittle, and you will be able to break off or carefully pull off the drippings.

◆ Cut off a section of a plain brown paper bag, and place it on top of the melted wax. With a medium-hot iron, press the paper for several seconds—long enough to soften the wax and have it transfer from the carpet to the paper. If you have to repeat the process a few times, always use a new piece of brown paper.

Removing Pet Urine

◆ Test carpet swatches or a tiny, inconspicuous patch of each carpet and rug in your home with distilled white vinegar. If the color of any of the test patches change, make note *not* to use the vinegar solution on that carpet or rug, if and when your pet has an accident on it. Be on the lookout for such accidents, because you'll want to deal with them immediately.

First, blot up as much of the urine as possible, and rinse the area with warm water. Blot again. Then, for a vinegar-safe rug, mix ½ cup of distilled white vinegar with ½ cup of water, and sponge it into the fibers. After a few minutes, blot it off and repeat the procedure. Then pour equal amounts of table salt and baking soda on the wet area. Wait until it dries—it may take a few hours—then vacuum.

◆ For a fresh accident, blot the spot, then cover it with a thick layer of table salt. More is better, since you want the salt to absorb all of the liquid. Wait until the salt has hardened—overnight if possible—then vacuum over the area.

See "Cleaning Carpets" on pages 4–5 for tips on removing a urine smell.

 CAUTION: There is ammonia in urine. Therefore, NEVER use ammonia or a spot remover that contains ammonia to clean urine. It will mislead your pet into believing that this is his/her marked territory. He will return to it on a regular basis, rewetting and restaining the spot.

 Dealing with Pet Hair
Give the vacuum a helping hand by sweeping the rug with a damp broom. That will loosen and/or pick up the pet hair. Then finish the job by vacuuming the rug.

Removing Chewing Gum

◆ Start by blow-drying the gum on the *warm* (not *hot*) setting on your hair dryer. You want the gum to melt, not the carpet's fibers. As soon as the gum seems real gooey, put a small plastic bag around it and gently pull off the bag, bringing the gum with it.

Repeat the process until all of the gum is out of the carpet, or there's just a stubborn little bit left. For that little bit, work in a dab of petroleum jelly, rolling the gum into it. Then wash the spot with a gentle laundry detergent formulated to fight grease, rinse with water and blot dry.

Petroleum jelly may stain carpet, so be sure to do a spot-test first.

◆ See the ice-cubes-in-a-plastic-bag remedy for candle wax removal on page 6.

Removing Coffee or Tea

Gulp! You might as well have spilled hair dye. Blot up as much of the spill as possible, as quickly as possible. *Then, depending on what is available to you at the time, use 1 of the following remedies…*

◆ Pour on club soda and blot. Then more club soda and more blotting. If the stain isn't fading fast, pour on a bit of 3% hydrogen peroxide and let it stay on for about 15 minutes. Then blot and rinse with either more club soda or some cold water.

◆ Combine 2 tablespoons of baking soda and 1 tablespoon of borax powder (available at supermarkets and drugstores) in 1 pint of water. Sponge the stain with this solution, then blot dry.

◆ Using a clean, dry washcloth, work a beaten egg yolk into the stain, and then rinse with warm water.

◆ Work a heaping tablespoon of foam shaving cream into the stain, then rinse with club soda or cold water.

Removing Crayon Marks

Put a strip of transparent tape on each crayon mark, then gently remove the tape. Hopefully some of the crayon will come off but none of the fibers.

Removing Fresh Fruit

Try to pick up all of the pieces of fruit and blot up the juice. Then combine 1 tablespoon of liquid laundry detergent, 1½ tablespoons of distilled white vinegar and 2 cups of water. Gently work the mixture into the fruit stain, and then blot dry.

Removing Grease/Oil

◆ Use a paper towel to blot up as much of the grease or oil as possible. Then pour cornmeal or cornstarch on the stain. Let it stay that way overnight and vacuum the carpet in the morning.

◆ Work a heaping tablespoon of foam shaving cream into the stained carpet fibers. Let it dry thoroughly, then vacuum the spot spotless.

Removing Latex Paint

Take action immediately! Make a solution with 1½ teaspoons of distilled white vinegar and 1½ teaspoons of laundry detergent mixed in 2 cups of warm water.

 NOTE: You should definitely test this solution on a carpet swatch or on an inconspicuous portion of the carpet *before* using it. If the carpet color is not affected by the mixture, then proceed.

Dip a clean sponge into the solution and use it to wipe away the latex paint. Once the stain is gone, rinse with cold water and blot dry.

If the carpet color on the test patch changed after you applied the vinegar solution, then just use the laundry detergent in warm water. You'll have to work harder to get the paint out, and it may not be as effective.

The Color Cure
Next time, consider using paint that's the exact same color as your carpet so that nobody will ever notice if you spill some.

Removing Mud

Let the mud dry, then use an expired credit card or a dull knife to scrape off as much of it as possible. If the rug is still a little muddy, mix 2 teaspoons of laundry detergent with 1 cup of water, and sponge it on the carpet. Blot with paper towels, rinse with a wet sponge and blot dry with more paper towels.

Removing Red Wine

◆ Open another bottle—seriously! Quickly blot off the red wine with a paper towel, then neutralize it with white wine. Next, wipe it clean with a cold, damp cloth.

◆ If you don't have any white wine, work some table salt or baking soda into the stain, and dab it off with club soda.

Getting Rid of Insects

◆ Moth larvae may be found in carpet fibers. Get rid of them by pouring a thick layer of table salt (a lot of salt!) on the carpet, wait 1 hour, then vacuum up the salt. The salt destroys the moth larvae and also brightens the carpet.

◆ This is a bit of an ordeal, but if you have an insect infestation (especially fleas or ticks) in your carpet, take the time to get rid of the little buggers. Buy boxes of table salt, enough to layer the entire carpet with it.

As you pour the salt into the carpet, use a broom or brush to work the salt down deep where the bugs nest.

Once the salt is in place, let it stay there for 2 to 3 days, giving it time to (somehow) dehydrate and destroy the insects. Then vacuum as usual. To prevent future infestations, it's a good idea to vacuum at least once a week.

Bug Off!
Printer's ink repels moths and silverfish. Put a layer of plain (non-colored) newspaper between the pad and the rug, and be bug-free.

Raising a Matted Nap

If you're into rearranging furniture on a carpeted floor, you'll want to know how to raise matted-down nap or *pile* (the cut or uncut loops of yarn that form the carpet's surface). There's the cold way and the hot way. *So take your pick…*

◆ *Cold:* Put an ice cube on each matted area—most likely where 4 furniture feet rested. Let the ice cubes melt on the dents overnight (just be sure nobody will be walking around the house). In the morning, fluff up the nap with your fingers or an old toothbrush.

◆ *Hot:* Hold a steam iron a few inches above the matted carpet area until the nap is mildly moist. *Do not touch the carpet with the iron.* Then scrape up the nap with an old toothbrush or the edge of a spoon's handle.

Removing Loose Threads

Never pull out threads, unless you want the carpet to unravel. Instead, use scissors to cut each loose thread, making it level with the pile (the surface of the carpet).

Dealing with Static Electricity

If you're tired of getting shocks each time you walk on your carpet, particularly in the winter months, try this solution…

Mix 3 tablespoons of liquid fabric softener with 1 cup of water in a spray bottle. Give the carpet a modest misting. If you wet the carpet too much, dirt will stick to the carpet. Allow it to dry thoroughly before taking a shockless stroll across it.

DID YOU KNOW?

If you get shocks even when you're not walking on carpeting, it's because the humidity levels are low or because you're wearing shoes. The soles of your shoes (especially rubber soles) do not allow you to release the electric charge. Prevent shocks by walking barefoot and discharging the static electricity through your feet. This isn't too practical, though, especially during the cold winter months.

You usually know when you're going to get a shock—when you touch a metal doorknob, the television set, a light switch or a faucet. You can discharge most of the static electricity in your body by touching whatever you want to touch with a wooden pencil *before* touching it with your fingers. You may get a little shock, but nothing like the jolt you would have gotten without the pencil.

Moving Heavy Furniture

On those rare occasions when you have to move a piano or another piece of heavy furniture on wheels, place a protective barrier—such as a piece of heavy cardboard or a plywood plank—between the wheels and the carpet to prevent damage to the carpet.

Anchoring Throw Rugs

If you don't want a throw rug slipping out from under you, make sure it stays put by sewing nonslip rubber rings from mason jars (available at hardware stores) on the underside.

Use strong cotton thread (doubled), and attach each rubber ring by tacking it in 3 or 4 places. Use your discretion as to how many rings to sew on each rug. If you have a rectangular throw rug, consider putting a rubber ring under each corner.

Bathtub decals are also a good idea, as is double-sided "carpet" tape.

Velcro adhesive strips (available at hardware, crafts and sewing-supply stores) are also an option. Velcro strips come in pairs…an upper strip and a lower strip. On the outside of both strips is adhesive…on the inside of both strips are the Velcro fibers that interlock with each other. Stick 1 side on the floor under where the rug is going to stay. Line the rug up and stick the other portion of the Velcro on the underside of the rug. Then lay the 2 pieces of Velcro (the 1 on the floor and the 1 on the underside of the rug) on top of each other.

This is sounding so complicated…if it's not making sense, but the thought of using Velcro appeals to you, go to a store that sells it and just look at it. You will be able to figure it out once you see it. And if you don't want to deal with that…just buy a nonskid rug.

Can't Beat It

Do you still beat your rugs to get them clean? Save yourself the trouble and toss the throw rug in a dryer on a "no-heat" setting. Let it run for its usual cycle. The rug should come out clean and lookin' good.

Vacuuming

Aside from the contents of accidental spills, have you ever wondered what exactly you're vacuuming up? Brace yourself for a surprise. Household "dirt" is about 75% to 80% sloughed-off human skin cells. Who would have thought that most of the vacuum cleaner dirt comes directly from the people who own the vacuum cleaner? The other 25% to 30% is hair, animal dander, dust mites and just a small amount of actual dirt—sand, earth and pollen—that has been blown in or tracked in from outside. *Now that you know **what** you're vacuuming, here are some ideas on how to get the best results…*

When vacuuming a carpet or a rug, use long, slow strokes. That gives the vacuum time to loosen the dirt and then let it be sucked up. For a lightly soiled area, try to make 3 passes with the vacuum…for a heavily soiled area, go over it at least 5 to 7 times.

 Best Time to Vacuum

When it's raining or humid outside, open the windows and vacuum. The moisture in the air helps prevent dust from flying up and landing on the carpet again.

Extend Your Reach

Figure out which outlet is most central in terms of the areas you vacuum. Next, measure the farthest distance the vacuum needs to go from that outlet. Then buy a lightweight extension cord that will accommodate that measurement, even if it has to be 50 feet long. Using the extension cord will save you the time and effort of going from one outlet to another.

Sweet Smells

Vacuum up a tablespoon of your favorite sweet-smelling herb—lavender, cinnamon, the contents of a spiced tea bag—or put the perfume strips from magazines or a scented fabric softener sheet in the vacuum cleaner bag. The

heat from the vacuum brings out the fragrance of the herb or perfume. It makes vacuuming a little more pleasant.

 Prep the Brushes

Go over the (unplugged) vacuum's brushes with a wet paper towel before you vacuum a carpet. It will help heighten its dirt-sucking power.

Finding Lost Beads

Necklaces break, containers of things fall over… it happens. And when it does, find a piece of old pantyhose (or use a knee-high stocking) and stretch it over the vacuum suction hose—you can keep it in place with a small rubber band.

Aim the hose at the little things on the floor, then turn on the vacuum and they will be sucked up against the pantyhose. Hold the vacuum hose over a shoebox or other wide, shallow container, and turn off the vacuum's power. The little things will fall into the box where they are easy to recover.

Changing Dust Bags

If you wait until the dust bag in your vacuum reaches its full capacity, you may notice a reduction in the vacuum's suction, and more dust in the room that you're supposedly cleaning. It's best to change the dust bag as soon as you can tell it's filling up. Check it every 3 or 4 times you vacuum—don't wait until it's bursting at the seams. (For bagless canister models, check them every other time the vacuum is used.)

To change the dust bag, spread out and spray a couple of newspaper pages with water. Put the vacuum on the wet paper and remove the old, filled dust bag. The loose dust will adhere to the wet paper.

Insert the new dust bag in the vacuum, fold up and discard the newspaper along with the old bag, and you're good to go.

Fighting Fleas

If you have a pet with fleas, your carpet may also have fleas. Fleas can be vacuumed up and continue living and multiplying in the vacuum's dust bag. If you're concerned that this may be happening in your home, place a commercial flea collar or a few mothballs in the dust bag to eliminate the problem.

Also, see the instructions for a do-it-yourself herbal flea collar on page 182 of "Pet Care," Chapter 8.

WALLS

 Walls are great. Without them, you would not know where a room starts and ends. Walls are there waiting for you to paint them, paper them, create wall arrangements or do any number of other things to make your living space a reflection of your taste and a happy place for you to be.

However you choose to decorate your walls, this section offers some basic cleaning, painting and wallpapering suggestions, which we hope will serve your walls well. Just keep in mind that you can always put on a new coat of paint or wallpaper if they don't work out.

> **NOTE:** It's not good to remove paint inadvertently while cleaning a wall, nor would you want to get rid of a stain and end up with a conspicuous light spot. So get testy! That is, test an inconspicuous part of your wall before you do a general cleaning or hone in on a smudge, stain or dirty area.

Cleaning Painted Walls

To prepare, it's important to protect the floor by putting down a fabric drop cloth…or an old bedsheet…or towels…or pieces of brown-paper bags…or newspapers. Don't use plastic drop cloths because they can get very slippery when they're wet.

Next, use a soft-bristled brush or a vacuum cleaner to get rid of any dust and cobwebs from the wall (especially in the corners or crevices, like near molding).

Clean off any marks from the wall (using our stain-removing tips—*see* page 12) in preparation for the overall washing.

Next, get 2 buckets. Fill one ¾ full with warm water, and add at least 1 tablespoon of liquid dish detergent (any other kind of soap or detergent may affect the color of the paint). Leave the other bucket empty.

Dampen a natural (better than nylon) sponge or sponge-mop or even a paint roller in the bucket with the soapy water, and wash the wall. As illogical as this sounds, always start at the bottom of a wall and work your way to the top. Trust the fact that it's easier to wipe off dirty streaks from a clean surface than from a wall that's dirty. Every so often, wring out the dirty water from the sponge into the empty bucket, then redip it in the soapy water.

> **NOTE:** Once you start, be prepared to wash the entire wall. Do not stop midway—when the wall dries, this will create a *tidemark*…a dirty line that shows where you cleaned and where you didn't. These types of marks can be difficult to remove.

After you've washed the wall, rinse it with a clean, damp sponge. Then dry the wall with a terry cloth towel. It's the best fabric to use for drying, and it has a minor loofah effect—so it will help to remove the last bits of gunk from the clean wall.

"Dry" Clean Your Walls

Do you have terry cloth sweatbands for your wrists, like tennis players use? If not, you can make wristbands by folding washcloths and securing them with not-too-tight rubber bands.

The wristband will help to prevent water from running down your arm while your hand is raised to wash the wall, even if you're wearing plastic gloves.

Cleaning Textured Plaster Walls

If you've stashed some small squares or swatches of leftover carpet in your junk closet or basement, dig 'em out—they are great to use to wash textured plaster walls (low-cut, thick piles generally work best).

In a pail, combine 1 quart of warm water with 2 tablespoons of liquid laundry detergent and 2 tablespoons of distilled white vinegar. Dip a piece of carpet in the solution and scrub the wall with the carpet square. It will get into the crevices and will clean the wall without scratching it. Wipe the wall down with a sturdy, wet sponge and dry it with a terry cloth towel.

Cleaning a Smoky Wall

If there's a smoker in the house, walls tend to get a dingy nicotine film—soapy water alone may not be able to cut through it.

Rather than subject your lungs to the strong fumes of ammonia, we recommend *trisodium phosphate* (TSP), which is available at most hardware stores. This ionic, water-soluble salt, used as a cleaning agent and degreaser, is also a food additive. That should be a good indication of how user-friendly it is. Follow the instructions on the package.

It's important to remember that, although TSP is safe, it can be *strong*. Wear protective gloves, goggles and even a nose/mouth mask for safety.

Removing Wall Stains

 CAUTION: Once you decide which ingredient is necessary to get rid of a wall stain, test that ingredient on a small, inconspicuous area of the stained surface. By doing this, you'll make sure it's not going to create a new (and possibly worse) stain.

◆ For grease stains, pour some baby powder on a soft, clean cloth—no water necessary. Wait a few minutes, then rub a cloth on the spots until they fade away.

◆ A baby wipe should remove most crayon marks. You can also spritz them with WD-40, then clean with a paper towel.

◆ If there are marker marks on the wall, put some rubbing alcohol on a cotton puff and wipe the ink spots. The marker should come off and the paint or wallpaper should stay on.

◆ To remove ballpoint pen marks, spritz any type of hairspray on the mark, then blot it with a clean, soft rag.

◆ For pencil marks—as well as fingerprints— use a gum eraser (available at stationery and art-supply stores). If all you have is a pencil eraser, that's fine. To make sure it's clean, erase with it first on a blank piece of paper.

◆ If you took pictures off the wall and are left with the sticky remains of the masking or transparent tape, get out your blow-dryer. Set it on *low* and, in one hand, let it heat up the adhesive, while in the other hand, carefully use a knife to scrape up the tape goo.

If you don't trust yourself with the knife, then press a bit of transparent tape on the heated residue and pull it off. (Hopefully, you will remove all of the sticky stuff, and not add to it.)

Magic Dirt Erasers!

We would be remiss if we didn't mention a product that we use and love for wall clean-ups—Mr. Clean Magic Eraser (available at supermarkets and home improvement stores).

Although these miraculous just-add-water sponges take off crayon, ink and grease stains, they may also remove dirt you didn't know was there. More often than not, you may have to clean the entire area so that there's not just 1 small yet conspicuous clean spot.

WALLPAPER

Putting wallpaper in a room is a great way to make a creative decorating statement. Depending on your choice of wallpaper pattern, texture and colors, it can coordinate or dominate …or simply become a low-profile background.

Want your room to look taller? Consider using wallpaper that has vertical stripes. Want your room to look wider? You guessed it—horizontal stripes. If you have a high ceiling and want the room to look cozier, consider adding a border near the ceiling. The room will appear smaller if you choose wallpaper with dark colors and large patterns.

Selecting wallpaper is the first and the most fun step. Next comes the work of prepping the walls and applying the paper. *Here are some tips that will help you get to the final step, when you can step back and admire the new look of your room…*

Removing Old Wallpaper

This process can get messy, so be sure to move your furniture to the middle of the room (or to another room), remove all curtains and window treatments, and cover the floor with a drop cloth, tarp, some old bedsheets or lots of newspaper.

◆ First perforate the old wallpaper (you can buy an inexpensive scorer at hardware and paint stores). Then mix equal amounts of hot water and distilled white vinegar. Saturate a sponge with the mixture and wipe it on the wallpaper. (If you prefer to use a paint roller and tray or a spray bottle, that's fine. It doesn't matter how the solution gets on the wallpaper as long as it's HOT going on.) Allow it to saturate the paper for 10 to 15 minutes, then you should be able to easily peel off the paper.

◆ If you would rather not be around the smell of vinegar, use 1 part liquid fabric softener to 2 parts hot water. Apply the solution to the wallpaper with a sponge, roller or spray. Then about 10 minutes later, start peeling.

Preparing the Walls

Take the time to thoroughly prep your walls before putting up wallpaper. It will help keep you safe, help ensure that the wallpaper adheres to the wall properly and will make future wallpaper removal a lot easier. *Let's start with safety…*

◆ After you remove the switch plates, cover electrical outlets and switches with pieces of masking tape to protect them from exposure to sanding, priming, paste and water.

CAUTION: When the wallpaper is up, turn off the electricity in the room before cutting the excess wallpaper and cleaning around the electrical outlets and switches. You don't want there to be surging electricity when water and metal are involved.

◆ Before hanging wallpaper, be sure the walls are clean, completely dry and free of any residual paste, grease, mildew or other stains. Wait at least 1 hour after washing to apply new paper.

Use a spackling compound (available at hardware and home improvement stores) to repair small nicks or cracks in the wall, then use sandpaper to make it smooth. It also helps to sand away small bumps or protrusions.

◆ Apply a good acrylic-based primer/sealer (get one that is specially formulated for wall coverings) to protect the wall surface from paste damage, and prevent the wall from absorbing moisture from the paste. Primer slows the paste's drying time and makes it easier to position and reposition the paper as you work with it.

Also, priming ensures that the wall and the paper will form a strong bond and adhere better. And in the future, when you're ready for another decorating change, the paper will be easier to remove, thanks to the primer.

 Ask the Expert!
The best advice we can give you—without devoting half of this book to wallpapering—is to buy wallpaper from a knowledgeable salesperson. Tell him/her exactly what kind of walls (such as painted, papered, drywall or new plaster walls) you want to cover.

The wallpaper person should be able to offer valuable guidance in terms of your specific wall preparation and wallpaper application, and also suggest the proper tools you will need for each step of the process. Take notes.

Applying Wallpaper Paste

Keep in mind that it's better for wallpaper paste to be too thick than too thin. Thicker paste will hold the paper in place better than thin paste.

You can test the paste by dipping the paste brush into it. Then, lay the brush on the back of the wallpaper. Leave it there for 1 to 2 minutes. When you pick up the brush, the paper should be stuck to it. Then you can just peel it off, knowing the paste is ready to use.

 Clean as You Go
Keep a sponge and a bucket of clean water nearby. As you apply the paper to the wall, use the wet sponge to wipe off any globs of paste that land on the wallpaper.

The Case Against Seam Rollers

If you are applying embossed wallpaper, do NOT use a seam roller to seal the seams. The roller can crush the embossed pattern and give it a flattened look.

Even if you don't have embossed wallpaper, you may not want to use a seam roller. This type of roller seems to squeeze the paste out from under the paper.

 Prevent Wallpaper Peeling
If your cooking heats up the kitchen...or your hot showers steam up the bathroom, you may want to take a precautionary step.

After you finish wallpapering the room, paint the wallpaper seams with clear varnish (available at paint and hardware stores). Doing this should go a long way in preventing the paper from peeling.

Creating a Wallpaper Patch

If you need to patch a section of wallpaper months—or even years—after you originally wallpapered a room, you will want that patch to be totally unnoticeable. But chances are, if you take a patch piece from the extra roll you put away when you first wallpapered, the piece will be brighter—and therefore more noticeable—than the rest of the wall.

To prevent that from happening, as soon as you hang your wallpaper, also tack a leftover piece of the paper in an out-of-the-way place—for example, on part of a wall that nobody can see…maybe behind a piece of furniture. Since it will be exposed to light and air, it will match your hanging wallpaper perfectly, if and when you need a patch.

 Make Note of It

Write down all the details of the wallpapering job—for example, the wallpaper lot number, brand and name (go ahead and attach a sample), the store where you bought it, the price you paid, the size of each roll, the number of rolls you bought vs. the number of rolls you used, and the tools and supplies you needed to do the job.

Put the information in a computer document or attach it to something—in the back of a picture or on the bottom of a lamp—in the room that was papered. And make a note of where you put the note!

Using Leftover Wallpaper

Once you've saved enough wallpaper for patches that you may or may not need, think of creative ways in which you can use the rest of the leftover roll of wallpaper. *Here are some suggestions to get you started…*

◆ Line drawers and shelves.

◆ Let the pattern dictate shapes for you to cut out and use as place mats. Spray them with acrylic and set the table.

◆ If the paper is flexible, use it to cover books.

◆ Cover the mats on framed pictures in the wallpapered room.

◆ If the pattern lends itself, cut out appropriate designs and decorate furniture—such as cabinets, table tops and chair backs—with it. This usually works well with wallpaper in a child's room.

◆ You can cover kitchen windowsills with vinyl wallpaper.

◆ Use the wallpaper for scrapbooking activities.

Cleaning Washable Wallpaper

In a mixing bowl, combine ¼ cup of liquid dish detergent and 1 cup of warm water. Use a mixer to beat the solution until you get a stiff foam. Use the foam on a sponge or cloth to wash the wallpaper. The foam will clean the wallpaper without drenching it.

 NOTE: This tip is only applicable to wallpaper that is meant to be washed.

Cleaning Wallpaper Stains

◆ For stains on washable wallpaper, make a thick paste using 1 heaping tablespoon of either cornstarch or baking soda mixed with 1 teaspoon of water. It should be the consistency of oatmeal. Wipe on the paste, and wipe off the smudge with a clean cloth.

◆ For smudges and other unidentifiable spots on nonwashable wallpaper, use a gum eraser (available at stationery and art-supply stores). Make sure the eraser is clean before you gently rub it on the wallpaper. If the paper has a grain, rub with the grain.

◆ If there is a fresh grease mark on your wallpaper, blot off as much as possible with a clean paper towel. If the stain remains, cover it with 2 layers of plain brown paper from a grocery bag, and go over it with a warm iron. When the grease is transferred to the paper, use new pieces of paper. Continue doing this until the stain is gone.

◆ Gently rub a scrunched-up piece of fresh crustless bread—white or (seedless) rye—on the greasy stain. Think of the bread as an absorbent eraser with gluten, the substance that is said to be a cleaning agent.

◆ Use a soft brush to dust cornstarch or talcum powder on the grease spot. Let it stay on for 30 minutes, then brush it off. If it's not as clean as you hoped, repeat the process.

◆ To remove crayon marks from wallpaper, use a dry, fine-grade steel wool cleansing pad—the kind with soap in it. Gently rub the scribbles until they're gone.

◆ You can also dab on a dollop of non-gel white toothpaste to remove crayon marks. Leave it for 30 minutes, then wipe it off with a dry cloth.

Easier Kitchen Cleanup
If your kitchen is wallpapered and you have areas that are at high risk for stains (like behind the stove), cover the wallpaper in those areas with clear contact paper (available at paint, craft and some hardware stores). It's easier to clean contact paper than most types of wallpaper. Just be aware that it will look slightly different.

Cleaning Other Types of Wall Coverings

◆ Dyes in burlap-textured paper may run, so you don't want to clean it by wetting it. Instead, use an appropriate vacuum-cleaner attachment to dust it on a regular basis. If there's a stain, remove it by rubbing the spot with crustless white or (seedless) rye bread.

◆ As you may already know, grasscloth-textured paper is not the most durable paper to live with (especially if you have cats who like to scratch it!). It's not a good idea to place furniture—or anything else—against a grasscloth-covered wall. The grass will soon rub off and leave unattractive marks or bald spots. Dust grasscloth with a feather duster or, if you're brave and willing to take a chance, use a soft-brush vacuum-cleaner attachment on low suction.

PAINTING (Indoors)

Before starting any indoor painting project, it's important to make sure you are prepared. First and foremost, you need to use good paint—high-quality paint means the job will look better and last longer. When you're at the paint store, talk to the salesperson—he/she should be able to tell you which paint and tools are best for your specific job. *Then you're ready to get started…*

Preparing the Painter

◆ You can spare yourself the trouble of having to scrub your face and hands to remove any drips of paint—just cover up before you paint. Apply a thin layer of moisturizer…shaving cream…hair conditioner…petroleum jelly…or cold cream to any body parts that will be exposed to paint splatter.

◆ If you intend to wear glasses while you paint, cover each lens with a layer of plastic wrap. If you don't wear glasses, you may want to put on goggles to protect your eyes, especially if you are painting a ceiling.

◆ Cover your hair with a shower cap…swim cap…plastic bag…baseball cap…or paper bag. Or drape plastic wrap around your head to protect your hair.

◆ If you insist on wearing your watch while you paint, wrap plastic wrap around the face and band.

◆ Those dirty, should-have-been-thrown-out-years-ago sneakers are perfect to wear when painting. If you already threw away that pair, then put an old, stretched-out pair of socks over your new sneakers.

   Since the socks will be slippery, especially on waxed floors, wear them only in the area where the painting is to take place. That area should have a cloth tarp or newspaper covering the floor, making it less slippery and, of course, protecting the floor from any paint splatters. Please, be careful!

◆ Even if you plan on wearing old, ratty painting clothes, you should cover them by wearing a big plastic trash bag with holes cut out for your head and arms.

   When you're finished painting, throw the trash bag away and save the *clean* old ratty clothes for another messy job.

Painting Pointers

Here are a few things that you may want to consider before you paint…it never hurts to be prepared!

◆ While the light switch plate is off, make a note on the wall of the brand and exact color paint you're using, and the amount of paint it takes to do the room, so you'll know for next time.

◆ Sand the edges of any door that you are going to paint. This will help prevent eventual paint buildup, which can make the door hard to open and close. Be sure to wipe the sanded edges with a clean tact cloth (available at paint stores) to remove any debris.

◆ If you can't remove your doorknobs, cover them with plastic wrap, plastic sandwich bags held in place with rubber bands or aluminum foil.

◆ When you're going to paint cabinets or furniture and you take off their pull-knobs, fill the screw holes with matchsticks, toothpicks or cotton swabs so that they won't fill up with paint.

◆ Coat all door and cabinet hinges with petroleum jelly. It's a good lubricant, and you can easily wipe off any paint that gets on them.

◆ Before painting the ceiling, wrap a plastic bag around the chandelier to save yourself the bother of having to clean off paint splatters.

◆ Cover the blades of ceiling fans with plastic wrap or bags to prevent them being splattered with paint.

◆ Coat the edges around window panes with a bar of soap or a bit of petroleum jelly. It's also a good idea to cover the window panes with wet newspaper pages.

 NOTE: Be sure to keep the newspaper pages or the soap or the petroleum jelly on the window panes until all the paint is completely dry.

◆ If you're not planning to paint the baseboard, use painter's tape (available at hardware and paint stores) to cover it. Once the paint is just about dry, remove the tape. When you see the paint-free baseboard, you'll be happy you used it.

Preparing the Room

◆ Remove the light switch plate—not to paint the space underneath it, but to protect it from unwanted paint.

 Waxy Tape Hint

> If you don't have any painter's tape available, then—as temporary protection when painting—rub a candle around the edges of a masking tape roll. The tape will be easier to remove, thanks to the candle wax, and it will also reduce the chance of the tape taking off old paint when it's removed.

Preparing the Tools

◆ Make sure there are no loose bristles in the brush. Run a brush comb through it a few times before you use the paintbrush.

◆ To revive an old stiff paintbrush that has hardened paint on it, heat some distilled white vinegar on the stove...once it's hot, pour it into a clean, empty coffee can. Cut an X in the can's plastic lid. Push the handle of the paintbrush through the X, then put the bristle end of the brush in the can. This will allow the brush to hang down in the hot vinegar without resting on its bristles. Let the brush soak for about 30 minutes.

To finish the job, wash the paintbrush with warm soapy water. If the brush was in a really bad way, you may need to remove the loosened paint with a wire brush. Or you may need to buy a new paintbrush.

◆ If the brush is stiff but doesn't have much paint on it, add a capful of liquid fabric softener to a coffee can of hot water. Then push the paintbrush through the lid (as explained above) and let it soak until it's flexible—check it every 30 minutes. Rinse with clean water and let dry before painting.

◆ Line the paint tray with aluminum foil—that way, when you're finished painting, you can just throw away the foil. The tray will look like new, and it will be ready to be used again and again.

 Selecting the Right Roller And the Best Brush

> According to experts at Benjamin Moore & Co. (*www.benjaminmoore.com*), you should always use an applicator that is designed for the type of paint you're using. For latex paints, use a synthetic bristle brush or a shed-resistant roller with beveled edges to help prevent *lap marks*—lines formed where the paint overlaps.
>
> Brushes that have natural bristles or high-quality Chinese bristles (known as *China bristle brushes*) and *phenolic-core* (treated cardboard) rollers are recommended for use with oil-based or alkyd paints. (Of course, most paint manufacturers have their own line of custom-blended brushes and rollers that are specifically made for use with their paints.)
>
> Once you decide on the paint you're going to use, check the label on the paint can. In most cases, it will advise you as to the best kind of brush (such as natural or synthetic) or roller (including the pile height) to use. And chances are that the same paint company also makes the type of applicator you will need.

Preparing to Paint

◆ Enamel paint spreads more smoothly when it's warm. Fill a pot with hot water and put the enamel paint can in it. Once the paint has had a chance to warm up, start using it.

◆ Always stir your paint to adequately mix its compounds (even if the can was "stirred" where you bought it). Pick up a few complimentary wooden stirrers when you buy paint, or use a special paint-mixing drill bit (available at home-improvement stores). In a pinch, a food skimmer or draining tool does the job, but plan on thoroughly washing the utensil if you plan to reuse it—or, better yet, just toss it.

◆ After you open a can of paint, but before pouring it into a tray, put tape (masking or transparent) around the entire rim of the can. When you're finished painting, take off the tape and close the can. The rim of the can will be paint-free and the lid will not get stuck the next time you need to use the can of paint.

◆ If you're using spray paint, place the spray-paint can into a pail of lukewarm water. After 3 minutes, take it out and spray away. Warming the spray will produce a finer mist and a smoother-looking finish.

◆ If a can of spray paint seems to be clogged, turn the can upside down and spray it into a plastic bag for 2 or 3 seconds. (Be sure you're in a well-ventilated area.) That should clear the nozzle, and once again you'll be ready to spray away.

 How Much Paint Do You Need?

One gallon of paint covers about 375 to 400 square feet. To find the total square footage of the room (not including the ceiling), multiply the perimeter of the room (the width of each wall, including doors that will be painted) by the floor-to-ceiling height.

For example: The room has 4 walls that are each 10 feet wide...4 x 10 = 40. If the floor-to-ceiling height is 8 feet, then 8 x 40 = 320 total square feet.

To find the number of gallons of paint needed for that room, divide the square footage by 375—in our example, that would be 320 ÷ 375 = 0.85, or less than 1 full gallon. (Be sure to account for the application of second or third coats of paint, if necessary.) To calculate the paint needed for the ceiling, multiply the length by the width of the room to get the square footage, then divide by 375.

If you don't want to fuss with the math, then take the measurements of the room(s) you want to paint and visit *www.glidden.com.* Click on "How-To," then "Paint Calculator"— the online calculator will do the math for you.

Paints That Let You Breathe Easy

A newly painted room can please the eye but offend the nose and lungs. If you want to avoid that too-familiar odor that accompanies most fresh paint jobs—or if you are decorating near infants, seniors, asthmatics or other people who have respiratory problems—consider using low VOC-emitting paints.

Volatile organic compounds (VOCs) are released by certain solvents, such as formaldehyde (used as a preservative), that are found in most commercial paints—these solvents are what causes odor. Benjamin Moore & Co. (*www.benjaminmoore.com*) was the first manufacturer to offer low VOC-emitting paints—its Eco Spec line contains no solvents, and therefore, it has virtually no residual odor. This line of paint was awarded certification from the GREENGUARD Environmental Institute (*www.greenguard.org*).

Other manufacturers also supply these paints, which are primarily used in hospitals, motels, schools and businesses that can't be easily emptied when a paint job is scheduled to take place. But low VOC-emitting paints are also recommended for residential painting, especially for those who may be sensitive to fumes. Figure on paying 10% to 20% more for this type of no-smell, fast-drying paint. It comes in the same finishes as other brands...and they are available in white and more than 1,000 custom colors.

Doesn't that thought make you breathe easier? *Ahhh...*

Painting Doors

Before installing a new door, be sure to paint all surfaces—including the bottom. This is especially important on new wooden doors that haven't already been primed or otherwise sealed.

If the door is already hung on its hinges, a toothbrush is great for painting the underside of the door.

 White Paint That Never Yellows

Many experts believe that by adding a few drops of black paint to a gallon of white paint, it will keep from yellowing. WRONG!

We talked to sources at Benjamin Moore & Co. and also at Glidden. They told us that nothing keeps oil-based white paint from yellowing. If the painted room gets lots of sunlight, the ultraviolet rays will slow down the yellowing, but eventually, the paint will turn yellow. (However, by then, it may be time for another paint job.)

Instead, use latex (water-based) white paint, which will not yellow unless there is a heavy smoker in the house.

Painting Stairs

♦ If you want to paint the steps of a staircase to which people must have access, paint every other step. The next day, when the first set of painted steps are dry, go ahead and paint the other set of every-other steps.

♦ If people in your home can't manage climbing over every-other step, then put a strip of masking tape down the middle of each step. Paint one half of each stair, allowing people to use the unpainted half to get up or down the staircase. The next day, when the first half is dry, remove the tape, then paint the other half of the steps. (Be sure to let people know which half is wet and which is dry!)

Painting Closets

Consider painting the inside of a closet with white enamel paint. With or without a light in the closet, the white enamel should help you see the closet's contents more easily.

Painting Radiators

Paint adheres better to warm (not hot) metal. If you plan on painting the radiator, do it when the radiator is warm.

Painting Baseboards

Make it easy on your knees when painting a baseboard—borrow a kid's skateboard and sit on it. Merrily you'll roll along as you paint.

 Painting a Small Object

When painting a small object, the first thing most of us do is to put down newspaper and work there. And then the object gets stuck to the newspaper. So forget newspaper! Use waxed paper instead.

If you don't have any waxed paper, then rub a candle on pieces of brown paper grocery bags, and use them when you paint objects and leave them to dry.

Easy Drip Catchers

♦ Attach a paper plate—use double-sided tape or glue—to the bottom of the paint can. All drips will stay on the plate, keeping the bottom of the paint can clean. The can will not stick to the floor, a ladder, a tarp, a table top or any other surface.

♦ Carefully cut a tennis ball in half with a sharp knife or scissors. Even more carefully, in the middle of 1 of the halves, cut a slit a little bigger than the width of the paintbrush handle. Stick the paintbrush handle through the slit and push it toward the bristles. The half-ball will catch drips from the brush when you raise your hand to paint overhead.

♦ Make a slit in the middle of a small paper plate or paper cup and push the paintbrush handle through it. It will act as a drip catcher (but you'll have to watch that the drips don't roll off the plate).

◆ To minimize paint smell, mix 1 teaspoon of peppermint extract or 1 tablespoon of vanilla extract into 1 gallon of oil-based paint. This solution will help reduce the strong, relentless smell of paint.

◆ To eliminate strong paint odors, the obvious thing to do is to open a window and air out the smell. But you may not want to open windows and run the risk of bugs and dirt coming in and messing up your newly painted walls. So keep the windows closed—instead, cut 1 or 2 big yellow onions into chunks. Put the chunks on dishes and place them around the room. They will absorb the paint smell.

By the way, don't keep the onions out for more than a day, or you'll need something to get rid of the obnoxious onion smell.

◆ Charcoal briquettes placed around the room will help absorb paint smells. So will a few plates or cookie trays filled with a layer of table salt.

 No More Wasted Paint!

If you have the most common kind of paint can, where the rim collects excess paint from your brush, carefully drill a few holes in the rim. The paint that comes off of your brush will go back into the can through the holes. When you put the lid on the can, it will cover the holes and keep the paint from drying out.

Dealing with Paint Problems

◆ If you have a *new* can of paint that has lumps in it, take it back to the store. If you have an *old* can of paint that has lumps, get a piece of screen from the hardware store—it should be about the size of the can. Put the screen on top of the paint and let it settle to the bottom of the can, taking the lumps with it.

◆ Sometimes, a can of paint that has been stored away for a while will develop a layer of "skin" on its surface. Get a large wide-mouthed jar (or a clean, empty paint can), stretch a piece of pantyhose across the mouth, and keep it in place with a rubber band.

For safety's sake, in addition to the rubber band, make sure the pantyhose stays secure by putting duct or masking tape around the can. Then carefully and slowly pour the paint from the can into the jar. You may have to pause for a few seconds to give the paint time to pass through the pantyhose. But in the process, you will be straining away the skin.

Straining paint through a screen will also work to get rid of the skin.

⭐ **Prevent Paint Skin**

Put the can of paint on a piece of waxed paper or aluminum foil, trace the can's circumference, then cut out the circle—it should be a tad smaller than your outline. Place the waxed paper or foil circle on the surface of the leftover paint, and put the lid on. The next time you're ready to use the paint, there will be no layer of skin on top...just the waxed paper or foil. Then remove it when you're ready to paint.

Saving Leftover Paint

◆ If you don't finish painting in a day, instead of cleaning the brush or the roller, just wrap it in aluminum foil, put it in a plastic bag and put it in the freezer. The next day, thaw out the brush or the roller at least 1 hour before you're ready to start painting again.

 NOTE: A wrapped paintbrush or roller can be stored in the freezer indefinitely.

◆ Put some paint in a small baby-food jar and keep it handy for minor touch-ups...the kind you can do with a cotton swab or a clean makeup sponge.

◆ With a magic marker, draw a thick line on the outside of the can that shows how much paint is left inside the can.

◆ Empty clean, plastic laundry-detergent bottles make great containers for leftover paint. They have a dripless pouring spout, a handy handle and if you close them tightly, the paint won't dry out in them.

 Paint Color Keepers!
On a 3" x 5" index card, write the paint brand, color name and the room you used it in—you may even want to paint a color swatch on it. Then attach the card to the paint can or laundry-detergent bottle, sticking it in place with transparent tape.

   While you're at it, paint an additional index card or dip half a popsicle stick in the paint. When it is dry, write the paint brand, color name and the room you used it in, so that you will have the color handy for matching and decorating purposes.

Cleaning Up After Painting

◆ Pour distilled white vinegar into a pot and heat it up (don't boil it). Then pour the hot vinegar into a pail or can, and soak your paintbrush or roller in it.

   In 10 to 15 minutes when the vinegar has cooled off, take out the brush or roller and wash it in lukewarm soapy water, then rinse it in clear water. There shouldn't be any paint left in the roller or brush, and when it is dry...it will be good to go.

 Keep Brushes Longer
You may want to rub a few drops of vegetable oil into the bristles of a clean, dry paintbrush. This will keep them soft and reuseable.

◆ If paint splattered on your tile floor, warm up some distilled white vinegar in a pot on the stove, and sponge it on the tiles. Let it sink in for 1 to 2 minutes, then wipe it off with a clean cloth.

◆ Nail-polish remover will also do away with dry paint splatters on a ceramic tile floor. Dab it on the tiles, and rub it off with a clean, dry cloth.

✎ **NOTE:** These tile tips—hot vinegar or nail-polish remover—will also work for paint that has splattered on window panes.

◆ If you want to scrape dry paint specks off your windows, use the edge of a penny or a razor scraper.

◆ For skin-so-painted with latex paint, use Avon's Skin-So-Soft lotion to remove it. For oil-based paint, gently rub your skin with baby oil, olive oil or foam shaving cream. For a stubborn paint spot, dab it with a bit of nail-polish remover.

◆ If you get paint in your hair, rub the painted strands with a little baby oil or olive oil, then comb and shampoo as usual.

PAINTING (Outdoors)

Tom Silva, a member of the home-improvement team on the television program *This Old House*, says, "A good paint job protects the outside of your house like a thin, waterproof raincoat."

Mr. Silva also believes that a good paint job should last at least 10 to 15 years, depending on the location of the house and how well it is protected from the elements—such as sun, wind and rain. He suggests you follow 2 simple rules—prepare the surface well, and buy the best paint you can afford.

Here are more suggestions to get the job done efficiently...

When to Apply the Brush

The best time of day to paint outdoor surfaces is in the early afternoon, after the morning dew has completely evaporated.

Painting a Deck

It has been reported to us that it's best to paint a deck using a broom that has nylon bristles with "flagged tips" (these are essentially split ends, which is a good thing for broom or brush bristles to have). Using the broom is easier and more efficient than using a paintbrush.

Repelling Insects

Since bugs can't read a "Wet Paint" sign, add 1 tablespoon of oil of citronella (available at health-food and some hardware stores) to each gallon of paint, and stir it well. Your paint job should be bug-free thanks to the citronella.

Prepping Metal Surfaces

To reduce the possibility that paint will peel off a metal surface, wipe the clean, to-be-painted metal with a mixture of 1 part distilled white vinegar to 5 parts plain water. Let it air-dry, and then paint.

Painting Wrought-Iron Furniture

Dab paint on wrought-iron furniture with a regular kitchen sponge. You will be able to get the job done faster.

Painting Odd-Shaped Things

If you're painting unusual configurations, like intricate stair railings or wrought-iron gates, it may be easier to use your hand than a paintbrush. Put on a long plastic or latex glove and wrap an old hand towel around your hand. Keep it in place with rubber bands. Dip your fingertips into the paint, distribute it over the rest of your palm and then massage/paint the odd-shaped whatever. ■

■ Products ■

HANDy Paint Pail

Why did it take so long to come up with something so useful for the do-it-yourself painter? This pail holds up to 1 quart of paint, and it can be secured on a belt for hands-free use.

Source: Bercom, 877-464-1170 (or in MN, 952-448-7766), *www.handypaintpail.com*.

Fantastic Furniture

When humans decided to settle in homes, giving up their nomadic lives, they began to make furniture. After all, they needed to sleep...to eat...and to kick back and relax in front of the TV.

Through the ages, people have continued making their own furniture. Recently, a man made news for furnishing his entire apartment with a bed, a corner desk, a table and chairs and a couch—all created from Federal Express boxes and packing supplies.

Chances are, you acquired your furniture through traditional means and simply want to know how to take care of it, so that you'll have it to enjoy for a long time. *Well, here's how...*

WOOD FURNITURE

We spoke with J. Michael Flanigan, owner of J.M. Flanigan Antiques in Baltimore, Maryland. He is a fine-furniture expert who specializes in classic American furniture. After college, he spent 8 years repairing, restoring and conserving antique furniture. Several of those years were spent at J.W. Berry & Son, a company that has done conservation work for almost every museum, historical society and historic home in and around Baltimore.

Mr. Flanigan is also the former administrator of the Kaufman Americana Foundation, where he oversaw the exhibition of the collection at the National Gallery of Art in Washington, DC. Since the close of the exhibit, Flanigan has been a private dealer and lecturer.

You may also know him as one of the guest appraisers on the popular PBS television program *Antiques Roadshow* (*www.pbs. org/wgbh/pages/roadshow*). He graciously agreed to share his expertise with us.

And Flanigan's advice is thrilling. It turns out that all the time we were feeling guilty about not taking care of our 10-piece dining room set, we were in fact treating it right...by not treating it at all. *We want you, too, to know what to do—or what not to do—so here is advice direct from the expert...*

Flanigan's Furniture Philosophy

What's the best way to take care of furniture? Flanigan believes in an idea that was suggested by the late Daniel Patrick Moynihan, a revered

US Senator from New York—"benign neglect." Flanigan feels that if you leave something alone, it will be fine. In other words, you will cause no harm by doing *nothing* to your furniture.

The Best Way to Protect Furniture

Give fine wood furniture a good environment. That means keeping it out of direct sunlight. Also, keep the temperature relatively constant and without humidity fluctuating quickly or radically. *That's 99% of what needs to be done...*

The Other 1%—the Finish

Furniture comes with a finish. The finish is put on to protect the wood. The worst thing you could do for finished furniture is to put oils on it too often. If you want a little more sheen, put a small amount of beeswax on a soft cloth and massage it on your furniture once or twice a year. Buff it with a clean cloth, going with the wood grain. And that's it! Just beeswax once or twice a year.

If you have modern furniture, chances are it has a modern finish, such as a catalyzed varnish that you really don't have to wax...ever. Just dust the furniture when it gets dusty.

Thank you, J. Michael Flanigan!

 Do-It-Yourself Furniture Polish
For those of you who insist on polishing your wood furniture—regardless of what Mr. Flanigan advises—here are 2 formulas from which to choose...

- Mix ⅓ cup of distilled white vinegar with 1 cup of olive oil.
- Mix 1 cup of mineral or baby oil with 3 drops of lemon extract.

  Rub the homemade polish on the furniture with a soft, lint-free cloth, and then wipe it off.

Remove Polish and Dirt

If you watch *Antiques Roadshow*, you may know that many pieces of furniture go down in value (and price) because they've been cleaned, polished and/or refinished. Therefore, consider that you have been warned, once again, to practice "benign neglect."

To remove old polish and dirt, place 2 bags of black tea (such as Pekoe) in 1 quart of water and bring it to a boil. Once the tea cools to room temperature, dampen a cloth with the solution and wipe the furniture. Then buff it dry with a soft cloth. Hopefully, you will have gotten the furniture down to its original finish and will stop there.

Remove a Water Mark/ White Ring

A water mark or white ring is caused by moisture that's trapped between the finish and the wood. To get rid of the mark, the finish needs to be opened up so that the moisture can be released.

There is no way for us to tell you what will work best on your furniture. *Assess the level of damage, decide on a course of action and then proceed cautiously with 1 of the following...*

- Mix cigarette ashes with an equal amount of mayonnaise, butter or vegetable oil. Carefully rub the mixture on the water mark. Let it set for about 1 hour, then wipe it off. If the mark or ring didn't disappear, you may need to gently sand the mark with #000 (extra fine) steel wool, and reapply the ashes and oil.

- Rub the ring with a dab of non-gel, plain white toothpaste on a damp cloth until the ring is gone. Then wipe and buff with a soft cotton cloth.

- For a major water mark, mix non-gel, plain white toothpaste with an equal amount of baking soda, then massage the mixture into the problem area. Then wipe and buff dry.

Removing Scratches

◆ On dark wood, fill in a scratch or nick with a paste made from a bit of cooled instant coffee mixed with 1 or 2 drops of water. Use a cotton swab to apply.

◆ Cover up a scratch on varnished wood by using an appropriately colored eyebrow pencil, shoe polish or crayon. You can also try rubbing a pecan, walnut, Brazil nut or peanut into the scratch.

◆ On mahogany, a little iodine will hide most scratches. Apply with a clean cloth or a cotton swab.

◆ If you have wrought-iron furniture that stays indoors, fill in scratches with black shoe polish. If the wrought-iron is subject to wet weather outdoors, rub a black crayon on the scratch and blend it in with a soft cloth.

Prevent Tabletop Scratches

Put small pieces of felt on the bottoms of lamps, vases and other decorative pieces that sit on top of furniture. It's easy to do—just attach the felt with plain white paste (school paste) or double-sided tape. Your tabletops will be better for it.

UPHOLSTERED FURNITURE

The furniture industry created a common cleanability code in 1969. The code is made up of 4 letters—W, S, W-S and X. Each letter stands for the recommended care and method of cleaning the specific fabric. The code assigned to each type of upholstery is usually found on the furniture label—check under a seat cushion or on the frame that the cushion sits on.

But here is a brief summary of each code, so that you can coordinate the code on your upholstered furniture with the cleaning suggestions that follow…

◆ **Code W**—Use water-based cleaning agents or foams only.

◆ **Code S**—Use only mild, water-free dry-cleaning solvents.

◆ **Code W-S**—This fabric may be cleaned with water-based cleaning agents and foams, as well as with mild, water-free dry-cleaning solvents.

◆ **Code X**—Do not use foam or liquid agents on this fabric. Vacuum or brush lightly to remove soil.

 CAUTION #1: Before cleaning any upholstery, test a small, inconspicuous portion of the fabric to be sure the color stays the same and doesn't run, and that the fabric doesn't shrink.

 CAUTION #2: Do not remove the cover from a foam cushion, even if it has a zipper that seems to be there for the purpose of removing the cover and throwing it in the washing machine. That would probably be a big mistake. Even if the cover doesn't shrink after being washed, it's almost impossible to get it on again properly. We know…we've tried. Also, chances are that once the covers are washed, they will not match the rest of the upholstery that wasn't washed.

Cleaning Upholstery (By Code)

Cleaner for Upholstery (Codes W and W-S)

In a big mixing bowl, combine 1 part mild laundry detergent with 4 parts water. Use a hand mixer or a whisk in the mixture and create as much foam as possible. Do one small, manageable section at a time. Brush on the foam, then wipe off the dirty foam with a spatula or an index card. The goal is to clean the fabric without drenching it. Next, blot it with paper towels.

Once you've cleaned every section of the entire piece of upholstered furniture, use a hair dryer to dry it thoroughly, or let it air dry. Be sure no one uses it before it's completely dry.

Remove Grease Stains (Codes S and W-S)

Apply a layer of dry cornmeal to the stain, and let it stay on overnight. The next day, vacuum up the cornmeal—and the stain.

Remove Musty Smells (All Codes)

If your furniture smells musty or has the lingering scent of cigarette smoke, just sprinkle baking soda or natural clay kitty litter on the upholstery. After a few hours, vacuum up the baking soda or litter, and the smell should be gone.

Pick Up Pet Hair (Codes W and W-S)

Use a damp sponge, microfiber or chamois cloth to wipe the furry upholstery clean. You can also use a strip of sticky tape to pick up the hair.

Removing Candle Wax

Put ice cubes in a plastic bag and place the bag on top of the wax. Keep it there until the wax is frozen. Then break off as much of the frozen wax as possible. If all of the wax comes off—great. If not, cut pieces of paper from a brown grocery bag (make sure the pieces are print-free). Place a piece of brown paper on top

of the remaining wax. Then press over it with a medium-hot iron. After the paper absorbs some of the wax, place a new, clean piece of brown paper on it. Keep repeating the process until the wax is gone.

Even after the wax is gone, a wax stain may remain. If that's the case and you're brave enough to try something that may bleach out the stain, get some 3% hydrogen peroxide. Dip a sponge in the peroxide and gently sponge it on the stain. After 15 minutes, blot the stain with a dry paper towel. If the stain is lighter but still there, repeat the process again and again until the stain is gone.

Cleaner for Leather Upholstery

If there's a wax buildup on your leather furniture, rub it with stale beer...or a solution made from ¼ cup of distilled white vinegar combined with ½ cup of water. Then wash the leather with saddle soap (available at tack stores where saddles and other equine supplies are sold, as well as some shoe-repair stores) and water. Complete the job by buffing the upholstery with a soft cloth to bring out the leather's shine.

Cleaning Vinyl Upholstery

Oil from the human body and hair can stiffen vinyl and cause it to crack. That being the case, you should clean vinyl arm- and headrests fairly often if they get lots of use. Wipe them with a sponge that's been moistened with distilled white vinegar, or use a damp sponge sprinkled with baking soda. Follow that with a sponge dipped in a sudsy solution of water and a couple of drops of dish detergent. Then rinse and dry the vinyl.

WICKER (CANE) FURNITURE

By definition, *wicker* is anything that is woven—reeds, rush, willow…even paper. Most wicker furniture is made from the long, tough, slender stems of rattan climbing palms. *Cane* is the skin of the rattan pole and is used for certain parts of furniture—most often for seats—and for wrapping the joints of wicker furniture.

Now that you have a better understanding of what wicker furniture is, here's how to care for it…

Preventing Yellowing

If you have new natural-colored wicker furniture, sponge it down with a solution made from ½ cup of table salt mixed in 1 quart of warm water. Let it air dry.

Fixing a Sagging Seat

To firm up a sagging cane seat, turn the chair bottom-side up and sponge the seat's underside with hot water. The seat will shrink if you let it air dry, preferably in the sun.

DUSTING

The average American home generates about 40 pounds of dust every year for every 1,500 square feet of space. In only 1 ounce of that dust, there are about 40,000 dust mites, which may be the cause of many people's allergy problems.

A lot of dust comes into the house from the bottoms of people's shoes. It's a good idea to put rubber-backed, bristly mats near every door that opens to the outside world, and to make sure everyone does the *brush-brush-clean-your-shoes* dance before entering.

Here are some other ways you can deal with dust…

Inexpensive Dust Cloths

In addition to (or instead of) buying a microfiber dust cloth, recycle old pairs of cotton socks or gloves and use them to dust. Old, cut-up cotton T-shirts and discarded shoulder pads also make good dust rags. Snagged pantyhose and used fabric-softener sheets are excellent lint-free dust collectors. And they're all washable.

Shake That Dust Mop

To clean a dust mop easily and efficiently, put the dusty mop head in a plastic or paper bag, scrunch up the neck of the bag, hold it tight and shake it vigorously.

Dusting High-Ups, Unders and Behinds

Clean those hard-to-reach places with any or all of the following…

◆ **Broomstick**—Wind tape (transparent, duct, masking or any other kind)—sticky side out—around the end of a broomstick. Or put a net pouf or scrunched-up mesh onion bag on the end of the broomstick, securing it with string or rubber bands. You can then use the broomstick to clean cobwebs out of corners easily.

◆ **Long-handled automotive snow brush**—This long, slim brush is the answer for cleaning in and around a household radiator.

◆ **Yardstick**—Put a sock on it! Or wrap an old pair of pantyhose around it. Keep the sock or hose in place on the yardstick with string or rubber bands. Then you can dust high up, under or behind everything that is otherwise out of reach.

◆ **Golf club or hockey stick**—Wrap a cloth or hand towel around the head of a golf club or the blade of a hockey stick, and secure it with string or rubber bands. Both club and stick are perfect for dusting the tops of picture frames, high shelves, the tops of doors, near ceiling wall molding and the top of bookcases.

METALS

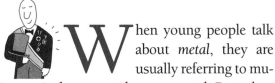

When young people talk about *metal*, they are usually referring to music—as in *heavy metal* or *rap metal*. But when we talk about *metal*, we mean the shiny *metallic* items in your home. *And if they're not shiny, here are some great ways to fix them up...*

Cleaning Metal Objects

Rule #1 for cleaning metals—*test, test, test!* Do not use any mixture or solution unless you try it first on an inconspicuous part of the metallic object. Wait a little while to see if anything unintended happens, such as discoloration, rust, tarnish or bubbling.

Also, keep in mind that cleaning some pieces may reduce their value. The appraisers on *Antiques Roadshow* have talked many times about how an item could have been worth thousands of dollars more...if only it hadn't been cleaned...if only it still had its natural patina. Don't let this happen to you!

If you have any doubt about cleaning a special *objet d'art*, seek the advice of a credentialed specialist at a museum, auction house or antiques gallery.

 Great Use for Wine Corks
Most metals will shine like the sun if you rub them with cork.

Removing Tarnish

If you have a wood-burning fireplace (or know someone who has one), collect some wood ashes in a glass jar. Add 2 tablespoons of baking soda for each cup of ashes, then shake the jar until the ashes and baking soda are fully integrated.

When you are ready to clean a tarnished metallic object, take a scoop of the mixture and add enough water to form a mildly abrasive paste. Use a damp cloth to gently rub the paste on the metal. Use a soft cloth to wipe off the paste, then rinse and dry.

 NOTE: Damp metal tarnishes quickly, so immediately after cleaning, dry the object thoroughly.

Silver

You are not the only person who appreciates the beauty and durability of silver. Silver has been mined for at least 6,000 years. It's easy to mold and shape. In fact, 1 ounce of silver can be drawn into 8,000 feet of thin...very thin...wire. For more information about this amazing ore, visit *www.silverusersassociation.org*.

Here are some ways to treat your silver as though it's worth its weight in gold...

Caring for Silver

◆ Put baking soda on a damp cloth and massage the silver with it. Then rinse and buff dry. Baking soda will remove tarnish and enhance the silver's patina.

Quick Silver Cleaner—and an Alternative

The following remedy is a popular cleaning method that cleans lots of silver pieces quickly and easily…

Line the bottom of a heatproof glass pan (Pyrex works well) with aluminum foil, shiny side up. Put the pieces of silver on top of the foil. Add 1 heaping tablespoon of baking soda, then pour in just-boiled water—enough to cover the silver items. In minutes, right before your eyes, the tarnish will disappear from the silver and end up on the foil. As soon as the silver is totally tarnish-free, rinse everything thoroughly, then buff the pieces dry with a soft cloth.

This easy and fast method magically removes the tarnish from silver—lots of pieces at once.

And although it works well, it may also remove dark accents in design crevices. That's not always a good thing. And it may also soften the cement of hollow-handled flatware. *Definitely* not a good thing. And, based on our experience, it may leave silver with a lackluster finish.

So, if you like luster…and the dark accents in design crevices…and you want to hang on to your flatware's hollow handles, then we have something that may be a better idea, especially if your silver pieces are heirlooms. *Try this…*

Rub each piece of silver with baking soda sprinkled on a moist, soft cloth. Then buff dry. It may take a little more elbow grease to clean your silver this way, but your heirlooms will be better off—and eventually, so will your heirs.

◆ Cut the hard ends off a banana peel, and purée the peel in a blender or a food processor. Then, using a soft cloth, rub the silver with the puréed peel. Wipe, rinse and buff dry with a clean soft cloth.

◆ Coat the silver with a thin layer of non-gel white toothpaste, and gently rub the object with a damp cloth. Once the tarnish is gone, wipe off all of the toothpaste, rinse and buff dry with a soft cloth.

◆ Got sour milk? Pour it in a glass pan and soak the tarnished silver pieces in it for 30 minutes. Then wash the silver with dish detergent, rinse and buff dry with a soft cloth. (Throw out the rest of the sour milk.)

⚡ **CAUTION:** Do not rub the silversmith's markings too hard. They will fade away, along with the value of the piece.

◆ Moisture causes silver to tarnish. So, whether you store or display your silver objects in

a case, a credenza or a cabinet, add things that will help to absorb moisture, such as little pieces of blackboard chalk…a handful of uncooked rice…a few charcoal briquettes…or the small silica gel packets or drums that come in vitamin bottles.

◆ Exposure to moisture and air causes silver to tarnish. If you're not displaying your silver, store it in acid-free tissue paper or in specially treated tarnish-proof bags (available at some hardware and houseware stores). You can also look for bags that are made of *Pacific cloth* (also called *silvercloth*), which is available at some hardware, houseware or fabric stores, including Hancock Fabrics (*www.hancockfabrics.com* or 877-322-7427).

◆ Never let rubber bands or any rubber come into contact with—or even come close to—silver. The sulfur in the rubber can cause tarnishing and corrosion.

- Wrapping silver in newspaper is a no-no because the paper is acidic—it will cause silver to tarnish.

- Oak is an acidic wood. It's not a good idea to store silver in oak drawers or cabinets unless you wrap the silver or line the drawers with Pacific cloth or acid-free tissue paper.

- Plastic bags are better than nothing at all, but moisture can get locked in, and it will cause tarnishing. Find another way to store your silver.

Not Just for Special Occasions!
If you have silverware, use it! The more you use it, the less it will tarnish, and the better the patina will be. If you're saving it for special occasions, make every occasion special by bringing out the good stuff.

Silverware—Dos and Don'ts

- According to the experts at Tiffany & Co., even though silver is dishwasher-proof, it's better to wash silverware by hand in hot sudsy water as soon as possible after use. Doing so will prevent food from causing tarnish stains. Rinse well in clear warm water, dry thoroughly (do not let silver air-dry) and put it away.

- Foods that contain sulfur, like eggs, and mild food acids, like those found in vinegar, mustard and salt, will make silverware tarnish and/or corrode faster than alkaline foods. That's not to say, don't eat those foods. It's just to emphasize—wash silverware as soon as possible after use.

- If you insist on putting silverware in the dishwasher, OK. Just don't put it in with stainless steel. An electrolytic action takes place when silver and stainless steel interact. The action causes pitting on the stainless pieces and leaves black spots on the silver.

Pacific Cloth/Silvercloth

Some smart cabinet and jewelry box manufacturers are now lining drawers with Pacific cloth (also known as silvercloth). If you have treasured silver, consider buying some Pacific cloth by the yard to line the drawer or wherever you keep your silver pieces. It is available at most hardware, fabric and housewares stores.

David W. Stevens, owner of Stevens Paint and Wallpaper (*www.stevenspaintandwallpaper.com*) in Baton Rouge, Louisiana, agreed to share with us his method of applying a Pacific cloth lining…

"From my experience, doing one surface at a time works best. That way, you complete the job in manageable sections.

"When you cut each piece of Pacific cloth, over-measure the cloth by an inch or so on all sides.

"Before applying the dry fabric, thin down white glue [school glue] with plain water. The glue should be thin enough to brush on but not so thin that it will soak through the fabric. Brush the glue on the surface area. Wait a few minutes until the glue is slightly tacky but not completely set.

"Keep the fabric taut—you don't want wrinkles as you lay it down—but don't over-stretch the fabric. [*You may need someone to help you, especially if you're covering a sizable area.*] Once it's down, use something with a flat surface, like a spatula, to smooth it out completely. It can be problematic to turn corners with the fabric, so you may want to carefully trim the fabric in corners with a sharp razor blade, or you can have a little ruffle.

"Now that you have the basics, and you begin to work with the Pacific cloth, the best way to cover your space will become clear."

◆ Salt should not touch silver. Salt will make silver tarnish and/or corrode within no time. Be sure your shaker has a glass lining. It's also a good idea to remove the salt after each use, even if there is a glass lining.

Caring for a Silver Coffeepot or Teapot

◆ In between uses, keep the lid off and put lumps of sugar or a charcoal briquette inside. It will prevent the pot from developing a stale smell.

◆ To clean stains from the inside of a coffeepot, use fine steel wool that has been dipped in distilled white vinegar and table salt.

◆ To clean tea stains from the inside of a teapot, fill the pot with just-boiled water and ½ cup of washing soda (available at most supermarkets). Let the solution soak overnight, then rinse the pot and wipe it dry.

Caring for Silver Candlesticks

Remove wax by pouring just-boiled water over the candlesticks to melt off the wax. A hair dryer set on *hot* will also melt the wax. But be careful. You don't want to melt your fingers in the process!

Caring for Silver Jewelry

◆ Clean your silver jewelry by placing it in 1 cup of water. Add 2 Alka-Seltzer tablets and wait for the *plop, plop, fizz, fizz*. After 5 minutes, rinse the jewelry and dry thoroughly with a soft cloth.

◆ Tarnish on the posts of silver earrings may cause an ear infection. Prevent that from

happening by painting the posts with a tiny bit of clear nail polish—unless you're allergic to nail polish.

 Go Easy on Silver Plate

Treat silver-plated things as if they were solid silver, but with even more care—the coating on silver plate can come off if it is rubbed too vigorously.

Mixed Metals

If you have household objects or furniture details that are made from a "mixed metal" (such as brass, copper, bronze or pewter—*metal alloys* that are made from more than 1 type of metal), these pieces require special cleaning and care.

Caring for Mixed-Metal Objects

You can safely use this cleaning formula on most mixed metals. But please do a test spot first…just to be sure it's safe!

Mix 1 tablespoon of plain bleached or unbleached flour with 1 tablespoon of plain table salt. To that blended mixture, add 1 tablespoon of distilled white vinegar, and stir it all into a thick paste. Dip a damp sponge or cloth into the paste and rub it on the metal piece. Then rinse thoroughly and buff dry.

 CAUTION: This formula should *not* be used on silver or silver plate. It will scratch the finish.

Cleaning Brass and Unlacquered Copper

◆ Put a few drops of Worcestershire sauce on a dry cloth and rub the tarnished object. It's said that the *ethanoic acid* in the sauce helps cut through the grime and tarnish. Once the brass or copper item is clean, rinse with warm soapy water and dry thoroughly.

◆ Make a paste by adding water to a powdered fruit juice like Tang. Rub it on with a damp cloth and wipe it off with a damp cloth. Rinse and buff it as you dry it with a soft cloth. (Rumor has it, this is what the US Navy uses to clean their brass.)

◆ Non-gel white toothpaste will act as a mild abrasive. Apply it with a damp cloth, gently rub the object, then rinse and buff dry.

◆ Dip a wedge of lemon into plain table salt, and clean the copper or brass item with it. The citric acid in the lemon helps dissolve the tarnish as the grains of salt scrub it away. Rinse thoroughly, then use a clean, soft cloth to buff it dry.

◆ Make a paste with plain table salt and distilled white vinegar to clean severely tarnished copper or brass. Be sure to rinse and buff dry.

Removing Bronze Patina

Corrosion can cause a thin greenish copper sulfate layer (*patina*) on some bronze pieces. It can be removed by making a paste with 1 tablespoon of baking soda and 1 teaspoon of lemon juice. Rub the paste on with a cloth, and keep rubbing until the green disappears. Rinse the piece thoroughly and buff dry.

You can also pour the baking soda straight onto cut lemon wedges and rub them directly on the bronze.

Cleaning Aluminum

◆ Use the juicy side of a lemon wedge to rub aluminum clean.

Aluminum or Stainless Steel? A Test

If you want to know what you are buying at a flea market—or what you already own—here's a simple test. Take a knife and carefully scrape along an edge of the item. If some of the metal flakes off, the piece is aluminum.

Cleaning Stainless Steel

◆ Gently rub any marked-up stainless steel fixtures and appliances with a used fabric-softener sheet from your laundry.

◆ Pour some club soda on a sponge to wipe stainless steel appliances clean. Be sure to dry them with a soft, clean cloth.

◆ If your stainless steel flatware is dull or streaky, pour a little baking soda on each utensil, add 1 or 2 drops of water and rub it shiny clean. Rinse and dry—you should be able to admire your upside-down reflection in a spoon.

◆ To clean a stainless steel teapot, just drop a denture-cleaning tablet into the pot, add warm water and let it stay that way for a couple of hours. Rinse thoroughly, and you're ready to make afternoon tea.

Caring for Stainless Steel Sinks

It's simple to clean a stainless steel sink. Just mix a little baking soda and water to create the mildest abrasive cleaner around. Use it to clean the sink without scratching it. Dry the sink thoroughly to prevent water spots and rust.

◆ To clean water spots from stainless steel, make a paste out of 1 part 3% hydrogen peroxide to 3 parts cream of tartar. Put it on the water spots, and when it dries, wipe it off with a wet sponge or cloth.

◆ Remove rust from your sink by rubbing the corroded areas with rubbing alcohol.

◆ Use distilled white vinegar on a damp cloth or sponge to get rid of your sink's unsightly rust and water spots. And, since the vinegar will brighten up the stainless steel, you may want to wipe the entire sink with it.

◆ When in doubt, use baking soda. Add water to baking soda to make a thick paste. Apply the paste on the stains and let it stay for 1 or 2 hours. Then, with a damp cloth, wipe off the paste and rinse the sink clean.

◆ If the hairline scratches in your sink really bother you, get rid of them by gently rubbing the entire sink with #00 (very fine) steel wool. Then buff the sink with a soft cloth.

◆ Once you're finished washing dishes, use a damp paper towel to wipe the sink. Then wipe it with a few drops of baby oil. The coating of oil will keep your stainless steel sink shiny and rust-free.

Cleaning Chrome

Just as there are different qualities of chrome, there are several chrome cleaners. Here's a selection, but it's up to you to test and determine which of them will get the job done.

◆ Use rubbing alcohol on a soft cloth or paper towel. If you don't have alcohol, you can use vodka to clean chrome.

◆ Baking soda on a damp cloth will get chrome clean. Wipe it on, then wipe it off with a damp paper towel.

◆ Rub a hard-to-get-off smudge with the shiny side of a scrunched-up piece of aluminum foil. After using foil on chrome, wipe the chrome with a damp paper towel—you'll actually see the dirt on the towel.

When you scrunch up the foil, make sure there are no sharp points sticking out that might scratch the chrome.

◆ In some Chinese restaurants, the waiters pour leftover tea on the table to clean it. They know that strong black tea at room temperature is a good cleaner. You can use it on chrome to cut grease and add shine.

◆ Rub a damp and crunched-up piece of plain newspaper on chrome-trimmed glass fixtures or furniture, and clean the glass as well with the wet page. Both the chrome and the glass will be clean and lint-free.

◆ Remove rust stains from chrome by rubbing them with distilled white vinegar on a soft cloth.

Cleaning Pewter

◆ Use mild soapy warm water to wash off surface dirt. Rinse thoroughly to be sure there's no soap film left on the pewter.

◆ Use a large, outer leaf of a cabbage as you would use a cloth to rub the pewter clean. Then buff the pewter with a soft cloth.

◆ Boil eggs and keep the water. Once the water cools down, let the pewter sit in it for about 10 minutes. Rinse and buff dry.

◆ If a pewter object is badly tarnished, use #0000 (super fine) steel wool dipped in olive oil and cautiously scrub off the tarnish. Then wash, rinse and buff dry with a soft cloth.

◆ Pewter items will take a lot longer to tarnish if they are kept in a glass enclosure and in a warmish place.

◆ Put baking soda on the stain. Then, with a cloth that's been moistened with vegetable or olive oil, gently rub the stain away.

◆ Remove wax by placing the candlesticks in the freezer long enough for the wax to freeze. Then flick it off.

 CAUTION: Pewter has a low melting point. Do not EVER put pewter objects in an automatic dishwasher.

IVORY & BONE

 How many animals can you name that are the source of ivory? Think about it for a minute…of course, you probably said elephant and maybe walrus. What about the elk, hippo and boar as well as sperm and killer whales? Ivory pieces are carved from the tusks and/or teeth of all those animals.

Now that you know where ivory comes from, here's how to take care of it…

Piano and Organ Keyboards

It's best not to keep the fallboard (the cover) over the keyboard. Let the piano or organ keys be exposed to air and light. The light helps prevent the keys from yellowing, and the air helps prevent warping.

Cleaning an Ivory Keyboard

Using a soft cloth, apply small amounts (you don't want any of it getting between the keys) of 1 of the following ingredients…

◆ Yogurt
◆ Milk
◆ Paste of baking soda and water
◆ Rubbing alcohol
◆ Non-gel white toothpaste
◆ 2 parts table salt to 1 part lemon juice

Carefully rub each key until it's clean, then wipe each with a clean, damp cloth.

If the keys are very yellow, mix equal parts of hydrogen peroxide and water. Use a damp sponge to apply the mixture. Give it some time to bleach the keys…about 10 minutes. Then wipe the keys with a damp cloth.

MARBLE

 When limestone is exposed to the extremes of pressure or temperature, it undergoes a process known as *metamorphism*, and the limestone becomes crystal by nature, transforming into *calcite* or *dolomite*—the main materials in marble.

All you really need to know is that marble is considered to be an extremely sophisticated stone—used in art, architecture and for making home furnishings more beautiful. *That said, we're sure you want to know how to take care of it…*

Caring for Marble

Since marble is a porous stone and is at risk for holding stains, you may want to consider sealing it with a stone sealer (available at most paint and some hardware stores). If you do not have stone-sealer protection on your marble surface and you get a stain, it's important to tend to it as soon as possible. *You can try 1 of the following remedies…*

 NOTE: Be sure to test a small, inconspicuous spot first to make sure the cleaning solution won't damage the stone.

◆ For stains caused by beverages—such as coffee, tea or wine—mix 1 part 3% hydrogen peroxide to 4 parts water. Dip a cloth in the solution and rub the stain, then wipe it quickly. If the stain doesn't go away, repeat the process.

◆ Make a paste by combining baking soda and equal amounts of water and lemon juice. Dip a cloth in the paste and rub the stain with it. Then rinse and dry.

◆ For non-beverage stains, spill table salt on them. After 1 or 2 minutes, brush off the salt and then spill some more. If the salt doesn't soak up the stain after 3 or 4 tries, then pour sour milk on top of the salt. The milk will keep the salt damp. Leave it that way for 2 or 3 days. Then use a damp cloth to wipe up the milky salt. Hopefully, there will be no trace of a stain.

 FYI: Slate Solution

You can also clean slate with the baking soda, water and lemon juice mixture. Dip a cloth in the paste and rub the slate with it. Then rinse with water and dry.

MIRRORS

 Everyone has heard that old superstition about breaking a mirror and the 7 years of bad luck that supposedly follow. *If you buy into that, then you'll be happy to know that there are 3 ways to counteract that curse…*

◆ As soon as you realize that you broke a mirror, turn around 3 times counterclockwise. (Be careful not to step on the broken pieces of mirror. Now *that's* bad luck.)

◆ When it's dark out, light 7 white candles. At midnight, take a deep breath and blow them all out at once.

◆ Take a piece of the broken mirror to a cemetery and tap a gravestone with it.

Any of the above counter-curses should do it—or, rather, undo it.

Chances are you won't break a mirror, but you will need to clean the mirrors in your home. *Here are some suggestions that will help…*

Cleaning a Mirror

◆ Mix equal parts of distilled white vinegar and water in a bowl. Scrunch up a piece of (non-colored) newspaper, and dip it in the mixture. Wring it out, then wipe the mirror with it. Wipe the mirror dry with a soft cloth, soft paper towel or dry newspaper page. (Be sure to wear rubber gloves to keep the newspaper print off your hands.)

> ⚡ **CAUTION:** Do not spray water or liquid of any kind on a mirror. When moisture seeps into the edges and back of the mirror, the silvering gets spoiled…which causes dark spots.

◆ Wipe the mirror with a used, wet bag of black tea, then dry it with a paper towel or newspaper. The tea's tannic acid will leave the mirror sparkling clean.

◆ To get a lint-free shine, go over the mirror with a used sheet of fabric softener…or a dry coffee filter…or a pair of old pantyhose…or gift-wrapping tissue.

Creating Fog-Free Mirrors

◆ Apply a thin layer of glycerin (available at most drug stores) to the mirror to prevent it from fogging up in the shower.

◆ Before you shower, spray a dollop of foam shaving cream on a cloth and wipe the mirror with it.

◆ For longer-term defogging—2 to 3 weeks at a time—put a generous amount of foam shaving cream on the entire mirror and leave it there until the foam just about evaporates. Then wipe it off.

Removing Hairspray

Give your mirror the once-over with a cloth dampened with rubbing alcohol. Doing this will take off hairspray as well as any thin film that's left over from a cleaning agent, an aerosol product or from shaving cream.

Alcohol will evaporate on its own, which saves you the job of wiping it dry.

✳ Mirror Touch-Ups
- ◆ Most mirrors consist of 3 layers—a dark, protective bottom layer...a layer of metal (aluminum, silver or tin)...and a plain, glass top layer. If there are scratches in the metallic layer, and you can get to it, tape a piece of non-creased aluminum foil to the back of the metallic layer to hide the scratches.
- ◆ Put 1 or 2 coats of metallic silver auto paint on the scratched silver backing. Then seal the spot with clear shellac.

FISH TANKS

Keeping fish in an aquarium can be a wonderful, relaxing hobby. Fish tanks also make great conversation pieces! And it may surprise you to know that they don't take as much work to maintain as you might think. Actually, the bigger the fish tank, the easier it is to maintain. You won't have to change the water as often because the waste from the fish will stay stable longer.

When you buy a fish tank, look for the safety sticker on the glass (or ask someone at the fish and aquarium store). The sticker means that the tank has been tested for safety and has been caulked with a special silicon that will last for many years.

DID YOU KNOW?

The dirty water from a fish tank makes a wonderful organic fertilizer for houseplants.

Also—does your aquarium have a cover? A cover is a good thing. It helps prevent water from evaporating, and keeps your fish from leaping out.

Once you're squared away with a safe, covered tank, here's how to clean it...

Cleaning a Fish Tank

Put your fish in a temporary holding tank...put the tank's furnishings in a plastic shoebox...fertilize your plants (see above)...and you're ready to clean the tank. Soap or detergents of any kind may leave a residue that could be harmful to your fish, so get out the table salt instead.

Pour table salt on a sponge and pretend it's scouring powder. Once the tank is scrubbed clean, rinse it thoroughly and you're ready to set up the tank and move your fish back home. ■

■ Products ■

MAAS Polishing Crème for All Metals
Magic in a tube. We tested this crème on many household objects and had the most startling results with our grandmother's candlesticks. The silver was restored to what must have been its original beautiful patina, and it astounded us. The cleaning took some elbow grease (along with the polish) to remove the years of residue, but the outcome was worth it.

This crème restores and polishes just about all nonporous surfaces—all metals, fiberglass, Plexiglas, mirrors, crystal, ceramics, tile, porcelain, enamel, marble, linoleum, plastics, solid vinyl, polyurethane...and more. The results are long-lasting, too. Also available in a liquid.

Source: MAAS International, Inc., 630-654-4743, *www.maasinc.com.*

CHAPTER 3

Loads of Laundry Care

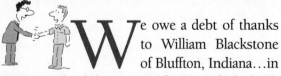

Today's average family generates approximately 50 pounds of laundry every week. If you are the person who gets stuck doing the wash, and there are kids around, get them to help you. Turn sorting, folding and putting away into a race. Time them and keep track of their performances. Encourage them to beat their own records. If you don't have children, you won't have nearly as much laundry, but it's still not always a fun job.

In any case, we hope the following solutions will help make cleaning your clothes easier, faster and more efficient.

WASHING MACHINES

We owe a debt of thanks to William Blackstone of Bluffton, Indiana…in 1874, as a birthday present for his wife, he built a machine that removed and washed dirt from clothes. That was the first washing machine designed for home use.

In 1908, the first electric-powered washing machine was introduced by the Hurley Machine Company of Chicago, Illinois.

And it just got better and better from that point. We've certainly come a long way from pounding clothes with a rock by a stream.

If you're in the market for a new washing machine, you may be interested to know that front-loading machines use 40% to 60% less water…30% to 50% less energy…and 50% to 70% less detergent than top-loading models.

If you're keeping the washing machine you have, here are some tips for making your machine perform at its peak.

> **FYI: Heavier Than It Looks!**
> A normal-sized load of wash is approximately 6 pounds of dry laundry. Who says doing chores isn't exercise?

Maintaining a Washer

Built-up detergent residue may be preventing your washing machine from doing its best. At the start of each month, clean out that residue by letting your machine run without laundry, but with a cup of distilled white vinegar.

Prevent Residue Buildup

Vinegar is not strong enough to harm fabric, but is strong enough to dissolve the alkalies in soaps and detergents. Get rid of detergent residue with each load you wash by adding 1 cup of distilled white vinegar at the start of the washing machine's final rinse cycle.

 CAUTION: If you use chlorine bleach in your wash, do not add distilled white vinegar. The combination will produce vapors that are extremely dangerous.

LAUNDRY SORTING & PREPPING

Doing a little bit of preparation *before* starting a load of wash will save you lots of work afterward. *Here's what to do…*

Sort Socks in the Hamper

Collect the plastic caps from gallon-sized jugs of spring or distilled water or from milk containers. Carefully cut an "X" in the middle of each cap. Place these cut caps wherever sock-wearers tend to take off their socks—in the bathroom, bedroom, den, etc.

Each time a pair of socks is taken off, the wearer should push a small part of the 2 socks through the cut in the cap, which can then be tossed in the hamper.

Just think of the results…each pair of socks will stay together through both the washer and dryer cycles—no sorting necessary, and no more missing socks.

Know Your Colors

There are 3 color categories—whites, pastels and darks. You may be someone who insists on separating clothes according to color. As long

as we know that a colorfast garment won't run (*see* "Test the Colorfast Claim" on page 40), then we're lenient when it comes to mixing light and bright colors.

DID YOU KNOW?

Soils can travel from one garment to another in the washing machine. That being the case, you should always separate heavily soiled clothes from not-so-soiled clothes.

Delicates vs. Indelicates

It's always a good idea to separate delicate fabrics from heavier garments that would not get as clean with the gentle cycle.

Lint Producers

Fabrics like terry cloth and chenille produce lint. It's wise to put linty robes, towels, blankets and spreads in a separate load.

But if you insist on throwing these items in with the rest of your wash, add 1 cup of distilled white vinegar in place of fabric softener. The vinegar will help prevent the lint from attaching to other clothes in the machine. (You also might want to invest in a lint roller to clean your clothes.)

Sorting Things Out

- Zip all zippers closed. Hook all hooks. That will prevent zippers and hooks from snagging or attaching to other items in the wash.
- Remove all items from pockets, particularly tissues. You don't want tiny bits of tissue all over every item in your wash.
- Button the cuffs of a blouse or shirt to the front of the garment. It will keep it from tangling in the washing machine.
- To machine-wash your delicates, put them in a pillowcase, tie it closed and then toss it in the machine.
- If you turn clothes inside out, it can help reduce wear-and-tear on them. Knits, permanent-press and quilted fabrics may have less fading and pilling, and corduroy won't pill, gather lint or flatten out.
- If you don't turn pants inside out, then at least pull the pants' pockets inside out. They will dry much faster that way.
- If you're washing a garment that has a drawstring waistband, make a knot or sew a bead or button at both ends of the drawstrings to prevent them from disappearing into the waistband during the washing process.
- If you have a drawstring that needs restringing, tape one end to a chopstick—or attach an end to a long safety pin—and patiently push the string through. Be sure you have a knot, bead or button at the other end.

Going to the Laundromat

Lighten your trip to the laundromat by putting each wash load in a pillowcase, along with 1 cup of powdered detergent, instead of lugging a big box or bottle with you. Empty the pillowcase plus detergent into the washer, and you're ready to go.

Disinfect a Laundromat Machine

If you are troubled by the thought of who used a public washing machine before you, you can disinfect the machine and your clothes by adding ½ cup of mouthwash to the wash cycle.

Colorfast Garments

If clothing is labeled as "colorfast," it means that the colors should not run or fade from washing or wearing them.

There has been an occasional instance when we didn't realize that a garment was NOT colorfast, and we threw it into the washing machine with other clothes. When that happens, you have to be flexible. If a red shirt turns your white towels pink, consider changing the décor of your bathroom. Better yet, follow the advice here and you won't have a problem with non-colorfast clothes.

Test the Colorfast Claim

If the care label says "colorfast," chances are the colors will not run. But if the label doesn't address this (or it says "do not use detergent" or "wash only in cold water"), you can test a garment's colorfast-ability before throwing it in with other clothes.

Test: Take a clean, white, wet washcloth, and rub an inside seam of the colored item with it. If the white cloth becomes stained, the garment is not colorfast. Which means that if you throw it in with light-colored clothes, everything will come out the color of that garment.

The good news is, once you've discovered that a garment is not colorfast, you can then lock the color so that it won't run or fade. *To do this, keep reading…*

Make a Garment Colorfast

Fill a basin with 1 gallon of water and 1 teaspoon of Epsom salt (available at drugstores). Soak the non-colorfast garment in the basin overnight. The next day, wring out the garment, then thoroughly rinse it with a mixture of ¼ cup of distilled white vinegar mixed with 1 gallon of water. Let the garment dry.

Next, do the colorfast test again, rubbing the wet, white washcloth on an inside seam. When none of the color comes off, you can then consider the garment colorfast.

HARD WATER

ard water is water that contains salts—such as calcium and magnesium—that limit the formation of lather with soap. If you have hard water, there may be an easy solution.

Does This Apply to You?

If your clothes don't seem to be getting clean, it may mean that you have hard water.

Test: Add ½ teaspoon of detergent to a 1-quart jar filled with warm water. Close the jar and shake it vigorously. If it doesn't get real sudsy—or if the suds that are there just disappear quickly—then, we hate to be the people who tell you, but you've got hard water.

Hard-Water Remedy

Did you think we were just going to leave it at that? *Of course not…*

Clean out a few empty, plastic detergent jugs…big enough to hold more than ½ gallon of water. In each jug, combine 4 ounces of washing soda (a natural detergent booster and freshener, available at supermarkets) with 2 ounces of borax powder (a chemical compound used as a cleansing agent and water softener, available at supermarkets and drugstores) and ½ gallon of warm water. The water must be *warm* for the washing soda and borax powder to completely dissolve.

CAUTION: The solution that's in the jugs should be labeled clearly and kept with your other clothes-washing supplies—out of reach of children and pets.

To soften the water, add 1 cup of the solution to the wash water, along with your regular laundry detergent—every time you do a wash. This *solution* is the solution!

DETERGENT

owder…liquid…with bleach …for whites…for colors… for black clothes…with fabric softener…allergen-free—decisions, decisions, decisions. We may not help you decide exactly which product to use, but we will give you some hints for getting your clothes their cleanest.

Use the Right Stuff

For best results, adhere to the manufacturer's recommendation for the proper amount of detergent to use—based on the size of the wash load. Remember, when it comes to detergent… more is *not* better.

Avoid Overload

Oops! Did you spill in too much laundry detergent? Quick—add 2 tablespoons of distilled white vinegar…or a capful of fabric softener…or 3 tablespoons of table salt to the water. Any of these additives will deactivate the extra suds.

Get a Brightness Boost

In addition to your regular detergent, pour ½ cup of baking soda into the load. Clothes should come out smelling fresh and looking cleaner, since the baking soda helps get rid of soap residue.

Keep Children's Clothes Flame-Retardant

Children's clothing is required by law to be flame retardant. But be sure to use a phosphate detergent to launder children's clothing. The label should clearly state that the product contains phosphates. If you use a detergent with a label that says, "contains no phosphates," the fabric may lose its ability to be fire-resistant.

If you use a non-phosphate detergent, boost the flame-retardant property of the fabric by adding 1 cup of white vinegar to the cold rinse water. Let the clothes soak in it for 30 minutes before continuing as usual with the spin cycle.

Detergent Extender

If you must do a wash, but you don't have enough detergent, add ¼ cup of baking soda to make up the difference. You may be so pleased with the results, you'll start doing every wash this way!

Detergent Substitute

In an emergency, when you *must* do a wash and you don't have any laundry detergent (or baking soda), use shampoo...that is, if you have shampoo. About ⅓ cup will do a full load.

 NOTE: In case you were wondering, dishwashing liquid is NOT a good idea as a laundry-detergent substitute.

The amount of liquid that is needed to launder clothes clean would create enough suds to float the Titanic.

Bleach Substitute

Instead of using harsh bleach, try one of these safer, gentler—and more effective—alternatives. Use ½ cup of lemon juice...or 1 cup of distilled white vinegar...or 6 ounces of hydrogen

peroxide (make sure the label says 3% hydrogen peroxide) in your wash.

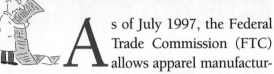

WASHING INSTRUCTIONS

As of July 1997, the Federal Trade Commission (FTC) allows apparel manufacturers to use symbols instead of written washing instructions on the care labels of garments. So the American Society for Testing and Materials (ASTM) developed a simple system...for details, visit the Web site of the Soap and Detergent Association, which publishes "Fabric Language Made Easy," a listing of the symbols and their meanings. The page is at *http://cleaning101.com/laundry/fabricsymbols.html*.

And see the following for more helpful washing instructions...

Dry-Clean Only...or Not

In our experience, many clothes that are labeled "Dry-Clean Only" can actually be washed at home. If you're willing to take a chance with your silk nightgown, chiffon wraparound, cashmere vest, angora scarf or lace bustier, put a few drops of clear dishwashing liquid into a basin of cold water and add the garment.

Swish around the water so that the detergent can do its job. Then gently rinse the suds out, shake off the excess water and let the garment dry flat on a sweater-drying rack or on a clean white towel.

Permanent-Press Clothes

If your permanent-press clothes need an energy boost, pour in 1 cup of powdered milk during the rinse cycle. This should give the clothes more body and help bring them back to their original shape.

 NOTE: Rinsing with powdered milk helps to remove chemicals, so it can be helpful to people who have allergies. Double-rinsing is recommended.

Silk and Other Fine Washables

◆ You can wash washable silk with shampoo. But make sure its first ingredient is water, *not* oil. Silk is a delicate fabric that must be treated gently. Don't wring it out. Instead, let it drip-dry, and keep it out of direct sunlight.

◆ To clean your other fine washables, add 1 tablespoon of hair conditioner to a sink or basin full of water. After 10 minutes of soaking, gently rinse the garment and drip-dry.

Think about it…the amino acids in hair conditioner make hair clean and soft, so they should make your delicate garments clean and soft as well.

Wool

Some interesting wool facts…

◆ Sheep are sheared (shaved) once a year for their soft woolen fleece.

◆ One pound of wool can be spun into 20 miles of yarn.

◆ A woolen sock was found buried on the banks of a river in England. The sock was perfectly preserved and estimated to be about 1,000 years old.

Here are ways to take care of your woolens so that they'll last—well, maybe not 1,000 years, but for as long as you enjoy wearing them.

Resize Snug Sweaters

Shampoo and hair conditioner soften and loosen knit fibers, which allows them to return to their original size. If your wool sweaters have become too snug, shampoo can help bring them back to their original size.

Put a couple of capfuls of shampoo—or ⅓ cup of hair conditioner—in a sinkful of warm water. Add your tight sweater, and let it soak for about 10 minutes. Then lay it flat on a towel. While it's still wet, reshape it by holding each side and pulling the sweater, making it larger. Pull it even in this way—both sides at the same time—all around the sweater.

Shrink Stretched Sweaters

Don't you hate it when a turtleneck looks more like a hippo neck? When this happens, it's easy to shrink a sweater's stretched-out neck, cuffs and waist back into shape.

Dunk the sweater in a sink filled with hot water. Shake off as much water as possible, then blot the sweater with a clean, dry towel. Once the sweater is no longer dripping wet, dry the stretched-out part(s) with a blow-dryer set on *hot*.

 CAUTION: Do *not* touch a wet sweater with a plugged-in dryer.

Remove and Prevent Pilling

◆ Turn the garment inside out when washing. Although there's no guarantee, doing this will go a long way in helping to prevent *pilling*—the formation of those unattractive balls of fabric on the surface, which is caused by abrasion from wear and washing.

◆ Put wool clothes in a pillowcase, tie the case closed with ribbon or string, and then wash.

◆ A wig brush—the kind with the little plastic balls at the end of the bristles—helps to depill wool clothes. Brush gently while constantly changing directions.

Soften Your Sweater

If a sweater is stiff or rough, wash it with your usual detergent plus 1 teaspoon of olive oil to soften the wool. Add the oil *after* the washer has filled with water.

Prevent Itchiness

If you are super-sensitive to wool, add 1 or 2 tablespoons of glycerine (available at drugstores) to a warm-water wash. Doing this should make the garment become less scratchy on your sensitive skin.

Avoid Moth Holes

If you suspect that moths have invaded your wool clothes, you can kill the eggs—just place the garment in a plastic bag, seal it closed and put it in the freezer for 24 hours. Then launder as usual.

Drying Sweaters

See "Speedy Sweater Drying" on page 48.

Whites

Whiter than white. That's what some laundry products—or their advertising agencies—promise. We don't know what it means, and we certainly aren't going to promise it, but we can tell you that the following ideas should work wonders to lighten and brighten your whites.

Hung Out to Dry

This suggestion may not be practical for most apartment dwellers, but for house owners—get out the clothesline. Hang your white clothing and linens outdoors to dry, and take advantage of the sun's bleaching power.

Cold Weather Clothesline

◆ To prevent wet clothes from freezing when hung outside to dry, pour ¼ cup of table salt into the last rinse cycle. (The salt will also help brighten your wash.)

◆ To prevent clothes from freezing onto the clothesline, sponge the clothesline with distilled white vinegar before you hang out the clothes to dry.

Lemony Fresh

In a basin of just-boiled water, add the juice of a small lemon. Let your white clothes soak for at least 30 minutes, then launder them as usual. For super-grungy sweat socks or other very soiled whites, let the clothes soak overnight before laundering.

An Aspirin a Day...

Dissolve 5 adult aspirin tablets (325 milligrams each) in a basin of hot water, and soak your white clothes in it. When you're ready to do the wash, pour the contents of the basin in the washing machine—the clothes along with the aspirin-water. The aspirin helps to remove perspiration stains.

Bright-White Maintenance

Add 1 cup of distilled white vinegar during the washer's rinse cycle to wash away soap residue, which is often the yellow-causing culprit.

Get Out the Yellow

Wash your clothes as usual until the last rinse cycle. Then dissolve 1 tablespoon of borax powder (available at supermarkets and drugstores) in 16 ounces of hot water, pour it in the machine and continue laundering as usual. This will remove any yellow dinginess in your clothes.

Boost for Whites

Fill a basin or sink with warm water and add ¼ cup of powdered, automatic dishwasher detergent. Add your socks, underwear or whatever else needs whitening. Swish them around, and let the garments soak for 1 hour.

Wring out the sopping clothes—enough to get them to the washing machine without making a mess—and then launder as usual.

Colors

People wear colored clothes for many reasons —because the colors enhance their skin tone and make them look good…cheery colors make them happier…or maybe the clothes don't show dirt as much. Whatever the reason, even if the dirt doesn't show, colored clothes need to be cleaned. *These hints will help…*

Set Bright Terry Cloth

The first time you wash those new towels, or that flashy bathrobe, pour in 1 cup of table salt along with your detergent, and it will set the color.

Perk Up Deep Colors

When colored fabrics start to fade, add 1 cup of table salt to the wash to help restore the color's original vibrancy.

Get Black Clothes Blacker

When doing an all-black wash, add 2 cups of strong, brewed black tea or coffee into the washer during the rinse cycle.

Jeans

Only a teenager, an immigrant tailor named Levi Strauss designed a pair of coveralls out of canvas. His target market for these coveralls was the miners in San Francisco during the 1850s. Those men were tired of their trousers wearing out and welcomed the change of clothes.

Some 10 years later, Strauss switched from canvas to a softer fabric—denim. To help decrease the appearance of soil stains, he dyed the denim dark blue. And, as they say, the rest is history.

Levis, dungarees or jeans…no matter what you call them, here's how to care for them.

Soften the Fabric

Soften jeans by tossing them in the washing machine with your usual detergent plus ½ cup of table or rock salt. You may need to double-rinse them.

Prevent Fading

Although the current trend is the more faded, the better, there are still some people who like a fresh, strong denim look. *Here's how to keep that look…*

Before you wash them for the first time, soak the jeans for 1 hour in a mixture of 2 tablespoons of table or rock salt and 1 gallon of cold water, or ½ cup of distilled white vinegar in 2 quarts of cold water.

After the soak, turn the jeans inside out and run them through the washing machine as usual, using a cold-water setting.

> **NOTE:** To prevent streaking and fading, always wash your jeans turned inside out.

Other Fabrics

Sheets and baby items—such as diapers, blankets and changing-table pads—all require special treatment because they come into contact with your delicate skin. *Here are some ways to make these items more comfortable and cleaner...*

Get Sweet-Smelling Sheets

To enjoy a special sensory treat at bedtime, add a small amount of your favorite bath salts during the rinse cycle when you launder your sheets.

Cleaner Baby Diapers

If you're using cloth diapers and the baby keeps getting diaper rash, separate the diapers from the rest of the laundry, and add 1 cup of distilled white vinegar during the rinse cycle.

In general, when washing any items the baby has soiled, it's smart to add 1 cup of distilled white vinegar during the rinse cycle. Vinegar is great at breaking down uric acid and puts the laundry's pH in balance. Your baby's clothes, sheets and blankies will all come out clean, soft and smelling good.

 It's Easy to Change

Use a pillowcase for a baby's changing-table pad cover—it's easy to put on and take off. When it gets dirty, you can easily throw it in the washing machine.

Plastics

Since 1976, plastic has been the most used material in the modern world. Plastics is a major industry, and plastic can be found in all or part of many products that are used in our daily lives...for example, clothing, televisions, cars, computers, packaging and even body-part replacements.

Here's how to care for the plastic products (excluding the body-part replacements) that we have come to depend on...

Tablecloths, Mats, Curtains

If a plastic item is machine-washable, add a couple of bath towels to the wash with it. The towels will help buff and scrub the plastic clean.

When drying plastic, put the towels in the dryer with it, and let the dryer run for only a few minutes so that the plastic item doesn't melt. It should come out practically wrinkle-free.

Floor or Bath Mats (Rubber and Vinyl)

Toss the mat in the washing machine along with a couple of bath towels. The towels will help scrub the rubber or vinyl mat.

Do not put rubber or vinyl in the dryer. Use another towel to wipe the mat dry or hang it on a clothesline.

Curtains (Dacron and Nylon)

After you launder as usual, soak the curtains—1 panel at a time—in a basin or sink filled with at least 1 cup of Epsom salt (available at drugstores) and 1 gallon of water (the ratio should be 1:1 for each gallon of water needed). Let each panel soak for about 5 minutes, and then hang them up. They should dry wrinkle-free.

 NOTE: Be sure to put something on the floor underneath the wet curtains—such as a towel on top of a plastic shopping bag—in order to catch the dripping water.

DRYERS & DRYING

If you're still using an old clothes dryer, you may want to consider replacing it with a new model. Newer dryers have better insulation and use much less energy.

The newest clothes dryers on the market do not have the yellow Energy Guide label that helps you compare similar models, nor do they have the ENERGY STAR label (provided by the US Department of Energy and the Environmental Protection Agency)—this is simply because there's now very little difference in energy use from model to model.

Regardless of the age of your dryer, here are some ideas for how to make it perform at its very best...

 Cut Down on Drying Time

◆ The more crowded the dryer, the more wrinkled the clothes—and the longer it takes them to dry. Consider dividing a big wash load into two drying cycles.

◆ Cut drying time considerably by tossing in a dry hand towel with each dryer load. The dry towel will keep absorbing water from the wash, then dry quickly and continue to absorb more water.

Lint Catcher

Cut an old pair of pantyhose in half, and tie 1 side in a few knots. Then toss it in the dryer to collect lint.

Wash-and-Wear

Do your so-called "wash-and-wear" clothes need ironing? If they do—and you don't feel like getting out the iron and setting up the board—just throw the garments in the dryer

with a damp towel, and let it run for about 10 minutes. Make that—wash-*and-dry*-and-wear!

Safer Dryers

A friend of ours, artist Bon Gordon, drew our attention to the fact that dryer sheets create a film over the dryer's lint-screen mesh. This film can cause the heating unit to burn out or—even worse than that—catch fire. You can't see the film, but it's there.

The dryer repairman told Bon the best way to keep a dryer working well for a long time—and to lower your electric bill—is to wash the lint filter with hot soapy water and an old toothbrush at least every 6 months.

Test your lint screen by running water over it. If the water runs through, then it's as clean as it needs to be. But if the water collects on it, prepare some hot soapy water and get a toothbrush...and then get busy cleaning the filter.

Drying Delicates

Give your hand-washed scanty undies a drying head-start by swirling them around in a salad spinner (you might want to designate a spinner just for this purpose). Once the excess moisture is removed, they'll dry a lot quicker when you hang them up.

Drying Wet Sweaters

If you don't use a drying rack for your wet sweaters, then consider the ol' pantyhose trick to avoid shoulder *pupkees*. (That's our family's word for those stretched-out, epaulet-type of shoulder bumps that result from hanging wet—and sometimes dry—sweaters on hangers.)

Take a pair of clean pantyhose and thread the legs through each arm of the sweater—1 leg in 1 arm, and the other leg in the other arm.

Bring the waist of the pantyhose up through the sweater's neck.

If you use a clothesline, attach clothespins to the waist and each of the 2 feet. If you want to use a hanger or a hook, tie the 2 pantyhose feet together, forming a loop, and then put it on the hanger or hook. This method puts no stress on the shoulders.

Speedy Sweater Drying

After you hang up your sweater to dry—or before you spread it out to dry—cut a brown paper bag down the seams, crinkle it and stuff it into the sweater. The paper stuffing will speed up the drying process.

Revive Stored Woolens

When you take sweaters and other wool clothing out of storage, throw them in the dryer with a couple of fabric-softener sheets. Dry on low heat for 30 minutes. The sheets absorb odors and the dryer action fluffs up fibers. The wool items will come out looking and smelling good.

Try to Be Static-Free

Crinkle up a piece of aluminum foil, and toss it in the dryer with your clothes. It will help eliminate static cling.

 CAUTION: Do not include sheer fabrics, silks or delicates that can get snagged on the aluminum foil.

Down-Filled Drying

◆ After washing a down-filled item—such as a coat or comforter—put it in the dryer along with 3 or 4 tennis balls. The balls will do a good job of fluffing up the down item. (They will also do a good job of waking up anyone who is taking a nap.)

◆ You can also put new life into an old, flattened-out feather or down pillow by letting it toss and turn for 10 minutes in a warm dryer with 3 or 4 tennis balls and a fabric-softener dryer sheet.

Unwrinkle Your Sheets

When you take a bedsheet out of the washing machine, shake it out a bit, then fold it before you put it in the dryer. The folded sheet will dry faster and come out less wrinkled.

Slipcovers

◆ After you've washed a slipcover and tossed it in the dryer, do not wait for it to finish the drying cycle. Instead, remove the slipcover while it's slightly damp. Put it back on the furniture, and let the material finish drying as it conforms perfectly to whatever it's covering. Use a hairdryer set on low heat to dry any lingering wet spots.

Be sure that people and pets keep off the just-washed-and-still-drying slipcovers.

◆ Once you've washed and dried a cushion's slipcover, it's usually difficult to put it back on the foam cushion...especially if the cover has shrunk a little. To remedy this problem, put the foam cushion in a dry cleaner's plastic bag, cut off the excess plastic, then slip the cover on the plastic-covered cushion.

This makes all the difference in getting it on. And if someone accidently spills something on the cushion, the spill won't go through to the pillow.

FABRIC SOFTENER & STARCH

Many fabric softener sheets have chemicals that eliminate static cling in the dryer, help soften clothes and make them somewhat wrinkle resistant, and produce a fragrance that makes clothes smell fresh. The down side is that the chemicals used in the production of the sheets may cause allergic reactions in people who are sensitive to them.

But don't fret! There are all-natural (chemical-free), nontoxic dryer sheets available. They cost about $20 and are reusable for about 500 loads of wash (which means that by using them, you can save money in the long run). One company that sells them is Nirvana Safe Haven, based in Walnut Creek, California (800-968-9355 or *www.nontoxic.com*).

Another company that produces excellent hypoallergenic, reusable fabric softener sheets (which also work wonders at removing pet fur from laundry) is Real Goods...877-989-6321, *www.gaiam.com/realgoods/*. Just click on "Shop Now," then type "static eliminator" in the product search box for more information.

However, if you do use regular, commercially produced fabric softeners, here are some helpful hints...

Suffering Sneezes?

An allergic reaction—possibly even an asthma attack—can be caused by fabric softeners when they are used on bedding and clothing.

If you (or someone for whom you do the laundry) are sensitive in this way, you may want to skip the softener.

Save on Softener!

◆ Buy liquid softener instead of expensive fabric-softener sheets. Dilute the liquid with water and pour 2 capfuls of the mixture on a clean washcloth, then toss it into the dryer with your wash load.

◆ If you don't want to use liquid softener, hair conditioner will also work—just use the same directions as above.

Less Cents and Less Scents

During the last rinse cycle, add ¼ cup of distilled white vinegar. It's a good and inexpensive fabric softener, and it will make your colored washables more vivid. It will also help eliminate bacteria, mold and fungus.

The wash will not smell like vinegar...but it won't have a nice, fresh-air fabric-softener smell, either.

 Smart Hint for Towels

Do not use fabric softener when washing your kitchen towels—they will be more absorbent and your plates don't care if they feel rough.

Starch

Starch is a complex carbohydrate that is mostly found in corn, potatoes, wheat and rice. For laundry use, starch is commonly prepared as a white, tasteless powder (but don't ever ingest laundry starch!). It is used to help clothes (especially shirt collars) retain their stiffness and shape.

If you run out of store-bought starch, you can make your own...

Make a Super Spray Starch

To prepare a super spray starch, you'll need a bowl, cornstarch, cold water and a 16-ounce fine-mist spray bottle.

For a light starch, combine 1 tablespoon of cornstarch with 2 cups of cold water in the bowl. For a heavier starch, use 3 tablespoons of cornstarch in the same amount of cold water. Mix well—making sure that the cornstarch is completely dissolved—then transfer the mixture from the bowl to the spray bottle.

To use the starch, shake the bottle, then spray the garment and iron immediately.

SMELLS

 According to the Sense of Smell Institute in New York City (*www.senseofsmell.org*), the average human being is able to recognize approximately 10,000 different odors—and tell where the odor is coming from because a nose can smell directionally. This is all the more reason to keep your clothes smelling clean and fresh. *Here are some tips for common scents…*

Steam Out Cigarette Smoke

If you've spent time in a smoke-filled room, chances are your clothes will reek from it. To get rid of the odor, fill a bathtub with steamy hot water and add 1 cup of distilled white vinegar. Carefully hang the smoky garment so that the steam envelops it.

Use a padded hanger so that the garment doesn't get *pupkees* (those unwanted epaulet-type shoulder bumps—*see* "Drying Wet Sweaters" on page 47). If you don't have a padded hanger, you can pin shoulderpads around the ends of a hanger to avoid getting the pupkees.

Booze for Cigarettes

Fill a plastic spray bottle with 1 ounce of vodka and 3 ounces of water. Mist-spray the smoky garment and hang it up to dry. The booze mixture should help to neutralize the cigarette-smoke smell. But you may still smell like a saloon.

Just Like New…

If you have a new washable garment that has an unpleasant chemical finish or dye smell, add ½ cup baking soda to 1 gallon of water in a sink or basin, and presoak the clothing for at least 2 hours.

After soaking, toss the clothing into the washing machine and wash as usual. During the rinse cycle, add ½ cup of distilled white vinegar.

 NOTE: This de-smelling process will also work if you (and your clothes) have been sprayed by a skunk.

Hinder Hamper Smells

Cut off the foot part of a pair of clean pantyhose and fill it with baking soda or kitty litter. Tie the open end closed and keep the soda- or litter-filled foot in your hamper. It will absorb moisture and help prevent stinky mildew from building up. Refresh the baking soda or kitty litter every month.

✱ **Hamper Freshener**
In addition to—or instead of the baking soda in a stocking—sprinkle a little baking soda on clothes that you put in the hamper each day. The hamper won't smell, and when you do wash the clothes, the baking soda will make them softer and smell fresher.

Scentsational Gym Bag

Place a fabric softener sheet in the bottom of a gym bag. This will help mask the smell of sweaty clothes and sneakers—and you'll know when it's time to put in a new softener sheet.

Managing Mothballs

If you store clothes in mothballs, let them air out for several hours when you first take them out. Then toss the clothes in a warm dryer for about 15 minutes. You may want to add a fabric-softener sheet, but check the information on the softener box to make sure the softener won't stain the clothes.

Tablecloths, Mats, Curtains (Plastic)

If a plastic item doesn't lose that yucky plastic smell soon after being unwrapped and out in the open, then help it along by soaking it in a sink with ½ cup of baking soda.

If the item also needs softening, add ½ cup of distilled white vinegar to the baking-soda water. Let it soak for 3 to 4 hours, then rinse and air-dry.

CLEANING NON-CLOTHING ITEMS

I f it's time for spring cleaning or you're expecting your in-laws for a visit, there are many things that perhaps you didn't think need cleaning... but they do. *Try these suggestions...*

Artificial and Dried Flowers

♦ Dust delicate blossoms with a hair dryer set on the lowest heat.
♦ If a hair dryer set on the lowest heat is too strong for fragile dried flowers, you can use an empty turkey baster, spray bottle or atomizer to gently blow away the dust.
♦ Wash plastic flowers in warm water with a mild detergent, then dry them thoroughly.

Once they're clean, help them stay that way by putting 1 or 2 coats of clear nail polish on the flowers.

Shake Yer Stems

If you want to clean sturdy fabric flowers, take a plastic or paper bag (big enough to hold the flowers), and pour in 1 cup of table salt. Hold the flowers by the stems and put the blossoms into the bag. Hold the neck of the bag closed around the stems, then *shake, shake, shake*, giving the salt a chance to clean the flowers.

When you take the flowers out of the bag, do it over the sink (or outside) and shake out all the salt that stayed on the flowers. The flowers should be clean and their colors fresh and bright.

Children's Toys

If a stuffed toy isn't machine washable, you can "dry-clean" it by placing it in a plastic bag and sprinkling in some baking soda or cornstarch. Shake the bag enough to evenly distribute the powder. Then seal the bag, and let it stay that way overnight. The next day, open the bag over the sink, shaking out most of the powder. Brush or vacuum off the remainder.

Removing Dust Mites

Those wonderful stuffed toys—which take up more room in the bed than the baby—are a breeding ground for dust mites. They can trigger allergic reactions, including asthma attacks.

Get rid of dust mites by placing the stuffed toy in a plastic bag and putting the bag in the freezer for 24 hours. Do this once a week with a child's most played-with stuffed toys, and there may be a noticeable difference in the child's health and well-being.

Cleaning Vinyl Toys

Use a damp sponge and some baking soda to wipe vinyl clean. Then rinse and dry.

Cleaning Hard Plastic Toys

Combine 1 tablespoon of liquid dish detergent with ¼ cup of baking soda to form a paste. Put the paste on a toothbrush and brush away the dirt. Use a clean, moist sponge to wipe the plastic clean. This works especially well on dolls with plastic faces.

STAINS A TO Z

STOP! PLEASE READ THIS BEFORE CONTINUING TO LOOK FOR A STAIN SOLUTION.

The stain removers described in this section are effective. That is, they've worked for the people who have passed them along to us.

Not knowing the extent of the stain and the quality of the fabric in question, we strongly recommend that—before trying any of these suggested stain removers—you test it on an inconspicuous area of your garment to prevent making a messy spot worse.

Thank you—now please continue…

The Simple Solution For UFOs

Before we get to specific kinds of stains, here's a basic formula for what we refer to as "UFOs"— "Unidentified Filthy Ooooooh…where did I get this spot?"

Invest in a new spray bottle, so that you can prepare this mixture and always have it on hand when you discover a UFO.

Combine 1 cup of filtered, spring or distilled water with 1 cup of rubbing alcohol and 2 teaspoons of liquid dish detergent (the stuff that breaks down the oil on dirty dishes) and you're good to go. Spray a bit to pretreat or spot-clean a UFO. Whatever you do, go ahead and launder the garment as usual.

 NOTE: The UFO solution can be used on many different stains. But, when in doubt, try it first on a small, inconspicuous area of the stained garment.

◆ The packaging on denture cleansers promises to dissolve tough stains. True, they don't necessarily mean food stains on clothing, but we've tried it and it worked 2 out of 3 times. If you like those odds and you have a stained garment, it's worth a shot!

Get a clean container (we used an empty, plastic shoebox), fill it with warm water and drop in 2 or 3 denture tablets. Leave the garment soaking for about 15 minutes—the same amount of time recommended for soaking dentures. When the time is up, launder the clothing as usual.

◆ If you find an unidentified stain on your furniture's upholstery, sponge it with distilled white vinegar and let it set for 15 minutes. Then wash the area, following the manufacturer's instructions.

 CAUTION: Check the upholstery's label for cleaning instructions (and do a spot test) *before* trying this suggestion!

 Cold Water Rules
Do not use hot or even warm water to get rid of a stain…not unless you want to set the stain permanently. Cold water will go a long way to prevent the stain from staying there forever.

Baby Formula/Milk

◆ Do not reach for the bleach to treat a baby-formula stain—it will set it. Instead, for colored clothes, use unseasoned meat tenderizer. It has an enzyme that breaks down the protein in baby formula and milk.

◆ After rinsing the garment in cold water, rub it in the tenderizer, completely covering the stain. Let it stand for 1 hour and then wash as usual.

◆ For whites, saturate the formula/milk spot with lemon juice, and leave it in the sun for 30 minutes, then wash as usual.

Ballpoint Pen

See "Ink" on page 56.

Barbecue Sauce

See "Tomato Sauce, Ketchup, Chili or Barbecue Sauce" on pages 59–60.

Beer

Wash out beer suds in warm soapsuds.

Blood

◆ If it's a small stain, and it's your blood, spit on it. The enzymes in your saliva should dissolve the stain.

◆ Do not use hot water on a bloodstain. It will set the stain. Instead, put the bloodied fabric in cold salted water—use 2 tablespoons of table salt for each cup of water. Strong salt-water breaks down the proteins that bind blood to fabric fibers.

◆ Let cold water run over the bloodied fabric. Then make a paste with unseasoned meat tenderizer and cold water, and put it on the stain. Let it sit and, after about 30 minutes, rinse off the tenderizer and wash the garment as usual.

◆ Try using 3% hydrogen peroxide to fizz away the stain. (Don't forget to test the fabric first.) Pour it on the blood, then rinse and wash the garment as usual.

◆ For a bloodstain on upholstery, cover the stain with a paste of cornstarch and water. Let it dry, then brush or vacuum it clean. If the stain is lighter but still there, repeat the procedure a second time.

 CAUTION: Check the upholstery's label for cleaning instructions (and do a spot test) *before* trying this suggestion!

Candle Wax

See "Chewing Gum" on this page.

Canvas

If you want to clean canvas, sailcloth or some other heavy material, use a gum eraser (available at office- and art-supply stores). It may not make the fabric spotless, but it should be better than it was.

Chewing Gum

◆ Put a few ice cubes in a resealable, plastic produce bag, and place it on top of the gum stuck to your garment. Leave the ice-bag in place for 15 minutes. Or, place the gummy garment in a plastic bag and stick it in your freezer for 1 hour.

   Gum shrinks and hardens when it gets cold, making it easy to peel away from fabric.

◆ Using a toothbrush and the white of 1 egg, scrub the section of fabric that has chewing gum stuck to it. After you remove as much of the gum as possible, let it stand for 30 minutes. Then flick off the rest of the bits of gum and launder as usual.

◆ Place a piece of waxed paper over the sticky spot (waxy side down), and go over it with a warm iron. The gum should adhere to the waxed paper and you should be able to peel it right off.

◆ Dip any gummy or sticky fabric in lemon juice and keep it there for about 5 minutes. Then rinse with warm water as you scrape off the stickiness.

Chili

See "Tomato Sauce, Ketchup, Chili or Barbecue Sauce" on pages 59–60.

Chocolate

Make a paste with borax powder (available at supermarkets and drugstores) and water—you can also use meat tenderizer and water—and rub it into the stain. Let it stay that way for 1 hour, then brush it off and launder as usual.

Cigars and Cigarettes

See "Tobacco" on page 59.

Coffee or Tea

◆ If you promise to be *very* careful, then consider this remedy for taking a coffee or tea splotch out of white fabrics.

 Stretch the stained area over an empty bowl or pot, and keep it in place using a rubber band. Then put the bowl or pot in the bathtub (it's safer than the sink). Boil a full kettle of water.

 From a height of about 2 feet—here's where you have to be careful!—pour the boiling-hot water through the stained fabric into the bowl. Then launder as usual.

◆ If you have a coffee or tea stain on colored fabric, soak the area in distilled white vinegar. Then launder as usual.

◆ For stains on white cotton, linen or lace—first dampen the stained area with warm water. Spread out the garment in a sink or basin. Drop 2 denture-cleaning tablets in ½ cup of warm water. Pour the fizzing liquid on the stain, and let it stay that way for 30 minutes. Then launder as usual. **Remember, this is for *white* fabric only.**

◆ When dining out, don't just let the stain sit there because you're embarrassed. In fact, you will gain everyone's respect when you show them that you know exactly what to do. And this is what to do—moisten a clean napkin with seltzer or club soda and gently wipe the stained fabric.

◆ If seltzer doesn't do the trick, rub table salt on the spill, and let it stay that way for 15 minutes. Then wipe it off. Needless to say, launder the garment as soon as you get home.

 If the stain remains and the garment requires a trip to the dry cleaner's, send the bill to the klutz who caused the spill.

Cola

Pour distilled white vinegar on the spot, then launder as usual. The secret to getting out a cola stain completely is to put vinegar on it as soon as possible...within hours (not days) after saying, "Oops! I spilled cola on my shirt."

Crayons

◆ Rub a few drops of liquid dishwashing detergent into the crayon marks, and then launder the clothing as usual.

◆ Lay the cloth stain-side up on a stack (8 to 12 sheets) of paper towel. Spray the stained area with WD-40 lubricant, and let it set for 3 to 5 minutes. Turn the cloth over and spray the other side, letting it set for another 3 to 5 minutes. Then launder as usual.

Deodorant Stick

If you accidentally get a bit of deodorant on a dark-colored shirt, use a clean pair of pantyhose to wipe it off. Those nylon fibers work like some kind of magic eraser.

Fruit, Berries and Fruit Juice

◆ If you spill grape juice on your shirt or drop a blueberry on your pants (at home or at a restaurant), first gently wipe the stain with cold water. Then, as soon as possible, prepare a kettle of boiling water. Stretch the stained area over an empty bowl or pot, and keep it in place with a rubber band.

　　　Then put the bowl or pot in the bathtub (it's safer than the sink). From a height of about 2 feet, pour the boiling-hot water through the stained fabric into the bowl. Then launder as usual.

◆ If you can act quickly, soak the stained area in distilled white vinegar, and then launder the garment as usual.

◆ If you get a fruit stain on a tablecloth or linen napkins, douse the spot with powdered laundry starch, and let it stay on for 3 to 4 hours. Then launder as usual.

Glue

If glue gets on your clothes in the middle of an arts-and-crafts project, this is one time you may want to come unglued.

　　　Simply place your shirt, smock or apron in a sink or basin filled with water, and add 4 tablespoons of distilled white vinegar. Let the garment soak for 1 to 2 hours…until the glue dissolves, and then launder as usual.

Grass

◆ If the stain just occurred, and you can get home quickly, squeeze out a portion of white, non-gel, non-whitening toothpaste and apply it to the stain. Work the toothpaste into the fabric until the grass stain is gone, and then launder the clothing as usual.

◆ You can also soak the stained area in distilled white vinegar, and then launder as usual.

◆ If the grass stain is old and set, cover it with rubbing alcohol and let it soak for 10 to 15 minutes. Rinse out the alcohol with warm water, and launder the clothing as usual.

Gravy

◆ For a major mess, sop up as much of the gravy as possible with napkins or towels. Then cover the stain with cornstarch…or flour…or baking soda…or table salt…or artificial sweetener. Once dinner is over and your company leaves, brush off whatever you put on the stain, and rub laundry detergent into the stain. Launder as usual.

◆ For a minor gravy stain, dissolve the gravy's starch by soaking the stain in cold water for 30 minutes. Then launder the clothing as usual.

Grease

◆ Absorb the grease by rubbing cornstarch, talcum powder or chalk into the stain. Let it stay that way for 15 minutes, then whisk off the powder. If the stain is gone, great. If it's still there but smaller than it was, repeat the process. If there's no change, then try the next remedy.

◆ Soak the grease stain in cola for 15 minutes. It should help loosen the grease. Then launder the garment as usual.

◆ Attention all you mechanics—if you're doing a greasy-clothes wash, pour a 1-liter bottle of cola in the washing machine along with the laundry detergent.

◆ Dish detergent cuts the grease on pots and pans, and it will do the same thing on fabric. Pour a little on the greasy spot, then launder the garment as usual.

◆ If you get a grease spot on your new couch, rub table salt on the stained upholstery as soon as possible. Give the salt at least 30 minutes to absorb the grease, then brush or vacuum the salt away.

 CAUTION: Check the upholstery's label for cleaning instructions (and do a spot test) before trying this suggestion!

Gum

See "Chewing Gum" on pages 53–54.

Ink

◆ If you get an ink spot on colored fabric, soak the stained area in milk, or sponge it out with milk.

◆ You can also douse an ink stain on colored clothes with rubbing alcohol. Let it stay that way for 5 minutes, then launder as usual.

◆ For ink stains on white clothing, combine 2 tablespoons of lemon juice with 1 teaspoon of table salt. Rub the mixture into the stained area, and then let it dry in the sun.

◆ If you get purple ballpoint pen on your white shirt, apply a dollop of foam shaving cream, and let it sit for a few minutes. Dab it off with a clean cloth, and the mark should be gone.

◆ For all fabrics, spray a 2-second spritz of hairspray on the ink mark, then launder the clothing as usual.

◆ Wet a cloth with vodka and rub the ink stain. It should make the permanent marker a temporary marker.

Ink Remover—The Formula

If our simple solutions do not effectively take out an ink stain, you may want to try the following formula…

In a bowl, combine 1 tablespoon of milk, 1 tablespoon of white vinegar, 1 teaspoon of lemon juice and 1 teaspoon of borax powder (available at supermarkets and drugstores) in a bowl. Put the stained area of the garment between 3 or 4 thick sheets of paper towel.

Dip a sponge in the mixture and pat it on the towel that's covering the stain. (You want the liquid to reach the fabric, but you don't want to put it directly on the stain.) After about 3 minutes, try sponging the stained area with cool water. Repeat the entire procedure until the stain is completely gone. When it is, launder the garment as usual.

Ketchup

See "Tomato Sauce, Ketchup, Chili or Barbecue Sauce" on pages 59–60.

Kitchen Curtains

To prevent stains from splatter and dust, starch your kitchen curtains before you hang them.

For simple spray-on starch instructions, *see* "Make a Super Spray Starch" on pages 49–50, or buy a box of starch in the supermarket and follow the package directions.

Lipstick

◆ Use a slice of white bread to blot off as much lipstick as possible, then launder the clothing as usual.

◆ Wet the lipstick-stained clothing with water, then rub on a little bit of dishwashing liquid. Thoroughly rinse the garment, and launder as usual.

◆ Brush white, non-gel, non-whitening toothpaste on the lipsticky clothing, and launder as usual.

◆ For lipstick marks on a cloth napkin, put several layers of paper towel under the stained area. Wet a clean cloth with rubbing alcohol and press down on the stain. Do that a few times to blot up as much of the lipstick as possible. Then launder the napkin as usual.

Makeup (Foundation)

◆ If there's a little smudge of makeup on your clothing, you may be able to make it disappear by rubbing the mark with a balled-up slice of white bread or stale rye bread.

◆ For a major makeup smear, cover the stain with baking soda. Then brush the area with a wet toothbrush. Keep adding baking soda and wet-brushing until the stain is gone.

Mildew

Put buttermilk in a basin and soak the mildewed fabric in it overnight. The next day, you can launder the garment as usual.

Milk

Meat tenderizer is effective on most fresh protein-based stains. Pour meat tenderizer on the wet milk stain. Let it stay that way for 1 hour, then brush off the residue and launder the clothing as usual.

Mud

Rub the mud-stained fabric with a slice of raw potato. Soak the garment in cool water for 15 minutes, then wash as usual.

Oil

◆ Drip a few drops of shampoo-for-oily-hair on the stained fabric. Let it set for 15 minutes and then launder as usual. Shampoo for *oily* hair…think about it.

◆ You can absorb a fresh oil spill with baby powder. Cover the soiled spot with a few shakes of powder. Let it set for a few minutes, then brush it off and wash the garment in warm water.

◆ If you get an oil spill on leather, clean it by covering the spot with cornstarch. Let it stay that way overnight. The next day, wipe the area clean with a dry cloth.

Perspiration

◆ For stains on cotton or polyester clothing, add 1 cup of white vinegar to a sink or basin filled with warm water. Soak the garment for about 1 hour, then launder as usual.

◆ For sweat stains on wool, mix ¼ cup of salt with 1 quart of cold water. Soak the garment in the mixture for about 30 minutes, and then launder as usual.

◆ If the wool still has a perspiration smell, mix 1 cup of water with 1 teaspoon of distilled white vinegar and gently sponge it on the sweaty areas. Let it stay that way for 1 hour, and then launder as usual.

Pillowcases

To help prevent stains caused by hair oil and face cream, lightly starch pillow cases.

For simple spray-on starch instructions, *see* "Make a Super Spray Starch" on pages 49–50, or buy a box of starch in the supermarket. Just follow the package directions.

Plastic Tablecloth

See "Vinyl or Plastic Tablecloth" on page 60.

Red Wine

As soon as possible once a spill happens, cover it with table salt or artificial sweetener. Then after dinner—or at least within 24 hours of the spill—brush off the salt or sweetener, and rub the clothing under cold water.

If the fabric is cotton, a cotton blend or permanent press, dab some distilled white vinegar on the fading stain, and launder as usual.

Ring Around the Collar

◆ First, check the ingredients in your shampoo. If the first ingredient is *water* rather than *oil*—that's good. Then look for *ammonium lauryl sulfate* in the list of ingredients. That's the ingredient that will help break down an oil stain.

Once you know that you have the right shampoo in hand, rub a few drops of it on the ring-around-the-collar (RATC) stain. Or you may want to brush it on with an old, clean toothbrush. Let the shampoo set for about 30 minutes, then wash the shirt thoroughly in warm water.

◆ If you don't have the right shampoo (to make the RATC solution), make a paste of baking soda mixed with distilled white vinegar. Massage the paste into the collar ring, then launder the shirt as usual.

◆ To prevent ring-around-the-collar on a clean, white shirt or blouse, sprinkle baby powder on the inside collar before you iron. The powder prevents the shirt from absorbing the wearer's body oil.

◆ In addition, you can use rubbing alcohol or witch hazel to clean off any oil or dirt from your neck before you put on clean, white, collared clothing.

Rust

◆ To remove rust stains from most colored and non-delicate fabrics, make a paste using equal amounts of table salt and cream of tartar (available in supermarkets) mixed with hot water.

Work the paste into the stain and let it sit for 15 minutes. Then launder as usual. For delicate fabrics—such as silk, satin, lace or organdy—proceed with caution...test the paste on an inside seam to be sure.

◆ On white clothing, douse the rust spot with lemon juice and leave it in the sun for a couple of hours. Then launder as usual.

 FYI: How Clothing "Rusts"

If you're wondering why rust stains pop up on clothing, it may be because you hung a garment on a metal hanger, and the garment or the hanger was wet.

Or, if you have hard water in your house and use bleach, the bleach's chlorine can leach iron out of the water, which contributes rust stains. Rusty pipes could also be at the root of the problem.

Scorches

The following remedies should work for all colors and most fabrics.

For delicate fabrics—such as silk, satin, lace or organdy—proceed with caution. Test the solution by first testing an inside seam with the ingredient you plan to use...just to make sure it doesn't worsen the problem.

◆ If you scorch the garment you're ironing, rub the scorched spot with an ice cube as quickly as possible. Most of the time, the scorch will disappear.

◆ Moisten a clean white cloth with distilled white vinegar and place it on top of the scorched area. Then cautiously iron it using a warm iron. Keep checking to make sure the scorch is disappearing, not getting worse.

◆ Take a piece of yellow onion and rub it on the scorched area. Make sure the onion juice soaks into the fabric. Let it stay that way for a couple of hours, then launder as usual.

◆ Mix equal parts of 3% hydrogen peroxide and water. Sponge it on the scorch and let it set for about 30 minutes. Then launder as usual.

Shower Curtain Liner

Put the shower curtain liner in the washing machine, along with 2 or 3 bathroom towels and start it going on *warm*. Then add ½ cup laundry detergent and ½ cup baking soda, and let the machine run its course.

The towels act as scrub brushes, removing soap scum and mildew from the liner. During the final rinse, add 1 cup of distilled white vinegar. When you take the clean-as-new liner out of the washer, hang it in the shower to dry and toss the towels in the dryer.

Suntan Oil or Lotion

Knead a little liquid laundry detergent into the stained area of clothing, then let cold water run forcefully through it.

Tea

See "Coffee or Tea" on page 54.

Tie Stains

If you are one of those men who is always staining his tie, you should consider making your ties stain-resistant. To do this, simply spray your neckwear with an upholstery guard (available at most hardware stores and some supermarkets).

Tobacco

Add ¼ cup baking soda to the wash along with your laundry detergent. It should help get out cigar and cigarette stains (not burns), and it will also take out any lingering smell.

See "Smells" on page 50 for more suggestions on getting rid of a tobacco smell.

Tomato Sauce, Ketchup, Chili or Barbecue Sauce

◆ Quick—get the shaving cream! Squirt a blob of plain, foam shaving cream on the saucy stain. Then wet a sponge with warm water and work the cream into it. Let the garment dry, and then launder as usual. The shaving cream's deionized water and alcohol should help dissolve a tomato sauce–based stain.

◆ Dip the stained area in cold water and then rub it with glycerine. Let it stay that way for 30 minutes, then wash it in warm water. If you can still see the stain from what you had for lunch, sponge it with 3% hydrogen peroxide, then rinse in cold water.

Urine

Babies and puppies are prone to pee-pee accidents on clothes, sheets, rugs, etc. This type of stain calls for soda water. Wipe the area with a sponge that's been dipped in soda water, then launder as usual.

If the urine is on a mattress or mattress cover, moisten the spot…this time with plain water. Work in enough borax powder (available at supermarkets and drugstores) to cover the stain, let it dry, then vacuum or brush it clean. You can launder the mattress cover as usual.

Vomit

This is possibly another form of "the hair of the dog that bit you"…sponge vodka on the stain, scrub it with a brush, and then launder as usual. This remedy can be used for bedding and removable slip covers or upholstery, as well as for clothing.

Vinyl or Plastic Tablecloth

Make a paste from 1 teaspoon of cream of tartar and ¼ teaspoon of lemon juice, and rub the stain with it. Let it stay that way for 15 minutes, then brush off the dried paste and rinse the tablecloth clean.

IRONING

At the end of the 1800s, women would iron their family's clothes using heavy irons that were heated near an open fire or on the stove. As you can imagine, the handles became red-hot and hands were burned. So…back to the drawing board.

Next came wooden handles and brass hotboxes that were fueled by charcoal and placed in the body of the iron, then lit. OK, so they sometimes caught on fire or simply exploded. Gas irons were the new-and-improved models to replace them. Talk about dangerous…! And this went on well into the 20th century.

We're telling you all this so that you'll appreciate the sleek and SAFE irons of today and will regard ironing as a pleasant chore…a task that might be made a bit easier and more efficient with the following hints.

Prepping Your Clothes

Dampen your clothes with warm water—rather than cold—which will help to make ironing faster and more efficient.

 Frozen and Fresh-Pressed
If you have already dampened your clothes but have to put off ironing them, put them in a plastic bag and place the bag in the freezer.

Doing this prevents mildew, and when you are ready to iron, you won't have to redampen them. You may have to thaw them out a bit, but otherwise they're good to go.

Supercharge Your Iron

Place one sheet of aluminum foil—uncoated, shiny side up—between the ironing board and the fabric ironing-board cover. As a result of the foil reflecting the heat from the iron, the ironing gets done faster and better.

All the Right Moves

Go with the grain of the fabric, using a back-and-forth motion to iron. A circular motion may stretch the fabric.

Keep the iron in constant motion without rushing. After completing a section of the garment, lift the iron and wait about 10 seconds... enough time to let the press set.

 CAUTION: Do not iron stained clothes. The heat from the iron can set the stain permanently.

Shine Prevention

Dark cottons, linens, rayons and silks should all be ironed inside out. Cover delicate fabrics with a sheet of tissue paper and use a cool iron.

Velvet and Velveteen

Do not iron directly on velvet or velveteen. Instead, use a pressing cloth (available at most supermarkets and hardware stores). Wet the pressing cloth, place it on the velvet and start ironing. Expect to hear a sizzling sound.

 NOTE: For a pressing-cloth substitute in a pinch...cut a panel out of a brown, paper grocery bag, moisten it and use it as you would the pressing cloth.

Ironing Sleeves

Slide a small rolled-up towel into the sleeve, and you may be able to iron it without creating a terrible-looking sleeve crease.

 Use a Broom to Sweep Up

To avoid sweeping the floor with clean clothes that you're ironing, use spring-type clothespins to shorten the hanging-down factor of shirt or blouse sleeves, full-skirt hems, tablecloths and scarf ends.

Pucker Prevention

Iron your cuffs, collars and hemlines on the underside first, gently pulling and stretching the fabric away from the iron.

Unsticking the Iron

If the underside of your iron is sticky, wait until it's cool (very important!), then put some baby powder on a cloth and coat the iron's bottom. Once it's coated with powder, turn on the heat and watch the powder disappear.

At this point, the iron should no longer be sticky. It should glide over silks and other delicate, catchy, clingy fabrics. To be sure, test the iron on an inconspicuous part of any delicate garment that needs to be pressed.

Scorch Prevention

If you don't want to risk scorching a special, potentially scorchable garment, carefully iron the item between 2 pieces of aluminum foil.

Pleats

You can use spring-type clothespins, bobby pins or the old hair-setting clips to hold pleats in place at the waist and/or hemline. Once you have ironed most of the pleats, just remove the

STEAM-IRON CARE
Cleaning the Water Tank

If you use a good ol' steam iron, you may need to clean out the built-up mineral deposits, which can create stains on clothes.

Mix ½ cup of distilled white vinegar with ½ cup of water (use distilled water if possible) and fill your iron with it. Let the iron steam until all of the liquid is gone. Once it cools down, rinse the iron's tank with water, and refill it with water. This time, shake the water through the steam holes. Before using the steam iron on wearable clothes, test it on an old cloth.

> **CAUTION:** Do not put your face or your hands in the path of the escaping steam.

Cleaning the Holes

When the steam iron is cold and unplugged, dip a small, fuzzy pipe cleaner in distilled white vinegar to clean its holes.

Mineral Deposit Prevention

◆ Here's a really easy way to prevent mineral deposits from forming—before ironing, put distilled water in the iron's water tank.

◆ If you do not use distilled water, then each time you finish ironing, while the iron is still warm, empty the water tank. Any remaining moisture will evaporate, thanks to the iron's heat. And, as long as there's no water left in the tank, there will be no mineral deposits —and no damaging spots on clothes.

Clean Off Starch

To clean starch off the bottom of an iron, heat the iron and then run it over a piece of aluminum foil several times.

Filling a Steam Iron

Prevent water spills by using a turkey baster to fill the steam iron's water tank.

---

holders and complete the job by ironing the waist/hemline.

Create a Permanent Crease

Put distilled white vinegar in a spray bottle. Lay out the pant leg on the ironing board, arranging the crease exactly where you want it. Spray the crease with the vinegar, then iron it. Let it set for several seconds and do the other side, then the other leg.

Buttons

Always iron *around* buttons, never *over* them. Otherwise, they may melt…they may break… they may discolor.

NO-IRON NEEDED

 Humorist and author Erma Bombeck once said, "My second favorite household chore is ironing. My first being hitting my head on the top bunk bed until I faint."

If you agree with Erma, here are some ways to avoid dealing with the iron…

Pants

After washing, hang your pants by the ankle end, not by the waist. The wet weight of the pants hanging down will take out most, if not all, of the wrinkles.

Vinyl Tablecloths, Shower Curtains, Shelf Paper

Set a hair dryer on high heat and hold it about 8" away from the wrinkled section of a vinyl tablecloth, shower curtain or shelf paper.

While the hair dryer is on, pay close attention. When the plastic seems soft and pliable, shut off the dryer and use your hand to smooth out the wrinkles.

Sheer Curtains

While your washable sheer curtains are in the wash, dissolve a packet of unflavored gelatin in a cup of boiled water, and add it to the final rinse cycle.

The protein in gelatin has a relaxing or softening effect on the fabric, doing away with wrinkles. (If only it worked that way with skin!)

Ribbons

When you have to wrap a gift and the piece of ribbon you want to use is creased, don't bother to take out the iron and set up the ironing board. Instead, carefully run the wrinkly ribbon over a clean, warm lightbulb.

Sheets

◆ Nobody likes to iron sheets. But you don't really have to if you take them out of the dryer promptly—while they're still warm—and put them right on the bed. They'll look and feel freshly ironed.

◆ If the sheets are cool by the time you make the bed, put them back in the dryer for a few minutes with a clean, damp washcloth. When the sheets are warm again, make the bed as soon as possible.

 Folding Fitted Sheets

If you have warm, hardly wrinkled, fitted sheets that you want to put away neatly, we're hoping this helps.

There are a few ways to fold fitted sheets, but none of them seem simple when you read the instructions. (If only this book came with a video!) The secret is to work with the sheet as you read the instructions and, sooner than later, you'll figure it out...or discover an even better way of folding the fitted sheet (in which case, please let us know!). *Here goes...*

Begin with the sheet inside out, then spread it on a bed with the pocket-sides up. (Tall people can do the folding while holding the sheet up in front of them. We find it easier to work with the sheet while it's on a flat surface.)

Place each hand in each of the top corner pockets. Bring your right hand to your left, and fold the corner pocket in your right hand over the 1 in your left hand. If you did it correctly, the corner on top will be right-side out.

Keeping your left hand in place, use your right hand to reach down to the remaining 2 corner pockets and tuck the corners into each other. Next, fold these corner pockets over the first 2 that are in your left hand.

All 4 corner pockets should now be tucked inside one another and the sheet should be folded in quarters. (Bonus points if you got it right on the first try!)

Put the sheet on the bed again, and fold the pocketed side over the flat part of the sheet. Now you should be able to fold it neatly to the size you want it to be without any elastic corners jutting out.

Pantyhose

◆ Strengthen the fibers of new pantyhose by soaking them in a basin of saltwater—about 4 quarts of warm water to ¼ cup table salt—for 15 minutes. Rinse them with cold water. It should make them more run-resistant.

◆ Picture yourself wearing your favorite sheer, black pantyhose. How unsightly is a run or a snag? Help prevent that from happening by lightly spritzing hairspray on the pantyhose as soon as you put them on. Hairspray stiffens the fibers, making them less vulnerable to average stocking abuse.

Keep Your Freshly Ironed Clothes Smooth

◆ Roll silk scarves around the empty cardboard tube from a roll of paper towel, plastic wrap, aluminum foil or gift wrap.

◆ Take a paper towel tube and cut a slit all the way across lengthwise. Slip the slitted tube on a hanger and hang any just-ironed linen or delicate article of clothing that's likely to crease.

◆ Hang 1 or 2 towel rods on the inside of your linen-closet door. It's perfect for storing tablecloths and keeping them wrinkle-free.

◆ When you rinse out your pantyhose, add a drop of liquid fabric softener to the water. The softener will lubricate the fibers, which is said to make them last longer.

Washing Hose

If you do not have a zippered laundry bag made for hosiery, this is a good alternative—put the pantyhose that need to be washed in the cut-off leg of an old, unusable pair of pantyhose (so if you get a bad run in your hose, don't throw them away—keep them for future uses!). Be sure to knot the top to keep the pantyhose from falling out and flailing around while in the washing machine.

Three for the Price of Two

Buy 2 of the exact same pair of pantyhose. When the leg of 1 pair gets a run, it still has 1 good leg. Set the run hose aside and wear the second pair. When the leg of the second pair gets a run, it still has 1 good leg.

Now, cut off the legs with the runs (and use them for machine washing!). You'll be left with 2 panty parts and 2 good legs. You can then wear them as a third, run-free pair of pantyhose.

SHOES & BOOTS

Before you criticize someone, you should walk a mile in his/her shoes. That way, you will be a mile away when you criticize him—plus, you will have his shoes! (Let's just hope they're nice ones.)

Here are some great ways to take care of all your shoes…

NOTE: Several of the hints that follow recommend that you polish, rub, massage or lightly coat your shoes or boots with a *soft* cloth. If you have an old, clean T-shirt that you're tired of wearing, cut it up and use it to spiff up your shoes.

Shining Shoes and Boots

If you do not have a commercial shoeshine product, you may want to use 1 of these—Coppertone Sunscreen (the SPF number doesn't matter)…lip balm, such as ChapStick…or a light coat of floor wax or furniture polish. With any of these, wipe the shoes dry and then buff them with a soft cloth.

Mold and Mildew

Mix enough fresh or bottled lemon juice with table salt, and use this mixture to wipe down a pair of shoes. You can use a soft cloth to wipe them clean. This will eliminate any surface mold and mildew.

Extend the Life of Shoes

◆ Take your new shoes to a shoemaker or shoe-repair shop, and have him/her add a thin piece of rubber to the sole of each shoe. The shoes may feel more comfortable, you'll be a teeny bit taller, you'll have more traction (especially in rainy weather and on slippery pavement) and the shoes should last longer.

◆ Human feet have 250,000 sweat glands. It's no wonder then that the sweat from an average pair of feet amounts to about ½ pint daily. *Phew!*

   With that in mind, it makes sense that 3 pairs of shoes worn alternately will last as long as 4 pairs of shoes that are not worn on a rotating basis. So, let the shoes you have on now air out for at least 24 hours before wearing them again.

◆ Cedar shoe trees are ideal for absorbing moisture and helping shoes keep their shape. Shoe trees are available at the Container Store (888-CONTAIN, 800-733-3532 or *www. containerstore.com*. Second best—stuff your shoes with a bit of newspaper.

Scuff Marks

◆ Prepare a paste made from baking soda and water—about 1 tablespoon of baking soda to 1 teaspoon of water. Use a clean cloth to apply the paste, and wipe off the scuff marks.

◆ Get a gum eraser (available at stationery and art-supply stores)—it is a very effective scuff-mark remover.

Dark Leather

Dip a soft, clean cloth in some lemon juice and rub it on your shoes or boots. Then buff it with another soft, clean cloth. The juice should make the dark leather glisten.

White Shoes (including Leather)

◆ Use an old toothbrush to scrub a little bit of white, non-gel toothpaste on your white leather shoes. Wipe off any excess.

◆ If the toothpaste didn't work on those stubborn scuff marks, cover them with correction fluid (such as Liquid Paper or Wite-Out). Afterward, you may want to polish the shoes to even out the color.

◆ If you don't have any correction fluid, rub the leather shoes with a piece of raw potato and then polish them. The potato will help the polish go on smoothly and the polish will cover the scuff marks.

◆ If you really love those old, dingy, used-to-be-white leather shoes and want to make them look like new, spray them with a couple of coats of semigloss white spray paint. Be sure to let them dry thoroughly between each coat.

◆ If you get grass stains on white leather shoes, rub the stains with molasses and let it set overnight. Next day, use regular soap and water to wash the molasses off the shoes. Your shoes should be white again and grass stain–free.

◆ Get your baby's white shoes clean—just use a bit of baking soda on a damp cloth and wipe off the dirt. Then rinse the shoes with another damp cloth and buff them dry.

Black Shoes

Touch up scrapes and nicks with a black permanent marker or India ink. Desperate times call for desperate measures—on occasion, we have even used mascara and liquid eyeliner.

Gold or Silver Shoes

Use white non-gel toothpaste on a toothbrush to brush away scuff marks. You may need to wipe off any excess paste.

Suede Shoes

Dip a clean sponge in glycerine (available at drugstores) to rub out grass stains. Be sure to test a tiny, inconspicuous spot on the shoes first.

Salt and Grease Stains on Leather and Suede

To remove salt and/or grease stains, a conservator at Toronto's Bata Shoe Museum (*www.ba tashoemuseum.ca*) recommends mixing a solution made from 1 cup of water and 1 tablespoon of distilled white vinegar. Dip a soft sponge in the vinegar-water, and gently wipe the stains off the leather or suede shoes.

This mixture will also remove salt stains and grease stains from suede. (Be sure to test an inconspicuous section of the suede before working on the stain.)

 Keep Your Boots Salt-Free

If you live in Salt Stain Country (meaning, anyplace that spreads salt on snowy, wintry roads and sidewalks), and you wear leather boots on a regular basis, here's a smart suggestion...

Smear petroleum jelly on a soft cloth and keep it in a closed container. Put the container in a closet or cupboard near the door you use to enter and leave your home. Each time you go out, give your boots a light once-over with the jellied cloth. Do the same thing when you come back in. Your well-nourished boots will never have salt stains.

This solution may also work on boots made from synthetic materials and imitation leather—but we can't guarantee it. Test a small, inconspicuous area before coating the entire boot.

Salt Stains

If you've been walking on wintry streets, you can wipe salt stains off your shoes with a piece of raw potato.

Wet Shoes and Boots

Let shoes or boots dry naturally, away from direct heat and out of the sun. You can speed up the drying process by stuffing them with newspaper (which will absorb odors, too).

When leather shoes or boots are completely dry, rub them with a piece of raw potato, then polish them.

Once-Wet-Now-Dried-and-Stiff Shoes

To recondition stiff leather footwear that got wet and then dried in direct heat, wipe them down with warm water and massage them with a little castor oil.

Buffing Shoes

Scrunch up a lint-free coffee filter and use it to buff your leather shoes.

Waterproofing Shoes... Sort Of

First, polish your leather shoes or boots...and then add a light coating of floor wax.

Let's put it this way—it's better than nothing, but we wouldn't recommend you try this on your pricey pair of Manolo Blahniks.

Patent Leather

Use a soft cloth dipped in a small amount of petroleum jelly, almond oil or baby oil to clean and shine patent leather shoes. Once you have gently massaged the oil into the leather, buff it with a soft, dry cloth.

Applying a bit of Pledge or Windex will also do the trick.

Shoe Polish Reviver

Some shoe polishes have a tendency to get hard. Make sure the bottle of polish is tightly closed, then place it in a bowl of hot water and let it stay submerged for about 5 minutes. After that, it should be liquid again.

Keeping Tall Boots in Shape

When you're ready to put your tall boots back in the closet, slide an empty, clean and dry 1- or 2-liter plastic bottle into each leg.

Safer Shoes

◆ New shoes, which have smooth soles, can cause you to slip and slide on slick surfaces, especially rain-soaked streets. To gain some traction, you can put a few small pieces of masking tape on the soles and heels of those new shoes.

◆ To help prevent baby shoes from sliding, lightly roughen the soles of the shoes with sandpaper or an emery board.

Squeaky Shoes

One of the many uses for the lubricant WD-40 is to take the squeak out of shoes. Spray it on the spot where the sole and heel meet, then enjoy your quiet steps (just don't walk on carpet immediately—wait for the WD-40 to dry).

Deodorizing Smelly Shoes

◆ You can prevent odor buildup by not wearing the same shoes every day. Give them at least 24 hours to freshen up.

◆ To deodorize a pair of shoes, put half of a scented fabric-softener or dryer sheet in each shoe and leave it overnight.

◆ Spread a few tablespoons of baking soda in your shoes and leave them overnight. In the morning, shake out the shoes over the sink or garbage can, and notice how great they smell.

◆ Take a pair of pantyhose, cut off the feet (at the ankle), then fill each foot with standard clay kitty litter and close it with a rubber band, ribbon or a twist-tie. Stick the litter-filled stocking feet in your smelly shoes and let them sit overnight. As you might imagine, kitty litter is a very effective absorbent.

◆ Place your shoes in a plastic bag (either separate or together) and put them in the freezer overnight. The cold temperature will kill any odor-causing bacteria. (Talk about *cold* feet...!)

◆ Crumple up a small piece of black-and-white newspaper and stuff it in your smelly shoes. The carbon in the newsprint absorbs odors.

Foolproof Storage

Put that old Polaroid or new digital camera to good use—take a picture of each pair of shoes that you own. Then tape, staple or glue the photo to the front of a box, identifying which shoes are kept in that box.

This system will make your shoe-storage more efficient. And you will save lots of time rummaging through boxes, looking for the shoes you want to wear.

Loosen a Tight Spot

To temporarily ease a shoe's tight spot, put rubbing alcohol on the inside part of the tight area.

Shopping for Shoes

Your feet tend to be 1 size in the morning and, as the day progresses, they get a little bigger. So it's a good idea to shop for shoes as late in the day as possible. That way, you'll be sure to buy shoes that will ultimately be more comfortable —day and night.

Cleaning Sneakers

◆ Give your white leather or canvas sneakers the once-over with a wet scouring pad and soap. Then dampen a sponge with a bit of lemon juice, and wipe the sneakers clean. (Windex also works.)

◆ To help your sneakers stay cleaner longer, once they are washed, allow them to dry, and then give them the once-over with spray starch. It will help them resist future dirt and grime.

Shoelace Maintenance

◆ If you're tired of having to retie your (or your child's) shoelaces, clamp a "claw clip" (the kind girls use in their hair) on the knot in the middle of the bow.

 NOTE: Because these clips come in many styles and colors, you may want to color coordinate them with your shoes or clothes.

◆ Shoelaces will stay tied if you dampen them before tying.

◆ The plastic tip of a shoelace is called an *aglet*, and these little pieces are prone to breaking and wearing out.

To structure a new aglet, simply dip the aglet-less end of the shoelace in colorless nail polish. As it's drying, use tweezers to shape the end into a point, then let it dry completely before retying your shoes.

Shoes on Ice—How to Make Tight Shoes Bigger

Everyone has a pair of killer shoes...the shoes that were most likely bought on sale and/or impulse. You don't wear them much because they're too tight, but you won't throw them away because you love them. Help is here!

First, you'll need 4 plastic produce bags, the size that you get at the local fruit stand or in a supermarket's produce aisle. Make sure the bag has no holes or rips, then place 1 bag in each shoe, pushed all the way down into the toe area.

Next, pour water into the plastic bag so that the shoe area is filled with the plastic bag of water. Then seal each bag securely so that there's no chance of water spilling out. Put each shoe into 1 of the other empty plastic produce bags, and close it securely with a twist-tie.

Let's review: You put a water-filled, plastic bag in each shoe. And each shoe is in another plastic bag. Right? *OK, let's continue...*

Place both shoes (plastic bags and all) in the freezer and keep them there for 24 hours. Now here's the secret—as the water inside the shoes turns to ice, it expands, which stretches the shoes!

The next day, when you remove the shoes from the freezer, take them out of the plastic bag and let them thaw for a while, until you can easily remove the bag with the frozen shoe-cicle.

The shoes may have expanded ½ to 1 full size. But if the shoes are still not loose enough, repeat the process.

 NOTE: We've been told that this solution also works on boots. Of course, you may have to empty out your freezer to make room for them.

◆ You can also create a new aglet with transparent tape. Wrap a piece of tape tightly around the frayed end of the shoelace. If you can do this so that the tip comes to a point, so much the better.

◆ If you need to replace your shoelaces, measure the ones that came with the shoes and look for the same size replacement. Or just look at the shoe and count the number of *eyelets* (openings) that the shoelace goes into on both sides, and then multiply that number by 3.

So, for example—say your sneaker has 10 eyelets (5 shoelace openings on 1 side… and 5 on the other). Then 10 x 3 = 30, so you will need 30" shoelaces for those sneakers.

LEATHER ACCESSORIES

 Leather has always been fashionable in this country. In fact, many Native American tribes lived in tepees made from cow leather and wore clothes and footwear that were made from leather. And why not? Leather looks good, it's warm and it's durable. *Here are some tips for making it even more durable…*

Liven Up Leather Luggage

Dampen a cloth with an egg white and then lightly coat the leather with it. Wait a few minutes, then wipe off the egg and buff the leather with a soft cloth.

Remove Scuff Marks on Luggage

Wipe the scuff marks off your best leather luggage with a dab of lemon extract (available at

supermarkets) using a clean washcloth. Then wipe off any excess extract.

> **FYI: Extract…Defined**
> In case you're wondering, an extract is the distilled or evaporated oil of a food or plant, which is usually dissolved in an alcohol base.

Stains on Leather Gloves

You can erase practically any stain from your nice leather gloves with a gum eraser (available at stationery and art-supply stores).

For an oil stain on a pair of leather gloves, pack cornstarch on the spot and let it sit overnight. Whisk it off the next day with a soft brush or your hand.

Dirt on White Kid Gloves

Rub a bit of flour into the dirt, then whisk it off with a soft brush or your hand.

HATS

We've all heard the expression "mad as a hatter"— historically, hatters DID go mad from inhaling the mercury used in the process of making felt hats. But mercury is no longer used, and hatters are no longer mad. (Here comes the segue for this section…)

But if you're mad about hats, here are some ways to take care of them…

Clean and Brighten

In a clean, dry container, combine 1 cup of cornmeal with 1 cup of table salt. Cover the container and shake it until the ingredients are combined. Then, using a soft hairbrush, brush your felt hat.

With your hand, diligently work the cornmeal-salt mixture into the hat, then let it stay that way for a few minutes. Brush your felt hat again—removing all of the mixture this time—and you'll have a tip-top topper.

Revitalizing Your Hat's Nap

Use this hint only if you have a felt hat that looks like it has seen better days, and if you promise to be super-careful.

Boil water in a teapot, and when the steam starts pouring out, lower the heat so that the steam trickles out at a steady pace. Then, *using extreme caution*, hold the hat over the steaming spout, rotating it, and allow the steam to reach every inch of the hat. When you're done, let the hat air-dry and gently brush it with a soft hairbrush. (Easter Parade anyone?)

Drying a Beret

After you've washed your beret, help it keep its proper shape by letting it dry on a Frisbee or a dinner plate.

Wash Your Caps

Washing machines tend to be tough on baseball caps...so use the dishwasher instead. The cap will come out clean, and it will also retain its shape.

SEWING

Whether it's a torn hem or it's a popped button, our aim here is to keep you in *stitches*—ba-da-DUM! And these suggestions should help.

Needles and Pins

◆ Use a bar of soap or a thick candle as a pincushion. When you take a pin or needle out of the soap or candle, it should glide through the fabric with the greatest of ease.

◆ If you didn't do the soap or candle thing, and you have oily hair, carefully (*very* carefully) rub the needle or pin through your hair and see if that helps it glide through the fabric.

◆ Keep a magnet handy (you may want to glue it to the end of a yardstick), and use it at the end of a sewing session to attract any stray needles and pins.

◆ To sharpen the tip of a pin or needle, rub it with an emery board.

◆ Make a pincushion by stuffing a little drawstring bag or plastic bag with plain (no soap) steel-wool pads. Each time you stick pins or needles in or out, you'll be sharpening them.

Thread

◆ Dip the end of the thread in nail polish and let it dry. The dry thread will be stiff and easy to put through the eye of the needle.

◆ Squirt a bit of hair spray on the end of a piece of thread—this will stiffen it and make it easier to use.

◆ As soon as you've threaded the needle—but before you knot the bottom—sew through a fabric-softener sheet. This will make the thread behave better as you sew with it.

◆ Keep threads from unraveling and tangling by putting a rubber band around each spool of thread. Be sure to tuck the loose thread end under the rubber band to hold it in place.

Hems

Measuring and Marking

Whether you use a ruler to measure the number of inches to turn up a hem, or a yardstick to mark the inches from the floor to the hemline, make the marking process easier by placing a rubber band around the exact line on the ruler or yardstick.

No-Pins Pinning

Paper clips or spring-type clothespins can be more convenient than pins when pinning up a hem...and you cannot prick yourself with a clothespin.

Hemming Jeans

If your jeans are too long and you're not into the style of having shredded hems, consider an easy way out. Rather than dealing with the difficult chore of denim hemming (say that 3 times fast!), turn up each hem, iron the folded edge, and then put on duct tape.

Duct tape now comes in many colors, so you can match the tape to your jeans or other clothing...not that anyone will see it. The duct tape should stay stuck on your clothes through many washings.

Emergency Hemming

You pull an innocent-looking thread and half your hem comes down...or you get your heel caught in your hem, making that section of hem hang down. When these mini-emergencies occur, you can do a temporary repair, depending on what's available.

Double-sided tape is great, but chances are, you'd sooner have needle and thread around. There's always a quick fix with duct tape, safety pins or staples. If you're going to staple a hem, be sure to do it so that the open side of each staple is on the outside, rather than next to your skin where it can scratch you or snag your socks or hose.

The Ghost of Hemline Past

If you lengthen a hemline and don't want the previous hem to show, here's what to do—on the underside of the fabric, gently sponge distilled white vinegar on the old crease.

Fold the garment where you want the new hem to be, place a damp cloth over the fold, then press it with a hot iron. The old hemline will disappear, the new hem will be nicely set.

Basting—Just Thread Once

If you work off a spool of thread when *basting* (using long stitches to temporarily hold fabric layers or seams in place until the final sewing is completed...at which time the basting stitches will be removed), you won't have to stop to rethread your needle. This may be one of those "Hey, why didn't I think of that?" moments.

Waistband Expander

When your favorite skirt has gotten a bit too tight around the waist, get a piece of 1"-wide elastic. Determine how many inches you need to extend the waistband and cut the length of the elastic accordingly.

Then using a button that's the same size as the button that's already on the waistband, sew it on 1 end of the piece of elastic. On the other end of the elastic, cut a buttonhole-size slit. The waistband button goes through that slit, while the button on the elastic goes in the original buttonhole.

Of course, it may be easier to just go on a diet than to bother with all of this!

Sewing Machines

◆ It's important to keep your sewing machine well-oiled. It's also important to make sure the oil doesn't stain the fabric you're sewing. So, after each oiling, treat a few sheets of paper towel as if they're fabric, and stitch some rows until you're sure that all of the excess oil has been absorbed.

- To prevent the sewing machine pedal from sliding around on a hardwood floor, place the pedal on a computer mouse pad or on a drink coaster.

- To sharpen a sewing-machine needle, take a sheet of fine sandpaper and stitch a few rows of thread.

- For more accurate sizing, be sure to iron pattern sections *before* laying them on the fabric. A wrinkled pattern piece can change the size of a garment.

Buttons

- Double-over your thread before threading a needle. Next, using a big-eyed needle, thread it, then double the thread again and knot it.

     Think of the time you'll save. You'll be sewing with 4 strands of thread and will only have to go through the buttonhole a couple of times to secure the button in place.

Sewing Buttons on Thick Fabric

Do you know how, on some jackets or coats, it looks as though the buttons are falling off, but they really aren't? A bit of slack is purposely put between the button and the garment—it allows the garment to lie flat when buttoned.

Here's how to create that slack between the button and the fabric—first, anchor the thread starting from the underside. Pull the needle through the fabric and sew 2 tiny stitches on top of each other. Then place the button over the stitches and place a toothpick or kitchen matchstick on top of the button. Bring the needle up through 1 hole, over the toothpick and down through the other hole.

Repeat the "up, over and down" 2 or 3 times, ending under the button. Discard the toothpick and wind the thread around the underside of the button a few times. Push the needle through the fabric, make a couple of stitches, then knot and cut the thread.

- Dab a little glue or clear nail polish on the thread in the middle of each button and it will be less likely to pop off—no matter how much you eat for dessert.

- Children's clothes and some types of work clothes often test the endurance of buttons. However, you can sew buttons on with dental floss, and they'll pass the test with flying colors (and no cavities!).

- When sewing 4-holed buttons, first sew 2 holes as though they were the only holes on the button. After you finish off these 2 holes with a knot, then sew the other 2 holes.

     That way, if the thread on 2 of the holes tears or comes loose, the other 2 holes (which were sewn separately) will keep the button from falling off.

- If you need to reattach a popped button and there's no needle and thread around, see if you can find a twist tie, like the kind used to close loaves of bread, garbage bags or supermarket produce bags.

     Let water run on the twist tie for a few seconds and remove the paper. If it's a plastic twist tie, cut off the plastic. The object here is to use the piece of wire. Thread it through the button's holes and twist it closed.

- To guard against cutting or tearing a garment when removing a button, slip a comb under the button. Then slide a knife, razor or box cutter between the button and comb to cut the thread.

- This is just plain ol' common sense—store buttons in a glass jar or plastic case so that you can see what you have.

- String all the same-color buttons on a long piece of dental floss…or put sets of buttons on big safety pins.

Zippers

- Replace a zipper's missing pull tab with a silver, gold or any other appropriately-colored paper clip.

- Squirt a small puff of foam shaving cream on your finger and spread it over the teeth of the stuck zipper. The cream should lubricate the area, allowing you to unzip the problem.

Patches

- To prevent a patch from shrinking after it's been sewn on a garment, wash the patch fabric before attaching it.

- Before sewing on a patch, attach it in place with a straight pin or a few dabs of water-soluble liquid glue (such as Elmer's). The patch will stay in place while you stitch it on. And the glue will wash away when the garment is laundered.

- If you want to cover a hole with an iron-on cloth patch, be sure to place a piece of aluminum foil under the hole. It will keep the patch from sticking to the ironing-board cover.

- How's this for *irony*? To remove an iron-on patch, just iron it with a hot iron—it will peel right off.

 Padded Patch for Work Pants

This is a good idea if you're doing any on-your-knees cleaning, gardening or just crawling around on the floor.

Take that old, comfortable-but-less-than-flattering pair of pants out of the thrift-store donation bag. Sew a patch on each knee, leaving the top side of the patch open...as though you've sewn a pocket on each knee.

Then, in each pocket, place a sponge...or a substantial shoulder pad...or a piece of foam rubber. These protective pads are easy to remove and will make a big difference in your on-the-knee cleaning or gardening endurance.

Pockets

At the first sign of a pocket wearing thin (you know that thin, threadbare feeling), reinforce it with iron-on tape (available at sewing-supply and crafts stores). ■

■ Products ■

Magnifying Finger Attachment

Here's a case where "little things mean a lot." This flexible 5x magnifying glass attaches to your finger—it makes sewing, knitting, crafts and hobby projects a lot easier and done more efficiently. It also comes in handy for removing splinters.

Source: Miles Kimball, 800-546-2255, *www.miles kimball.com*.

Oliso Steam Iron with Auto Lift

You'll want this iron if you have arthritis, carpal tunnel syndrome or any other pain-in-the-wrist condition. This is the first major innovation in iron design in over 60 years. And innovative it is.

Imagine—a handle senses your touch and lowers the iron onto the fabric. When you release the handle, it lifts the iron to protect the fabric. Therefore, you don't keep lifting the iron and standing it on its end. You won't burn the garment you're ironing (or your hand or arm), and the iron won't topple over. This smartly designed iron is safe, efficient, fun to use and it can cut down your ironing time by as much as 30%.

The steam iron is available at retail stores throughout the country, including Bed, Bath & Beyond, Fry's Electronics Stores and Hancocks Fabric Stores, as well as select Ace Hardware stores and online at Amazon.com.

Source: Oliso, 800-899-5157, *www.oliso.com*.

Dye Grabber

A terry-cloth panel lets you wash colored and white fabrics together. It helps both colored and white clothes keep their vibrancy. When you toss this item in with your wash load, it grabs hold of and absorbs loose dye and grime.

Dye Grabber starts out white, then changes—getting darker and darker with each wash load...proof that it does absorb the dye from clothes. It's available at supermarkets across the country.

Source: Carbona, 866-227-2662, *www.carbona.com*.

CHAPTER 4

Better Bath Basics

On the TV show *Family Feud*, the question was, "Which room in your house do you most hate to clean?" And the #1 answer was, "The bathroom!" While we don't have any magic solution for avoiding the ongoing chore of bathroom cleaning and maintenance, we do have some helpful hints on how to get satisfying results without too much work.

For starters…José Carreras, a member of the world-renowned "Three Tenors," says that he never sings in the shower, but he does occasionally sing in the bathroom. He notes that bathrooms usually have the best acoustics. If you like to sing, do it while you work. It will make you feel a lot happier as you get the job done.

TOILET

According to the World Toilet Organization (*www.worldtoilet.org*), the average person uses the toilet 2,500 times each year—that's about 6 to 8 times a day. And it will probably come as no surprise that women generally take 3 times as long as men to use the toilet.

With all that use, it's no wonder the toilet needs cleaning. *Here are some hints that will have your bowl gleaming as you flush with pride…*

Cleaning the Bowl

◆ For basic cleaning, just toss 2 or 3 tablespoons of baking soda around the bowl, then scrub with a toilet brush and flush.

◆ If you want a deodorizer and disinfectant as well as a cleaner, pour ½ cup of distilled white vinegar around the bowl, with or without the baking soda. Let it stay for a few minutes, then scrub with a brush and flush.

Bowl Brightener

Every now and then, pour a 1-liter bottle of cola—flat or fizzy, regular or diet—into the bowl. Let it stay there for an hour or so, then flush and notice how the porcelain sparkles.

Cleaning Toilet Rings

◆ A ring in the toilet bowl is usually because of hard-water buildup. Make a paste of borax powder (available at supermarkets and drugstores) and a few drops of lemon juice. Wet

74

the bowl by flushing the toilet. Then smear the paste on the ring with a sponge or plastic knife. Let it stay there for a couple of hours. Then scrub with a toilet brush and flush the toilet again.

◆ Wet a pumice stone (available at drugstores) with a bit of water, and then gently rub the toilet ring with the stone. Wetting the stone is important because a dry pumice stone will scratch the porcelain surface.

Basic Stain Removers

◆ Toss a couple of Alka-Seltzer or denture-cleansing tablets into the toilet bowl. Once the fizzing stops, scrub the stains with a brush and flush.

◆ If you have some Tang fruit juice powder, sprinkle ⅓ cup of the powder in the bowl. Leave it there for a few hours, then scrub with a brush and flush.

◆ If the stains are too tough for even Tang or denture cleanser, empty a few vitamin C capsules, or mash vitamin C tablets into a powder and drop it in the bowl. Let it stay that way for a few hours. Then scrub with a brush and flush.

Toilet Seat

You can clean and disinfect the toilet seat by using this simple formula. In a spray bottle, add ½ cup of distilled white vinegar, ½ cup of plain water and 15 drops of tea tree oil (available at health-food stores). Shake the bottle, then spray both sides of the toilet seat. Wipe the seat dry with a clean cloth.

The slight vinegar smell will disappear, leaving the unusual, fresh scent of tea tree oil.

 FYI: Keep a Lid on It

When you flush without closing the toilet seat lid, a polluted plume of water vapor and bacteria spews out of the flushing toilet bowl. The polluted water particles waft around the bathroom and eventually land. If there are toothbrushes out in a nearby cup or holder, they will be a landing strip for some of those particles.

Toilet Tank

The parts inside a toilet tank—including the flush valve and the ballcock—are constantly submerged in water and are used many times each day. There's a lot of wear and tear on these parts and, even though they're fairly easy to replace, you want them to do their job properly for as long as possible. *The following suggestions should help that happen…*

Cleaning the Tank

◆ Once a month, before you go to bed, pour half of a 1-pound box of baking soda into the toilet tank. The next morning, when you flush the toilet, the tank—and the bowl, too—should be nice and clean.

◆ Drop in a couple of denture-cleansing tablets. Wait 1 hour for them to stop fizzing, then start cleaning and flush.

Tank Leak—A Test

If you suspect that water is leaking from your tank to the bowl, test it by putting a few drops of food coloring in the tank. If, after flushing, the water in the bowl turns the color of the food coloring, it's time to call a plumber to repair the leak.

Overflow Prevention

If, after you flush, the water is rising higher than it should, quickly turn on the cold water in the sink as well as in the bathtub or shower. The cold water coming through the pipes will cause a vacuum that will suction the water in the toilet down the drain.

Commit this tip to memory. It's a great thing to know, especially when you go to somebody else's home.

Clogged Toilet

If you have a minor clog and no plunger, try squirting about 2 ounces (4 tablespoons) liquid dish detergent in the bowl. Give it at least 15 minutes to work its magic, then flush. (Keep in mind the overflow prevention method, above.)

DID YOU KNOW?

The cleanest toilet in a public rest room is usually in the stall *closest* to the door. It tends to be the least used.

BATHUB

Bathing began as part of a magical and religious ritual. Then, thanks to the ancient Romans' regard for physical cleanliness, luxurious public baths were built and became the rage. By 300 AD, there were more than 900 bath houses in Rome. Gradually, people realized the health implications of public bathing and, what started as a social event soon shifted to a personal experience in the privacy of a person's home.

Today, it seems as though we've come full circle. While a shower is for getting clean, a bath is a magical, relaxing indulgence...it's almost a religious experience. *But whatever the reason for using your bath, here are ways to make it the best it can be...*

Cleaning the Tub

◆ The best time to clean the tub is right after someone has taken a shower or bath, and the room is warm and humid. Get rid of the grime before it has a chance to cake on.

◆ When cleaning the tub, kneel on a couple of sponges or shoulder pads. Your knees will be glad you did.

◆ Try this for an easy cleanser—sprinkle baking soda around the tub, then wet a washcloth with distilled white vinegar and scrub, then rinse.

If you do this once or twice a week, chances are there will be no need to *scrub*. It will be more like "just wipe it down." Plus, it's great that you are not using harmful chemicals or drain-clogging cleansers. *And* your bathtub is so clean!

Bathtub Rings

To prevent bathtub rings, do not use any bath preparations (such as gels, bubble bath, salts, pearls, etc.) that contain oils.

But what if you don't use them, and you still have a ring around the tub? Then, as you're filling the bath, add ½ cup of baking soda to the running water. After the bath, let out the water, and there should be no ring around the tub.

As a bonus, the baking soda soothes, softens and conditions skin.

✱ **Remove a Ring with Hose!**
If you forgot to add the baking soda and the bathtub still has a ring, get a pair of old, clean pantyhose, cut off a leg, scrunch it up and use it to rub off the ring.

Chlorinated-Water Stains

◆ Put a few paper towels on the water stains, then pour distilled white vinegar on the towels. Let it stay that way for at least 30 minutes, until the towels are almost dry and the stains are gone.

◆ If the stains are stubborn and the vinegar alone doesn't make them disappear, sprinkle baking soda on the stains and wipe them away with the moist paper towels.

Discolorations

◆ Cover the discolored spots with lemon juice —enough to cover the spots—and let it stay there for about 30 minutes. Then sprinkle about 1 tablespoon of baking soda on a wet washcloth and scrub the discolored spots.

◆ If you're still seeing spots, take 1 tablespoon of cream of tartar and add a few drops of 3% hydrogen peroxide—just enough to make a paste. With an old toothbrush, rub the paste into the discolored spots and then let it dry. When it's dry, rinse it clean.

Rust Stains

◆ Does the can of shaving cream leave a rust ring in the bathtub or on the sink? Paint the bottom rim—the part that touches the sink or tub and leaves the ring—with colorless nail polish. Let it dry thoroughly and then give it a second coat.

◆ Mix 1 teaspoon of table salt or cream of tartar with ¼ teaspoon of lemon juice to make a paste. Put the paste on a soft cloth and rub the rust stain away. (Then be sure to paint colorless nail polish on the bottom of the can that caused the rust ring.)

Cleaning Bathtub Mats

If you have a rubber or vinyl bathtub mat, throw it in the washing machine with a load of towels. The agitating towels will scrub the mat clean.

 CAUTION: Do not put a rubber or vinyl bath mat in the dryer.

Removing Nonslip Bathtub Appliqués

◆ Put 1 cup of distilled white vinegar in a pan and heat it up. Once the vinegar is hot, soak a sponge or cloth in it, then use tongs to plop it on top of the appliqué. When it cools to room temperature, take it off…the sponge or cloth *and* the appliqué.

 CAUTION: Although distilled white vinegar should be safe for all shiny surfaces, check with the manufacturer before you use it—especially if you have a new bathtub that's made of fiberglass, Plexiglas or any other modern material.

◆ Cover the appliqué with a piece of aluminum foil. Then zap it with a hair dryer set on *hot*. The idea is for the heat to melt the glue that's causing the appliqué to stick. After 1 or 2 minutes, you should be able to peel it off.

◆ Dunk a straight-edged razor blade (it may help to use a blade holder) in liquid dish detergent and *very carefully* scrape off the appliqué. Keep redunking as you progress.

If some of the appliqué adhesive remains on the bottom of the tub, use nail polish remover to clean it off.

Cleaning Whirlpool Tubs

It's important to prevent soap scum and anything else that might build up and clog the jets of the whirlpool. Once or twice a year, pour 1 gallon of distilled white vinegar into the water and run the whirlpool.

SINK

Once considered utilitarian, bathroom sinks are now available in a wide range of colors, materials, shapes and sizes to match any décor. So if you want to wash your troubles down the drain, be sure to choose the right sink for the job.

Cleaning the Sink

See "Cleaning the Tub" on page 76.

Fixing a Faucet Drip

◆ If you can't stop the faucet from dripping, you might need to replace the washer (a flat, rubber disk that prevents leakage). Any hardware store should have them—be sure to ask a knowledgeable salesperson for instructions.

◆ Until you replace the washer, you can at least stop the drip from getting on your nerves… just place a sponge or washcloth in the sink, directly underneath the faucet.

◆ If you can still hear the *drip…drip…drip*, then wrap a towel around the faucet and keep it in place with a rubber band or piece of string. Or, just take the string and tie it around the spout—the water will run down the string noiselessly.

SHOWER

The average in-and-out-in-5-minutes shower uses almost 20 gallons of water… compared with 37 gallons for the average bath. Obviously, showering is a good way to get clean *and* save water. You can save even more water by showering "The Navy Way."

Because of the scarcity of fresh water on ships, sailors are taught to turn on the shower just long enough to get wet. Then they turn off the shower, quickly soap up and scrub, and turn the shower on again to rinse off. Fast and efficient!

Whether you "Go Navy!" or shower any other way, here are some helpful hints to increase your shower power…

Cleaning the Showerhead

◆ If you aren't getting enough shower power, it may be that mineral deposits (hard-water buildup) are clogging the showerhead and minimizing the spray.

Do you have a totally metal showerhead that can be safely detached from the pipe and then put back? If so, remove the showerhead, put it in a big pot with ½ cup of distilled white vinegar and 1 gallon of water. Boil it for about 15 minutes. Then, when the showerhead is cool enough to handle, reattach it and…have a nice spray!

◆ If the showerhead is not all metal—or if you cannot detach it from the pipe—pour about 1 cup of distilled white vinegar in a small, leak-proof plastic bag. Put the bag over the showerhead and secure it in place with a thick rubber band or piece of string. Let it stay that way overnight.

In the morning, remove the bag, scrub the head with an old toothbrush, rinse with clean water and enjoy your power shower.

Cleaning Glass Shower Doors

◆ While you're still in the shower, pour a little shampoo on a washcloth and wash the doors. Rinse them with the shower's spray. After you're out of the shower and finish drying yourself, wipe the shower doors dry with your used towel.

◆ That takes care of the inside-the-shower shower doors. Clean the other side—the outside —of the shower doors with 1 part distilled white vinegar to 3 parts plain water. Dampen a cloth with the mixture and wipe down the doors, then dry them with a few paper towels or a dry cloth.

◆ For really grimy glass shower doors—either inside or outside—pour some full-strength distilled white vinegar on a washcloth or sponge, and go over the doors with it. Wait 5 minutes, then rub a corner of the door with the cloth or sponge.

If the grime comes off easily, finish the job. If the scum and film don't come off, sprinkle a bit of baking soda on the cloth or sponge, and scour the doors until they're clean. Then rinse with plain water and dry with a clean cloth.

Keeping Shower Doors Clean

Once your glass shower doors are nice and clean, pour a few drops of baby oil on a soft cloth and apply a light layer of the oil to the doors. This will keep them free of soap scum, hard-water deposits and dirt for weeks at a time.

Cleaning Shower Door Tracks

Stuff up the drain holes in the door track with wadded-up pieces of paper towel or aluminum foil. Then trickle in distilled white vinegar so that it covers the entire bottom of the track. Let it stay that way for 30 minutes.

Then remove the paper or foil plugs and rinse the track with water. Wipe it with a clean cloth or paper towel to dry.

Smooth-Sliding Secret
Apply a light coat of petroleum jelly to the track—this will keep your shower doors gliding smoothly.

Cleaning a Plastic Shower Curtain

◆ Before you hang up a brand-new curtain, fill the bathtub with a few inches of water, then add 2 cups of table salt. Put in the new curtain, and let it take a saltwater bath for about 10 minutes. Shake off the water, dry with a clean cloth and then hang up your mildew-proof curtain.

◆ If the curtain has been used for a while and it has some mildew or soap scum on it, check to see if it is machine washable—lots of plastic curtains are nowadays.

If so, just toss it in the machine along with 2 or 3 towels. Add your regular laundry detergent and 1 cup of distilled white vinegar. The towels act as buffers against the machine's agitation, and they will scrub the curtain clean.

As soon as the curtain is machine-clean, it should be mildew-free, soft and pliable—dry it with a cloth and rehang.

◆ If your curtain is not machine washable, you can clean it with a cloth or sponge dipped in distilled white vinegar.

Slip-Sliding Away

If the curtain doesn't glide open and close as smoothly as you would like it to, coat the rod with a thin layer of baby oil or petroleum jelly, or rub it with a bar of soap.

Replacing Shower Curtain Rings

The next time you buy plastic shower curtain rings, consider buying 2 sets instead of just 1. That way, if a ring breaks (as plastic rings often do), you will have extra replacement rings handy, and you won't have to buy and change an entire new set of rings.

TILE & GROUT

Have you ever noticed that the interior walls of many highway tunnels are tiled? According to the International Bridge, Tunnel & Turnpike Association (*www.ibtta.org*), ceramic tiles have 2 big advantages—tiles are easy to clean (think of the constant fumes, dust, tire particles, and exhaust in a tunnel)...and tiles are durable (having to withstand grime, vehicle emissions, water leakage, temperature changes, artificial light, sunlight and vibrations).

Compared to the abuse tiles take in a tunnel, cleaning and maintaining your tiled bathroom should be a piece of cake...or a cake of soap...or all of the hints that follow...

Cleaning Solutions

◆ Wet a sponge with distilled white vinegar, wipe it over the tile and grout and then use an old toothbrush to scrub it. Rinse everything clean with plain water.

◆ Mix 1 part borax powder (available at supermarkets or drugstores) with 2 parts baking soda, then add enough water to form a thick paste. Dip an old toothbrush in the paste and scrub the grout and tile. Rinse it clean with plain water.

◆ Do you have an old-fashioned typewriter eraser at home—the kind that's round and has a brush attached? If so, rub the eraser on the grout, then brush away the eraser particles. (Aren't you glad you kept that eraser all these years?)

◆ The grungiest grout is usually underfoot between floor tiles. If you want to get the grout back to its original color and are willing to work hard to do it, stock up on sandpaper.

 NOTE: If fine (150 grit) sandpaper doesn't do the job, kick it up a notch and use medium (100 grit) sandpaper.

Cut the sandpaper into 2" strips. Sand the grout with a folded piece of the sandpaper strip. It's a tedious job, but if there's a big difference in the way it looks, and you love it, then keep it up!

Once you complete the sanding, wipe the floor clean. You may also want to apply a coat of tile sealer (available at hardware and paint stores).

Mold and Mildew

If you suspect a major mold problem is developing in your home or office (the first clue is that you feel sick only when you're in that moldy area), visit the Mold-Help Organization's Web site (*www.mold-help.org*) for more information, including an inexpensive method of mold testing.

In this section, we offer solutions for dealing with mild cases of mold and mildew...and ways to prevent a major problem.

Preventing Mold and Mildew

◆ Moisture is the primary cause of bathroom mold and mildew. To combat excess moisture, open the bathroom door right after you shower or bathe. Better yet, if you have an exhaust fan, turn it on right *before* you jump in the shower.

◆ When you're done bathing, wipe down the shower walls with a clean, dry cloth or towel. It should only take a minute or so, and it will save you the trouble of cleaning away mold and mildew later on.

◆ After you step out of the shower, close the shower curtain to help prevent mold and mildew from growing in the folds. (You may first want to wipe down the shower walls with a towel or cloth.)

◆ If you are going to be away from home for some length of time, leave an open bag of natural clay kitty litter in the bathtub (or put an old box top filled with litter in the bathroom). The litter absorbs excess moisture and helps prevent mildew.

◆ Hot showers or baths produce moisture that can cause mold and mildew. Absorb some of the excess moisture by keeping a few charcoal briquettes in the bathroom.

Preventing a Steamy Bathroom

Before you run a bath, fill the tub with about 1" of cold water—and *then* add the hot water. Doing this should prevent "steamy bathroom syndrome," which may stop mold and mildew from developing.

Remove Mold and Mildew

Add 1 cup of lemon juice and 1 cup of table salt to 1 gallon of hot water. Use this solution to wipe the moldy and/or mildewed areas thoroughly.

Then rinse with plain water, and dry with a clean cloth.

Cleaning Chrome Fixtures

◆ Clean anything made from chrome with distilled white vinegar or rubbing alcohol, dabbed on a cloth or sponge. Then dry and buff the chrome with a soft cloth.

◆ Fabric-softener sheets—before or after they've been used—give chrome a great shine.

DRANS

There are 2 kinds of drains—clogged and unclogged. The remedies that follow should work like magic to clear your drain without harmful fumes, harsh chemicals or—the best part—an expensive plumber.

Clean and Deodorize

Once a month—or anytime there seems to be an unpleasant smell coming from 1 of the bathroom drains—pour 1 or 2 cups of baking soda down the drain. Follow by flushing it with hot tap water.

Fixing Clogged Drains

◆ If the water in your bathroom sink or tub isn't draining as quickly as it should, chances are there is a tangle of hair that needs to be cleaned out. It's a simple yet disgusting job, but someone's gotta do it. You'll want to wear rubber gloves and have a plastic bag handy.

Twist and pull out the pop-up stopper. Remove the hair and put it in the bag. Then clean the gunk off the metal tube with

1 tablespoon of baking soda or 1 ounce of distilled white vinegar on a sponge. Then replace the stopper and see how quickly the water goes down the drain.

◆ Pour 1 cup of baking soda down the clogged drain of your shower or bathtub. Follow that immediately with 1 cup of table salt, then ½ cup of distilled white vinegar.

If there is foaming and fizzing and gurgling—that's good. Let the ingredients continue working their way through the sludgy clog, while you boil 2 quarts of tap water and set a kitchen timer for 15 minutes.

When the timer goes off, carefully and slowly pour the boiled water down the drain. Then let the hot tap water run for a minute.

If the drain isn't completely unclogged, repeat the entire procedure again.

◆ Toss 3 Alka-Seltzer tablets down the drain and add 1 cup of distilled white vinegar. Wait 3 minutes, then run the hot water.

Clog Prevention

Use a hair catcher over the drain every time someone showers or bathes. They are inexpensive and available at most hardware and drugstores—even some supermarkets.

Hair catchers generally come in 2 sizes, so measure the diameter of your drain before you go shopping.

SOAP

The innovative and influential artist Pablo Picasso once said, "The purpose of art is washing the dust of daily life off our souls." In that vein, we say, "The purpose of soap is washing the dust of daily life off ourselves." *Here are some very helpful ways to make the most of your bars of soap…*

Preventing Messes

◆ Keep a sponge on the soap dish and place the soap on the sponge. The sponge will absorb all of the soap's drippings. (You may want to forget about the soap dish and just use a sponge instead!)

◆ Place a small, waterproof object—the plastic cover from a prescription-pill bottle, or the round plastic core of a used-up roll of transparent tape—and keep it on the soap dish. Place the wet soap on top of the object, which will enable the soap to dry without soap mush getting stuck to the dish.

Soap Slivers

◆ Instead of discarding that last little sliver of soap, paste it onto the new bar of soap. Just suds up the new bar, and stick the sliver on top. The 2 soaps will dry as 1 bar.

◆ You can recycle slivers of soap by making slits in a bath sponge. Then stick the slivers into the sponge and enjoy a wonderfully soapy bath or shower.

Soap Life Extension

Keep a bar of soap unwrapped for a month before you use it—the air-exposed soap will harden and, once you start using it, it will last longer than usual.

If the unwrapped soap is scented, let it sit in your linen closet. It will make everything smell nice.

FRESHEN UP

 Our sense of smell is closely linked to our sense of well-being. Get a whiff of a pleasant scent, and we want to stick around. This section includes easy, healthful ways to keep the bathroom fresh and at its best, especially when *female* company is coming (women have keener senses of smell than men).

Safe and Natural Room Deodorizer

In a spray bottle, add 2 cups of distilled water (available at most supermarkets), 2 cups of rubbing alcohol and 3 drops of natural lemon oil (available at health-food stores). The lemon oil may seem pricey, but a 1-ounce bottle may last you a year or more.

A few sprays of the mixture will freshen the air without exposing you to the toxic risk of chemicals that are typically used in many commercial air fresheners. Inhaling certain chemicals has been linked to headaches, sinus infections and even asthma attacks.

Fresher Clothes Hamper

Sprinkle baking soda on the bottom of the hamper...or keep an open box in the hamper...or in some inconspicuous place in the bathroom. After a couple of months, change the box and pour the baking soda down the drain.

When Company Is Coming

◆ Right before your company is due to arrive, apply 1 or 2 drops of vanilla, almond or lemon extract (available at health-food stores) on

a bathroom light bulb. Turn on the light as you walk out. When the bulb heats up, the pleasant fragrance will permeate the air.

You can also give the warm bulb a spritz of your favorite perfume.

◆ Light scented candles to help eliminate odors and to create a more romantic or festive atmosphere.

> ✎ **NOTE:** If you haven't followed our other cleanup suggestions, soft candlelight can cover a multitude of sins. Just be sure the candles are in secure holders and placed in safe areas, away from children and pets.

Extra Towels

If you have counter space in your bathroom—and you want to have extra towels on hand for you or for guests—get a freestanding wine rack (available at household-supply stores). It's perfect to hold rolled-up towels.

Bathtub Toys

Get a mesh bag (available at most hardware and household-supply stores) to hold kids' favorite bathtub toys, and hang it on the tub's faucet. When not in use, the mesh bag will allow the toys to drain and dry. Besides, it's a neat way to keep them tidy and out of the way.

Guest Amenities

To make guests feel comfortable, hang a shoe bag over the bathroom door and fill the pockets with items they might need—for example, bars of soap, washcloths, body lotion, shampoo, a hair dryer, combs and brushes, hair ornaments, gel, mousse, toothbrush and toothpaste...even a rubber ducky. ■

■ Products ■

Bluefish Bath Alarm and Temperature Sensor

This item is wonderful for people who are not able to gauge water temperature accurately because of *neuropathy* (a disorder of the nerves).

This adorable Starfish Alarm helps put an end to bathtub overflow and accurately checks the water temperature. Features an LCD readout in either Fahrenheit or Celsius—your choice.

Batteries included…as well as free shipping from England.

Source: Byretech Ltd., +44 (0) 1527-522-522, *www. byretech.com.*

Aquasana Shower Systems

Removes chlorine, enhances pH balance and removes synthetic chemicals and volatile organic compounds from your water. Easy-to-install filter comes with a cartridge that filters up to 10,000 gallons. You can expect to save 20% to 25% on your water and water-heating expenses.

With chlorine filtered out and pH balance improved, your skin and hair will feel softer and healthier. The health benefit of no longer inhaling chlorine or absorbing it through your skin is far-reaching. Good for your health…and your pocketbook. What more could we ask?

Source: www.aquasense.com. 1-866-NOBOTTLE.

CHAPTER 5

All-Around-the-House Hints

eloved 18th-century author Jane Austen knew what she was talking about when she wrote, "Ah! There is nothing like staying at home for real comfort."

Although we do not want to encourage couch potato-ism, we do want you to thoroughly enjoy your home, both inside and out, each day of the week and every season of the year. With that in mind, we hope our suggestions help you with the basic maintenance and care of your humble abode.

INSIDE THE HOME

Instead of sitting in front of the TV or computer for the next few minutes, take a tour of your home with a pad and pen in hand. Pretend that the person or people who live there hired you to improve their living conditions. Look at each room as though you're seeing it for the very first time. Jot down all of the things that need fixing, moving, redecorating, reorganizing…whatever can be done to make it a more comfortable, convenient and attractive living space.

At the end of the tour, if you have a list of changes, set up a room-by-room schedule, and do what needs to be done within a reasonable amount of time—without putting pressure on yourself. (We're sure you'll find lots of ideas in this book to help get you through the list.)

If you couldn't think of any ways to improve your living conditions, it means 1 of 2 things—either everything is exactly the way you want it, which is great (and rare!)…or you couldn't be objective enough to see the need for improvement.

Regardless, we suggest that you check out the suggestions offered here for ways to organize everything that needs organizing…and to care for things you have.

⭐ What's in Store at Your New Home

- If you've just moved into a new home, ask the previous owner for the names of stores where certain household accessories were bought—such as tile, light fixtures, paint/wallpaper, carpeting, countertops, appliances and whatever else came with the house that may need repairing or replacing at some point down the road.

- If you had the house built for you, ask your contractor for the names of stores that he used as resources for your new home. You'll be happy you have the information—if and when you need it.

HOME OFFICE

Just about everyone seems to have a home office these days, whether it's a separate room, a computer work station or the dining room table.

Here are some helpful hints to help you organize your space and manage your clerical work more efficiently...

 Increasing Accomplishments
Studies have shown that making lists encourages productivity. Tack a to-do list up in your office. Once you've completed something on the list, put a line through it with an orange highlighter.

The color orange stimulates the involuntary nervous system. It should make you feel more alert and competent.

Pens and Pencils

◆ When you can't find your usual pencil sharpener, use a vegetable peeler instead. It's safer and more efficient than using a pocketknife.

◆ Store pens in a cup with the point down. They will last longer (and poke you less) than if they're stored with the point up, or lying down in a drawer.

◆ When a marker has just about had it, dip the tip in distilled white vinegar for a few seconds. Instead of diluting the ink, the vinegar will help bring out the marker's last drop of color.

 Better Business Cards
Before filing a business card, write pertinent information on the back of it so that when you come across it a few months or years from now, you'll know exactly who this card belonged to...where you met the person...and what you may have had in mind when you took the card. The more details you can jot down, the better.

Paper Shredder

To sharpen a paper shredder, take 2 pieces of aluminum foil about the size of an 8½" x 11" sheet of paper, and put them 1 at a time through your paper shredder. That should make the shredder's blades as sharp as new.

 Recycle a Slinky
Use an old Slinky on your desk to hold things like mail, CDs, Lotto tickets waiting to be checked or checks waiting to be deposited.

Correction Fluid Extender

If your bottle of correction fluid is too gooey to use, add 1 or 2 drops of nail polish remover. Shake the bottle vigorously until it sounds like there's liquid sloshing around.

 Easier Trash Cleanup
Put several liners in the wastebasket at once. When the basket is full, take out the trash in the top liner, leaving the liner underneath already in place.

Dry-Erase Board Cleaner

If you pick up the wrong marker—it's indelible instead of dry-erase—and write on the dry-erase board, try erasing the mark with some rubbing alcohol or non-dairy powdered creamer, such as Coffee-mate. Add a little of the powder on a damp cloth and wipe the board clean.

 Easy Tape Starter
Here's a great way to save time in finding the beginning of an already-started roll of tape—just place a toothpick under the end each time you finish using it.

Packing and Shipping Hints

Keep this tip in mind when you're packing and shipping books or any other printed material (as well as CDs, DVDs and video or audio cassettes)—the US Postal Service (USPS) offers a low "media mail" postage rate.

You can determine domestic and international postage rates online at *http://ircalc.usps. gov* or by calling 800-275-8777. Then compare the rates with UPS (*http://wwwapps.ups.com/ calTimeCost* or 800-742-5877)...as well as Federal Express (*www.fedex.com/ratefinder/home* or 800-463-3339).

Before you check out the cost of shipping a package, it's important to know the package's weight, its measurements and the sender's and recipient's ZIP codes.

Here are some other ways to help you wrap the package...

 Filling for the Birds

When packing a box to mail, use non-buttered air-popped popcorn to fill in spaces. It's inexpensive, weighs practically nothing, it's good for the environment and it does the job.

You may want to add a note from you, the sender, to the recipient—"This popcorn used for packing is safe for birds to eat."

Dealing with Packing Peanuts

As soon as you open a package and see those polystyrene packing peanuts sitting there—just waiting to attack you—rub your hands with an unused fabric-softener sheet. The peanuts will not cling to your fingers, and you'll be able to throw them away easily.

 FYI: Reuseable Peanuts

Although polystyrene packing peanuts are not recyclable, they are reusable. Oregon State University has a program where they will pick them up and redistribute them. If you're near OSU, call them at 541-737-2925 or e-mail them at *recycle@oregonstate.edu*.

You can also call the Plastic Loose Fill Council's Peanut Hotline at 800-828-2214 —they will tell you which businesses in your area are willing to accept used polystyrene packing peanuts.

Sealing/Unsealing Envelopes

◆ Lick the problem by *not* licking the envelope. Instead, use a glue stick or a small sponge and some water. It's fast, easy and sanitary.

◆ How many times have you sealed an envelope—and then realized that you forgot to enclose something...usually the whole reason you needed the envelope in the first place!

Place the sealed envelope in the freezer for about 3 hours. When you take it out, slip a knife under the flap and you should be able to open it neatly, then repackage it and reseal it.

Mailing Photos

Next time you use a new light bulb, keep the cardboard sleeve that the bulb was in. When you mail a photo, just slip it in the sleeve. It's the perfect protection for the photo (provided the sleeve and photo are compatible sizes).

LIGHTING KNOW-HOW

 How many readers of this book does it take to change a lightbulb? Just 1—you. That is, if you have a lightbulb that needs to be changed and if you turned to this page for advice. Well, go to it…and light up your life.

 Quieter Fluorescent Bulbs

The buzzing sound of a fluorescent lightbulb can be extremely annoying. Before buying a fluorescent bulb, discover how much noise it will make by looking at the bulb's box.

For a quieter bulb, look for the letter "A" on the box. Noisier bulbs have the letter "B" (as in buzzing) on the box.

Halogen Bulbs

When you acquire a halogen light fixture, chances are there will be a sticker on it that tells you that you need to use a specific type of bulb. Before you buy a halogen fixture, check it out with the salesperson…so that you know *exactly* what you're buying and what you will need in the way of replacement bulbs.

Halogen bulbs are generally more expensive than regular lightbulbs, but you make up the price because these bulbs are more energy efficient than regular incandescent bulbs.

Of course, halogen bulbs should *only* be used in halogen-approved fixtures. And never touch the bulb when it's on, or right after it has been turned off. Hot! Hot! Hot! *A few more cautions you may not know…*

◆ Always turn off the power source before removing, inserting or cleaning a lightbulb.

◆ DO NOT use halogen bulbs in close proximity to fabric, paper or any other combustible material.

◆ DO NOT look at the lit bulb for any length of time. It can be damaging to your eyes.

◆ DO NOT touch the halogen bulb's surface or inside reflectors with your bare hands—oils from your skin can shorten the life of the bulb. Wear clean, lint-free cotton or latex gloves or a lint-free cloth to install, clean or remove a halogen bulb.

◆ Any dirt, oil or lint that's on the bulb can also cause hot spots, resulting in lamp failure. If you notice dirt of any kind, turn off the electrical power. When the bulb is cool, put on gloves and clean the bulb with rubbing alcohol and a lint-free cloth.

 Spare Fuse-Box Fuses

Tape an extra fuse on the inside of the fuse box. When a fuse gets blown and needs to be replaced, you'll have a new one right where you need it.

GETTING ORGANIZED

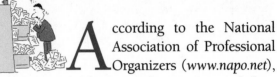

According to the National Association of Professional Organizers (*www.napo.net*), Americans are busier and more stressed than ever before, and they are looking for ways to better organize their lives—sometimes to the point of obsession.

There's no need to obsess! There are stores galore that cater to everyone's organizing needs—Bed, Bath & Beyond, Lowe's, Home Depot and the Container Store as well as discount stores, such as Target, Kmart and Wal-Mart.

Before you head out to the nearest mall, check out the following suggestions…they will show you how easy it is to begin organizing the disorganized things in your life. Once you start—and get the satisfaction of organizing a few small things—you will want to continue. And before long, you will be well on your way to having an orderly and organized home.

Storing Manuals, Guarantees And Warranties

Invest in a 3-ring, loose-leaf binder. Every time you buy something that comes with an owner's manual or instructions, punch holes in the paperwork and store it in the binder. Also, staple the purchase receipt and any guarantee or warranty (as well as replacement reorder instructions) to the item's manual.

If you ever need the proof of purchase ...or you have a question about using the item ...or need a replacement part—you will have all the information organized in the binder without going through a frantic sweat-and-search routine.

Of course, you should keep the binder in a special, within-sight and within-reach place so that you *always* know where it is.

Storing Take-out Menus

◆ Instead of having take-out menus floating all over your house, paste a manila envelope to the inside cover of the telephone book, and keep them in there.

◆ If you want to keep menus handy, put the menus in a large photo album that you can keep near the kitchen telephone (or wherever is most convenient).

When it's time to get take-out, flip through the pages until you reach the menu that whets your appetite and make your call.

Terrific Take-out Tip
Always put the date you got the menu right on the front of the menu. As prices and dishes change, you'll be able to keep tabs on the most recent menus of your favorite restaurants.

Storing Posters

Keeping posters flat seems better than rolling them up—and keeping them flat and protected seems best. Measure your posters, then get 2 pieces of clean cardboard from an art-supply or stationery store—you can also cut them out

of large cartons. But be sure that the cardboard pieces are larger than the posters.

Lay the posters between the 2 pieces of cardboard, put white tissue paper between each poster, and tape the sides closed. You can store about 6 posters this way.

Put the cardboard holder behind any piece of furniture that's against a wall and big enough so that none of the cardboard can be seen. Or slip the cardboard holder under a bed. Just remember where you hid it in case you want the posters.

The "What's Where" Book
It's a good idea to keep a "What's Where" notebook, especially if you are in the habit of putting lots of stuff away, then forgetting exactly where you put everything.

Of course, you must remember where you keep the "What's Where" book. How about keeping it on a bookcase or in a bedside drawer?

BOOKS

Francis Bacon—a prominent 17th-century statesman, philosopher and essayist—believed some books are to be tasted, others to be swallowed, and some few to be chewed on and digested. Of course, he didn't mean that *literally*...and certainly not by silverfish—those fast-moving little insects that feed on the starchy material in book bindings.

Here are some helpful ways to keep your books (including this book!) in good condition, so that you're the only living thing feasting on the pages.

Sticky Bookmark

It's so easy for a bookmark to slip out of a book, especially if it's the laminated kind. If you don't want to lose your place in the book you're reading, use a Post-it note instead.

You can either stick it directly on the page where you've stopped reading…or adhere it to the inside cover of the book—then, each time you stop reading, write the page number where you stopped on the Post-it note. It's an inexpensive, reusable and efficient bookmark.

Preventing Mustiness, Mildew and Silverfish

◆ Lack of circulating air around books encourages mustiness, mildew and silverfish. Resist the urge to stuff your books into the bookcase, and instead give them a little room to breathe by limiting your books to 1 layer per shelf, with enough room to add just 2 or 3 more books—but don't!

It also helps if you can keep books close to the front of the bookcase shelves, which lets more air get to them. Remember—no books behind books.

◆ If you're a real book lover, you may run out of bookshelf space and may have to store your excess books in cartons. Wrap a few charcoal briquettes in cheesecloth or in an old sock, and put it in the box along with the books. This helps to prevent mustiness and mildew. Store the carton in a cool, dry place, which will also help to keep your books in good condition.

Removing Mustiness

◆ Put the odorous tome in a brown paper bag, and fill the bag with crinkled pieces of plain (non-colored) newspaper, or 1 cup of natural clay kitty litter. Close up the bag, securing it with a rubber band.

After a couple of days, open the bag, take out the book and check to see if the smell is gone. If it isn't, replace the newspaper pages or kitty litter with a fresh supply, close the bag tightly again, and let it stay that way for 2 more days. Repeat this process until the book is odor-free.

◆ You can also place the book in a frost-free freezer overnight. In the morning, the musty smell should be gone.

 Best Book Duster!

Use a clean (never used) paintbrush to dust your books.

Removing Mold or Mildew

If you have a moldy or mildewed book that you treasure, and you have the patience to do a tedious job, try this remedy…

Get a soft toothbrush, and gently brush off the mold or mildew from each affected page. Then sprinkle cornstarch or baking soda between the dirty pages, and let it stay that way overnight.

The next morning, use a new, clean toothbrush to gently brush out the cornstarch or baking soda. The book may not be as good as new, but it will be a lot better than it was, and you will have stopped it from getting worse.

HOME ELECTRONICS

The home-shopping channel *America's Store* recently projected that the average American household will spend approximately $1,250 on consumer electronics this year. And that's just for batteries! (Only kidding.)

Actually, $1,250 seems conservative to us, considering all of the new and smaller versions of electronic gadgets that we see advertised on a daily basis.

Whether you're the first on your block to have the latest *whatever*, or you're happy hanging on to the older models of electronic products you've finally mastered, here are some ways to take care of them so that they will keep working for you.

Cleaning a Telephone

◆ Dampen a soft cloth with distilled white vinegar and wipe the telephone clean. Be sure to thoroughly clean the handset, earpiece and mouthpiece, where most germs congregate.

◆ For hard-to-reach areas around the buttons, use a cotton swab that's been dipped in distilled white vinegar. The smell will disappear in a few minutes.

Caring for a Computer

◆ Get the dust out of the keyboard crevices with a can of compressed air (available at hardware and art-supply stores).

◆ A hair dryer on *cool* can clean the keyboard.

◆ If the keys are the kind that don't pop off, you can use a portable vacuum cleaner on the keyboard.

◆ Use swabs moistened with water or rubbing alcohol to get at those hard-to-reach places. Lint-free (foam) swabs are best.

◆ If there's something stuck between 2 keys, press Silly Putty on it. When you peel off the Putty, the piece of dirt should come out with it. What? You don't have Silly Putty? *You can make your own using either of the following recipes...*

   ◆ In a cup, put 2 tablespoons of white glue. In another cup, dissolve 1 teaspoon of

Epsom salt in 1 teaspoon of water. (Don't worry if it doesn't dissolve completely.) Add the Epsom-salt liquid to the glue, and stir until it's the consistency of Silly Putty. Store the mixture in a plastic bag or other airtight container.

◆ Combine 1 cup of white glue with ½ cup of liquid starch. Stir until you have Silly Putty. Store the mixture in a plastic bag or other airtight container.

◆ An occasional swipe with a fresh baby wipe will work well to clean the computer's screen, keys and mouse.

◆ Wipe the monitor screen with a used fabric-softener sheet. The sheet helps repel dust by eliminating static cling. (You can also use this to dustproof your television screen.)

Cleaning a Spill on the Computer

Quick—turn off the computer! As soon as the power is off, turn over the keyboard to help prevent the spilled liquid from saturating circuits. Spread out paper towels in a dry area and shake the keyboard over them.

With the keyboard upside down, lift it high enough to clean it out with a microfiber or cotton cloth, and dry it as best as you can with paper towels. Once that's done, leave the keyboard upside down for at least 12 hours...even longer is better.

Meanwhile, check your newspaper for computer sales, because if it doesn't work when you plug it in again, you're going to need to buy a new keyboard.

 Preventing Spills
The key is to never eat or drink when you're working at your computer. Obviously!

Conserving Battery Power on a Laptop

◆ If you're not using your wireless card or the DVD player, switch them off.

◆ Use the battery until it's dead. Charge the battery completely, never partially.

◆ It's best to use and charge the battery at room temperature, definitely not in extreme heat or cold.

◆ Read the laptop manual and follow the suggestions for using your laptop's automatic function to save your work.

Keeping Computer Cables Neat

If you have an old telephone around—a unit you'll never use again—and it has a coiled cord, cut off the cord and gather up the messy computer cables. Wrap the coiled cord around the cables to keep all those loose wires together. It's so much neater to have 1 line of cables than several strands floating about.

If you don't have an old corded phone, you can also buy coiled telephone cord at the hardware store.

Keeping Electrical Cords Neat

Loose cords from extension cords and appliances can be kept together neatly—just thread the cords through a cardboard paper-towel or toilet-tissue tube.

 Clean Up Cord Clutter
Write the length of each extension cord and the appliance it fits on the storage tube as well as in the "What's Where" book (*see* page 89).

Electrical Connections— A Handy Guide

If you have several things (computer, printer, fax, speakers, etc.) plugged into a wall outlet or surge protector, take a picture of how the connections are set up.

Take a few photos—from the front, back and sides—so that if something gets undone, or if you have to move the equipment, you will know exactly what needs to go where.

 Dial, Switch or Knob Markings
When dial markings fade or are rubbed off by constant use, repaint those hard-to-see dials, switches or knobs with red nail polish.

Caring for Batteries

Battery manufacturers agree that refrigerating *alkaline* batteries—which are the most common household batteries—is not necessary or even recommended...and freezing alkaline batteries is definitely NOT recommended.

However, it IS a good idea to store alkaline batteries in a cool, dry place. They should retain 90% of their power while stored at room temperature, for a shelf life of 5 to 7 years.

Rechargeable batteries—either NiMH (nickel-metal hydride) or NiCad (nickel-cadmium)—lose their charge when kept at room temperature for a few days. If you store them in the freezer, they will retain 90% of their charge for several months.

When you take them out of the freezer, though, you will have to wait until they reach room temperature before using them.

NOTE: Always read and follow instructions diligently when using batteries and electronics equipment.

Caring for CDs, DVDs and Other Media

It seems like only yesterday that people were listening to music on the radio and watching films in movie theaters—and there were no other options. But today, people have a choice as to how they want their entertainment—either at home or in a public setting.

And technology is moving faster than ever—film reels and videotapes are being replaced by digital video disks (DVDs)...compact disks (CDs) have replaced record albums and audio tapes...and everybody seems to be connected to an iPod.

Here are some suggestions on how to care for your video/audio stuff...at least until it becomes obsolete.

◆ DO NOT touch the surface of a CD. Use only the outer edge and the center hole when you need to handle it.

◆ *NEVER* wipe a CD in a circular motion. It can—and most probably will—cause microscratches. If you do not have a CD-cleaning kit (available at electronics and music stores), then wipe the disk gently with a soft, water-dampened, lint-free cloth. Start in the center and work your way to the outer edge. Fight the urge to wipe in a circular motion.

◆ If the CD still skips after you wiped it with a dampened cloth, then combine 2 tablespoons of baking soda and 2 cups of water in a spray bottle. Shake well and spray the disk lightly. Then, with a dry, soft cloth, wipe it from the center outward in straight strokes.

◆ There's a rumor going around that peanut butter will clean CDs. We consulted with technicians and couldn't find anybody who thought this was a good idea. Eat the peanut butter yourself, and use baking soda and water on the disks. Just be gentle and use extreme care.

Storing CDs

Don't throw out cardboard shoe boxes. Paste attractive, room-matching contact paper on them and use them to store your CDs.

If you use clear (see-through) plastic shoe boxes, you can see which CDs are stored inside without opening them up.

Cleaning DVDs

Handle DVDs the same way you handle CDs...carefully. And NEVER wipe a DVD in a circular motion. Use a soft, cotton cloth or chamois to wipe the disk from the center straight toward the outer edge.

If the DVD is dusty, use an air puffer (available at art-supply and photography stores) to blow off the dust.

If a DVD has a somewhat heavy accumulation of dirt, rinse it with water. Remember—no rubbing or scraping. Pat dry with a cotton cloth. Do not use paper products, including lens paper, to wipe a DVD. They're too scratchy.

 Preserving Videotapes
You may be using DVDs now, but you're probably holding on to stacks of old VHS videotapes. It's important to store videotapes away from stereo speakers, which create a magnetic field that can actually erase the tapes.

Cleaning an Audio Cassette Recorder

It's important to clean the *play*, *record* and *erase* heads of your tape recorder. Cleaning will keep the heads free of dust and dirt that builds up (mostly from flakes that come off magnetic tape). If you use the recorder often—4 or 5 times a week—clean the heads about once a month using denatured alcohol on a cotton swab. The manual that came with the cassette player should have an illustration, showing you the exact location of the heads...or bring it to the store where you bought it and ask a knowledgeable salesperson for guidance.

Cleaning a Camera

◆ Use the soft, lint-free cloth with which you clean your glasses to clean your camera lens.

◆ Every time you change the batteries in your camera, clean all the contact points with a good, clean pencil eraser.

Cleaning Photos

After passing around traditional photo prints, you may want to clean off any fingerprints before putting them into an album. Lightly moisten a cotton ball with rubbing alcohol and gently wipe off the smudges. The isopropyl in the alcohol cleans off the oily residue that is left behind from people's fingers.

Test a tiny corner of the photo before you begin the cleaning process. Proceed with caution and care.

Unsticking Stuck Photos

You can separate photos that are stuck together by working a piece of dental floss between them. There's no guarantee that 1 or both of the pictures won't get damaged, but it's the best separating method we've come across.

 Safeguard Photos
Keep irreplaceable prints, disks of digital photos and copies of treasured family films/videotapes in a fireproof box.

AIR CONDITIONERS & HUMIDIFIERS

Think about it…air conditioners and humidifiers create man-made weather. The commercial use of air conditioners has changed the way we live, work and play—especially in Sunbelt cities like Miami, Houston, Phoenix and Las Vegas.

After World War II, air conditioning became a more common feature in the average American home. It was for the millions, not just the millionaires. *Here are some hints to help you chill out…*

Cooling a Room Efficiently

If your air conditioner is not doing its job as effectively as it should, and you have a furry pet, check the AC's filter. The animal's loose hair may be causing a blockage. Clean the filter often (according to the manufacturer's instructions) and, while you're at it, vacuum the air conditioner case as well as the area around it.

If you don't have a pet, you may have to call a repair service, or resort to using a fan. If you do that, put a bowl of ice cubes in front of the fan—the room's temperature will drop at least 10 degrees in a short amount of time. The ice increases the cooling output of your fan by 100%—especially if it's a stationary fan parked right behind the ice cubes.

Unclogging a Humidifier

If you use regular tap water to fill your humidifier, the water's mineral deposits will build up and eventually clog the machine.

If that has already happened, fill the humidifier bowl with warm distilled white vinegar, and let it soak for a couple of hours. Also, soak the *impeller* (rotating rod) in a jar with warm vinegar for the same amount of time. Then rinse and dry both parts. Be careful not to get the motor wet.

To prevent clogs, use only distilled water (available at supermarkets and drugstores) to fill your humidifier.

WINDOWS

Our mother used to say to us it was a sin to have dirty windows and not let the sunshine come in. *So all you sinners, atone— and here's how…*

Preparing to Clean Windows

If you have curtains, here is a way to prevent them from getting messed up while your windows are getting clean.

Without taking them off the rod, drape each panel on a hanger, then hang the hanger on the curtain rod—the panels on the right side of the window should, of course, be hung on the right side of the curtain rod. The panels on the left side of the window should be hung on the left side of the curtain rod. (We're sure you would figure that out for yourself.)

✦ Easy Window Cleaner
Combine 1 cup of distilled white vinegar with 3 cups of warm water. (If your windows seem extra grimy or greasy, add either 2 table-spoons of rubbing alcohol or 2 tablespoons of pulp-free lemon juice.)

Then, dip a scrunched-up piece of plain newspaper (no colored ink) into the mixture, squeeze it until it stops dripping, then use it to clean the window. (Be sure to wear rubber gloves so that the newsprint doesn't get on your hands.) Then dry the window with some dry pieces of scrunched-up plain newspaper.

 Better Window Washing
The key to getting clear windows is to use ei-ther a squeegee, pieces of scrunched-up plain newspaper (no colored ink), dry coffee filters, a clean blackboard eraser or any of the new microfiber cleaning cloths—they are available at supermarkets and hardware stores.

Window Cleaner And Primer

Mix ½ cup of cornstarch into 1 gallon of warm water. Dip a coarse washcloth into the solution, wring it out and use it to clean the window. Then dry the window with paper towel or plain newspaper.

After doing this a few times, the window should be primed, and all you'll need to clean it in the future is a dry cloth.

Window Caulking Needed? A Test

If your air conditioner and heater don't seem as effective as they should be, your windows may be to blame.

To test for air leaks, go outside and stand in front of the window in question with a plugged-in hair dryer. (You'll need an extension cord or a battery-operated dryer.) Meanwhile, have someone standing inside the house hold a lit candle in front of the window.

Turn on the hair dryer and hold it near the window, opposite the candle on the in-side. If the flame flickers because of the air coming from the dryer, then you'll know that the window needs caulking.

 Up, Down and Side to Side
When you wipe your windows, clean up and down on the inside, and from side to side on the outside. That way, if you do see a streak that you want to wipe away, you will know which side it's on.

Cleaning High Windows

If windows that need cleaning are too high for you to reach, get a water gun and a long-handled squeegee. Fill the water gun with a cleaning solution and spray it on the window pane, then squeegee it off. It's safer than climbing up on a stool or ladder…and it's more fun, too.

Cloudy Means Clean

If you clean your windows on a bright, sunny day, they will dry quickly, leaving those dreaded streaks. The answer? Clean windows on an overcast day so that they will dry more slowly, giving you more time to wipe them.

Preventing Window Frost

When freezing temperatures are in the forecast, dot the inside of your window with glycerin (available at drugstores), then use a cloth to spread the dots into a thin layer that covers the entire window.

Glycerin's moisture-binding ability helps prevent warm, moist air from seeping out and forming moisture on the outside window pane, which then freezes, causing the window to become frosted.

A Breath of Fresh Air

If you can't open your window because of the freezing cold weather, use a hair dryer to defrost it open along the edges. (But why do you even want to open your window if it's freezing cold outside?)

Windowsill Cleaner

Combine equal amounts of rubbing alcohol and water, then wet a soft cloth with the solution. Use it to wipe the sill clean.

Be sure to test a small area of the sill to make sure it's safe. DO NOT use this remedy on bare metal.

Keep Sills Dust-Free

To prevent dirt, paint the windowsill with high-gloss paint or clear polyurethane. Both will help prevent dust from sticking and are easy to clean.

Cleaning Window Screens

Before you wash the screen, vacuum up the dirt that's sitting there. Then you can get any leftover dirt by pressing a sticky lint roller over the screen's surface.

After vacuuming or lint-rollering, you may not need to wash the screen after all.

Cleaning Venetian Blinds

◆ Dust the slats with your hands—just cover them with either cotton socks or gloves.

◆ If the blinds need more than dusting, you can disassemble them, then wash them in the bathtub or hose them down outside on your porch.

◆ Keep the slats cleaner longer by giving them the once-over with fabric-softener sheets to help repel dust.

CEILING FANS

In 1882, Philip Diehl invented the first electric ceiling fan… and it was *fan*tastic. Diehl spent years improving his original model, and by the late 1920s, the ceiling fan was part of the décor and ventilating system of just about every public eatery—from elegant dining rooms to bawdy speakeasies.

If you have a ceiling fan, you're part of the ongoing history of this remarkable invention. *Here's how to take care of it…*

Dusting

Prevent the dust from flying all over the room by using a damp sponge instead of dry dust cloth to clean your fan's blades.

Smart Fan Use for Warm and Cool Months

You probably read the instructions when the ceiling fan was being installed. But if you're new to ceiling fans, you might not know that you can reverse the direction of the blades.

You may wonder, "Why would I want to do that?" Changing the direction of the blades helps circulate warm air during the cold months, which may cut your annual heating bills by about 10%.

When the blades are turning in a clockwise direction, they push the air against the ceiling and down the walls. The warm air gets recirculated without creating a cooling wind.

During cool months, turn on the fan and make sure the blades are rotating *counterclockwise* (the warm-weather setting). Turn off the fan and get a safe ladder—you need to reach the middle section of the ceiling fan. There's a switch that's located on the side of the section that houses the motor. Flip the switch to the opposite setting.

Once you've carefully climbed down off the ladder, turn the fan to its lowest setting. Check that the blades are now rotating *clockwise*. If they are, you're set for winter.

Be sure to reverse the switch and have the blades rotate counterclockwise during the hot summer months...or whenever you want to feel a cool breeze.

FIREPLACE

Comedian Ellen DeGeneres once said, "Go to bed in your fireplace—you'll sleep like a log." Although you shouldn't take Ellen's advice literally, you may want to follow through with some helpful hints to make your fireplace cleaner, prettier, safer and more efficient.

Read All About Substitute Firewood

If you want to light your fire but have no firewood (and it's too cold to go out and get some), finish reading your daily newspaper.

Then tightly roll up a couple of the plain (not colored) papers, and tie them securely with twine or wire. Use the paper-rolls in place of real or fake logs.

 CAUTION: NEVER burn colored newspapers or magazines in the fireplace. The inks and dyes used to make them contain lead—and that lead can be inhaled. This can be very dangerous, especially for children and pets.

Feeding the Fire Efficiently

By opening the window that is closest to the fireplace, the fire will use oxygen from outside, instead of taking it from inside the rest of the house. You only need to open the window an inch or even less.

Make a Scented Fire

◆ Spread the rinds from an orange or lemon on paper towels, and let them dry out overnight.

When the rinds are thoroughly dry, toss them on the fire to create a lovely citrus aroma.

◆ If you are not into a citrus scent, you could instead toss in a few pinecones for a more woodsy fragrance.

 Grate Idea!

If your fireplace has grates instead of andirons, you may be able to reduce the amount of smoke the fire emits—just place a brick under each leg of the grate.

Managing Soot

◆ Before lighting the fire, toss a handful of plain table salt on the logs (real, fake or made from newspaper). The salt will help to loosen soot from the chimney, and it will also give the fire a bright, yellow flame.

◆ If you don't eat a lot of potatoes, make a deal with a restaurant that serves french fries, and have them save the potato peels for you.

Put the peels on paper towel, and let them dry overnight. When the peels are dry, you can burn them in your fireplace. They burn with a gusto that sends the soot up and out of the chimney.

◆ If you're a tea drinker, tear open steeped, moist tea bags and sprinkle the tea leaves over the sooty fireplace remains. If you're a coffee drinker, you can use moist coffee grounds on the soot.

The tea leaves and coffee grounds help prevent the ash particles from flying up into the air when you clean up the soot.

 Soot Smell Absorber

After you've cleaned the ashes from the fireplace, fill a pan or a paper plate with baking soda and place it in the fireplace. Leave it for a day or so, and it will absorb the smell of soot.

Cleaning Glass Fireplace Doors

Use a wet sponge to rub on some wood ashes. Then use a clean sponge to rinse off the glass… along with the dirt.

Cleaning the Hearth

If you can regularly clean the soot marks off the hearth (the area surrounding the fireplace), the soot won't become ingrained and hard to clean off.

For light soot marks, dust them away with a vacuum cleaner attachment or a brush. For soot stains that can't be removed that way, try a gum eraser (available at office- and art-supply stores), or scrub them with a stiff brush and plain water.

For stains that don't scrub off that way, wet a sponge or brush with distilled white vinegar and go at it. Then, rinse the spot well with plain water.

EVEN MORE HINTS…

 If you've ever needed to know how to keep your magnetized cabinets closed…or how to see if things are level…or get back something you loaned out, here's how…

Cabinet Magnets

Do you have the type of cabinets that are held shut with a magnet in the corner? Do you have a wrestling match with your cabinet door each time you want to open it? If the magnet is too strong, just put a piece of transparent tape over it. The door will stay closed, yet opening it will be a lot easier.

On the Level...or Not

If you want to know if an object is standing level, use a measuring cup that has the same measurement markings on each side. Put water in the cup—enough to reach 1 of the marks.

Stand the cup on the object in question. If the water hits the same exact mark on each side of the cup, then the object is level. If the water level is different on each side, then the object is lopsided.

The Return of Your Stuff

At last, a good use for the return-address labels you get from charities! Put a label on each item of yours that friends or family may borrow. Let it remind the borrower to whom it should be returned.

What comes to mind? A stapler? A bottle of correction fluid? A bottle of nail polish? Tupperware containers? An umbrella? A tape dispenser? A videotape? A DVD? A book? Power tools? You bet!

CLOSETS

If you have used your closets as dumping grounds for stuff you do not want anyone to see, it's time to go through that stuff...then sell or donate to charity the things you don't need, and organize the things you still value and use.

There are stores that specialize in storage and organizational products—closet stores

have do-it-yourself kits that will help you reconfigure closet space for your specific needs. But before you can know what you *need*, you have to know what you *have*. Keep in mind that less is best.

Here are some suggestions to help you thin out the stuff in your closets...and to use the space more wisely. After you've done the initial thinning and organizing, you'll be able to determine whether or not a trip to a closet shop would be helpful.

Closet-Clutter Reality Check

Keep track of which clothes you wear—and, more importantly, which clothes you don't wear—using this simple method. First, start each new wardrobe season by hanging your clothes in the closet with all of the hangers' hooks facing you.

Then, each time you wear and wash an article of clothing, put it back with the hook facing into the closet. At the end of the season, you will be able to tell at a glance which garments were not worn simply by the way the hanger hooks are facing.

Now comes the decluttering part of this process. To thin out your wardrobe, select give-aways from the clothes that are on the hangers with hooks still facing you...the clothes that you didn't wear at all. And then, take it a step further. Review the clothes you DID wear and didn't like. Take them to a thrift shop and let them make other people happy.

Making Hangers Glide

◆ Rub your closet's clothing rod with a piece of waxed paper and your hangers will move along the rod smoothly and easily.

◆ Hardware stores have inexpensive plastic rod covers that come in a variety of colors.

The covers make it easy to slide hangers back and forth on the closet rod.

Extra Hanging Space

◆ Place a shower-curtain ring on the neck of a hanger, and then you can hang another hanger on it.

◆ Always hang your clothes facing the same direction—that way, there's less space between clothes. So, you'll have more hanging space, and your closet will look neater.

Hanging Accessories

If you have some extra shower-curtain hooks around, slip them on the closet rod, and use them to hang purses, belts or ties…or tote bags filled with stuff that would otherwise be floating around loose in the closet.

Shelves Made Easy

If you wish you had shelves in a roomy closet, visit a thrift shop or unpainted furniture store and look for an inexpensive bookcase.

Put the bookcase inside your closet—you will have your shelves and none of the bother of putting them up.

Entryway Closet Convenience

If you have a guest closet in your entryway, hang a shoe holder on the inside door. To store accessories that you may need before going outside—such as scarves, gloves, hats, sunglasses—assign compartments of the shoe bag for each of those things.

You can also store pet accessories in the shoe bag, such as your dog's leash or winter jacket, as well as a small flashlight.

Removing Moisture and Musty Smells

◆ Keep a few open boxes of baking soda somewhere in the closet.

◆ Put natural clay kitty litter in a shoe box or pie tin, and leave it on the floor of the closet…but NOT if you have a cat who has access to the closet.

If it's a walk-in closet and you don't want to step on the litter, put it in the leg of an old pair of pantyhose, knot it closed and hang it in a corner.

◆ Use chalk…or charcoal briquettes…or cedar chips to freshen your musty closet. Put them in a pie tin on the floor or hang them in an old pair of pantyhose.

 CAUTION: Do not let cedar chips come into direct contact with your clothes. They can cause fabrics to yellow.

Protecting Clothes

If you have louvered or slatted closet doors, you can keep your clothes dust-free and moth-free by covering the openings—just tape sheets of waxed paper on the inside of the doors.

Storing Blankets

If you're like everyone else, your closet space may be limited. Instead of taking up room storing blankets, put them on the floor under the beds on which they're used. That way, you save space in the closet, and it makes it easy to get to them on a cold night.

Sweet-Scented Moth Repellent

Ever make an orange-spice pomander ball? If not, here's your chance. *Start by gathering the following ingredients…*

1 thin-skinned orange (the peel stays on)

1 box of whole cloves

1 ounce ground orrisroot (available at some herb stores…or from Elizabeth Bradfield, *www.soapmoldsnmore.com* or 858-452-8980)

1 ounce ground cinnamon

½ ounce ground nutmeg

2 feet of ¼"- to ½"-wide ribbon (non-silky ribbon, such as grosgrain, works best)

Combine the orrisroot, cinnamon and nutmeg in a bowl and set it aside.

Take 1 foot of the ribbon and cut it in half. Then tie 1 strip around the orange and knot it on top. Do the same thing with the other strip of ribbon, so that the 2 strips criss-cross the orange. (If your ribbon is silky, you may want to stick a pushpin in on each of the strips to keep them from slipping.)

Next, stick the cloves all over the orange —but not in the ribbon. Then place the clove-stuck orange in the bowl with the spices, gently rolling it around. Let it sit in the bowl for about 5 days, turning it occasionally.

After 5 days, take the orange out of the bowl, hold it over the sink and, using a hair dryer set on a low and cool setting, blow off any excess spices. Now the pomander ball is ready to be hung in the closet.

Attach the remaining ribbon to the pomander ball, and hang it from the closet rod. This scented moth-repellent will last for years.

 NOTE: For a spicy-scented moth repellent, cut the leg off a clean, old pair of pantyhose and fill the foot with crushed peppercorns. Knot it closed, and hang it in the closet.

It smells better than mothballs and does the job as well.

DO-IT-YOURSELF SECRETS

 If you are (or want to be) a do-it-yourselfer, here are the top 10 categories of tools you should have to help you with most loving-hand-at-home projects…

- ◆ Claw hammer
- ◆ Level
- ◆ Pliers (tongue and groove long-handled pliers, needle nose, medium-sized locking pliers and slip joint)
- ◆ Screwdrivers (3 standard sizes and 3 sizes of Phillips head)
- ◆ Adjustable wrenches or 1 complete set of small-to-large wrenches
- ◆ Utility knife (average-sized and heavy-duty)
- ◆ Retractable, metal tape measure (make sure it's at least 12' long)
- ◆ Small all-purpose saw
- ◆ Small drill
- ◆ Safety goggles

You'll also need an assortment of nails, screws, nuts and bolts, electrical, masking and duct tape, sandpaper and glue.

As you get more and more into do-it-yourself projects, you will get a better idea of which tools you use most, and which need upgrading. At some point, you may want to treat yourself to a power saw or a sander…or whatever will make your workshop more complete. The main thing is to know what you're doing before you do it. *Be careful.* Oh yeah, and have fun!

Cleaning Rusty Tools

Author Robert Hughes once remarked, "A determined soul will do more with a rusty monkey wrench than a loafer will accomplish with all the tools in a machine shop."

As far as we're concerned, you can either get the rust off that monkey wrench or prevent it from rusting. *Just follow the advice below...*

◆ If you have a tool that is so rusty you're ready to throw it away, give it a final chance to unrust. Get a container—most tools will be able to stand in a wide-mouth jar—and fill it with apple cider vinegar. Put the rusty tool in, and let it marinate overnight. The next day, clean the tool with a cloth. It should be rust-free and usable again.

◆ You can also use sandpaper to take rust off a tool. Start with a fine grade, and if it doesn't work, use coarse sandpaper.

◆ Try getting rid of the rust with a moistened steel wool pad. If that doesn't work, you may have to replace the tool with something new...at least you know you tried.

★ **Keep Tools from Rusting**

To prevent rust, keep pieces of chalk or a few charcoal briquettes in your toolbox. This chalk or charcoal will absorb the excess moisture that causes rust.

If you don't use a toolbox, prevent rust from forming by cleaning your tools with steel wool, then applying a thin coat of petroleum jelly.

Removing Nuts, Bolts And Screws

◆ If you want to remove a nut, bolt or screw, but it won't budge, do the unexpected and try turning it to the right, tightening it a bit. If it gets tighter, chances are you can then undo it by turning it to the left.

◆ Pour a little cola on the culprit, wait 1 to 2 minutes for the soda to eat into the rust, then have a go at it.

◆ Distilled white vinegar, iodine or 3% hydrogen peroxide may help loosen a rusty nut, bolt or screw. Dab it on with a cotton ball and let it soak for about 5 minutes before turning it...yes, to the left.

 The Answer to "Which Way?"

When you need to remember which way to loosen or tighten a nut, bolt or screw, try this—"righty tighty, lefty loosey."

Tightening Loose Screws

◆ If the screw is just a little loose, dip it into a bottle of clear nail polish (or coat the screw's hole with a just-dipped nail polish brush). Let it set for a minute, and then screw in the screw.

This remedy is especially helpful if the screw is attached to a knob, like on a dresser drawer.

◆ Take a twist-tie from a loaf of bread, fold it over, then cut the unfolded, open ends so that the tie is the length of the screw's hole. Place the V-shaped end of the twist-tie into the hole, then put in the screw.

If there's not enough room for the screw, cut the twist-tie in half, reinsert only 1 side of the twist-tie in the hole, and then reinsert the screw.

◆ If the hole has gotten much too large for the screw, soak a piece of cotton ball in white glue (such as Elmer's) and stuff it into the hole. Let it stay that way until it dries—at least 24 hours—then screw in the screw.

Creating New Screw Holes

You can close up a large screw hole and start over—just get a little carpenter's glue or wood putty (available at hardware stores), a wooden golf tee (available from your neighbor, the golfer), a hammer and a saw.

Dip the tee in the glue or putty, hammer the tee into the screw hole and let it dry overnight. Then saw off the part of the tee that's jutting out of the wall, sand it flush, and you're ready to create a new hole for a screw or a nail.

Keeping Screws, Nails, Nuts and Bolts Together

When you take something apart, don't risk losing any of the hardware, especially if you will need to put the object back together again. As you remove them, stick all of the nails, nuts, bolts and screws on a thick piece of tape.

It's a good idea to stick the parts on the tape in the same order that you remove them (you may also want to write down the order as a backup).

Dealing with Drywall

◆ If you're putting up a shelf or a mirror or a towel bar, you'll want the solid backing of studs (the vertical 2' x 4' boards behind finished walls) to hang them securely.

If you do not have a battery-powered stud finder (available at hardware stores), you can use an electric razor. Plug it in and move it on the wall as though you were giving it a shave. When the razor passes over a stud, the sound will change from a hollow hum to an up-front buzz. Once you have found a stud, there should be another stud 16" or 24" away.

◆ When you know the exact spot on the drywall that you plan to hammer in a nail, place a piece of masking or transparent tape there. It should help prevent the plaster from

chipping off as the nail goes in. Once the nail is in the wall, gently and slowly peel off the tape so that the paint and plaster continues to stay intact.

Hammering Made Painless

If the nail in question is in an awkward spot and it's difficult to hold in place while you hammer (or if you hit your finger more often than the nail), the answer to the problem is a strip of clay (available at crafts and toy stores). Stick the clay on the wall, and let it hold the nail for you. Once you've nailed the job, peel off the clay.

 Hit the Nail on the Head

If you rub the head of your hammer with fine sandpaper every so often, it will help prevent the hammer from slipping off the nail and hitting your finger or the wall.

Using a Screwdriver

◆ To keep a screwdriver from slipping off the head of the screw, rub chalk on the end of the screwdriver before using it.

◆ Before screwing in a screw, screw it in and out of a bar of soap. The soap-coated screw should then screw into your target easier. (Easy for us to say, we know.)

 Shine a Light

If you need to use an electric drill in a dark area, tape a small flashlight (such as a penlight) to the side of the drill to make the work more visible...this will make it easier and safer to do the job.

Fixing Squeaky Hinges

If the hinges on a door or cabinet are *squeeeeeaking*, just dab a bit of petroleum jelly or foam shaving cream on the noisy part, or spray the hinges with nonstick vegetable spray.

Keep opening and closing the door until the jelly or spray works its way in and thoroughly lubricates the hinges.

Making Drawers Glide

Go over the tracks or runners of a drawer with a bar of soap or some leftover candle wax, and they'll practically open and close by themselves.

Smart Sandpaper Substitute

When a small job requires sandpapering, it may be more efficient to use an emery board than to try to maneuver a piece of sandpaper in a tiny or hard-to-reach place.

Fixing a Sticky Door

◆ Find the exact spot that causes the door to stick, then sandpaper it down a little at a time until it no longer sticks.

◆ If the bottom of the door is rubbing, wedge coarse sandpaper between the floor and the door, and open and close, open and close, until the trouble spot is sanded down.

NOTE: To make sure you sand the door and not the floor, staple a piece of thin cardboard on the bottom of the sandpaper—it should rest on the floor while the coarse sandpaper is up against the bottom of the door.

Hiding the Dark Marks

If there are annoying little marks throughout your home, consider covering them up with liquid correction fluid. Even though the white fluid may be whiter than most kitchen sinks or bathroom tiles, it will cover up a dark ding and make it a lot less noticeable.

If the surface on which you apply the cover-up is shiny, dab a little colorless nail polish over the correction fluid.

NOTE: In addition to white, Liquid-Paper correction fluid comes in several colors, such as ivory, blue, green, pink, ledger buff and canary yellow.

You can also get a matching paint sample from your local paint or hardware store.

PEST CONTROL

Would you believe that 95% of all the animal species on Earth are insects? Scientists have discovered over 1 million species, and there may be 10 times that many insects that haven't been named yet.

One out of every 4 animals on the planet is a beetle of some kind. (There are about 500,000 different species of beetle.) Social insects—such as ants and termites—make up about 20% of the total animals in the world.

We've given you these insect facts, not to gross you out, but to make your insect-control challenge seem minor when you realize that millions of insects can exist in 1 single acre of land. *And here are some solutions…*

Repelling Flying Insects

Many insects with wings are repelled by the smell of basil. If you're into growing herbs, be sure to feature basil in your herb garden, and you won't have to shoo-fly any flying insects.

If you don't grow your own basil, buy a bunch at the grocery store or flower shop…you can dry them by clumping 3 or 4 stems together with string or a rubber band. Once you have a bunch of clumps, hang them upside down in a place that's well-ventilated but that's not in direct sunlight.

When the leaves are dry, crumble them into small muslin bags or pieces of cheesecloth, and hang them all around your home, or wherever you suspect flying insects enter or where they like to hang out.

Battling Fruit Flies

◆ When you set out a bowl of fruit for company, just make sure your guests are not fruit flies—to repel these pests, just put a few sprigs of mint around the fruit bowl.

◆ If you have fruit flies hovering around the garbage can or your bunch of bananas, set out a small plastic container filled with a mixture of 1 tablespoon of apple cider vinegar, 6 drops of liquid dish detergent and ½ cup of water. The bugs will fly in, but they won't fly out.

Fighting Silverfish

◆ If silverfish are making their way through your books and important papers, clear out those shelves or boxes and thoroughly vacuum the entire area. Also vacuum the books and papers.

◆ If you have books that need special care, seal them in plastic bags and put them in the freezer for 4 days, time enough to destroy any insect infestation.

◆ Before putting your books and papers back on shelves or in boxes, get 1 of the following (or create a mixture of several)—dried lavender leaves, bay leaves, wormwood, tansy, mint leaves, cinnamon bark.

Silverfish hate all of these pungent smells and tend to be repelled by them. Put the leaves in muslin bags or in cheesecloth, and tuck them into the shelf corners. (The bags can also be used in the kitchen to repel silverfish.)

◆ If silverfish are in your kitchen, remove all utensils from drawers and food from the cabinets. Wash the drawers and cabinets with very hot water and dry it all with a blow-dryer set on *hot*, especially along the wall edges. The hot water and blow-dryer will help eradicate silverfish eggs.

◆ If you've had a severe silverfish infestation, wipe the cabinets and drawers with a potent lavender oil. That should keep them away for about a year.

◆ If you see a silverfish scooting across your bathroom floor, boil a pot of water, and carefully pour it down your bathtub and sink drains, which will hopefully destroy their hiding place. Then vacuum all of the room's corners and crevices.

When you remove the bag, it's best to do it outdoors. Once the bag is out of the vacuum cleaner, be sure to tape it closed, put it in a plastic bag, tape that bag closed and then discard everything.

 NOTE: When using the vacuum cleaner to get rid of insects, spill 1 cup of table salt on the floor and vacuum it up. The salt will help kill insect eggs and larvae that may be *inside* the vacuum cleaner bag.

Removing Bugs from Grains And Beans

◆ Place a dried chili pepper in the container with your dry grains or beans, and you will not be bothered by weevils.

◆ Weevils and meal worms are repelled by the scent of mint. Fresh mint leaves or strong-smelling dry mint leaves will keep the bugs away.

A stick of mint-flavored chewing gum in with flour or spaghetti will also get the job done. Each time you open a new bag of flour or package of spaghetti, put in a new stick of peppermint gum.

Dealing with Ants

Figure out the ants' main points of entry—windowsill, doorway, baseboards—and sprinkle those places with any of the following...

◆ cayenne pepper

◆ chili powder

◆ cinnamon

◆ sage

◆ whole cloves

◆ bay leaves

◆ cream of tartar

◆ salted cucumber peelings

◆ dried peppermint leaves or peppermint oil

◆ distilled white vinegar

◆ lemon juice and peel—mix it with water and wash the kitchen floor

◆ baby powder

◆ uncooked white or brown rice

You can also sprinkle the above items in food pantries, cupboards, cabinets or any other place you've seen ants scurrying around.

Rousting Out Roaches

There are various ways to get rid of roaches. The most successful methods use 1 of 3 ingredients—baking soda, borax powder or boric acid (which is a key element in most commercial roach products). The idea is to get the roaches to eat the bait, then go back to the nest and die. *Here is a selection of ways in which each of the 3 B's can eradicate a roach infestation...*

Combating Carpenter Ants

Black and red carpenter ants are found in woody environments. While they do not bite unless provoked, it's not fun to have them crawling around, chewing up your house or furnishings. *To combat these destructive pests, brew up this recipe...*

Carpenter Ant Bait

> 3 cups water
> 1 cup sugar
> 4 teaspoons boric acid powder
> several jar lids (shallow enough so ants can crawl in)
> wads of cotton batting

Heat water in a pot and then add the sugar and boric acid powder. Stir to dissolve. Place a wad of cotton on a jar lid, and soak the cotton with solution. Place lid in the area frequented by ants, and keep the solution replenished until ants disappear.

The ants are attracted to the sweet sugar ...and, because they will take it to their nests to share it with other ants, the deadly boric acid will reach ants you can't even see.

Source: Department of Conservation, Augusta, Maine.

 CAUTION: Boric acid is toxic. Use extreme caution when you're preparing this bait...wear rubber gloves and protect your eyes, nose and mouth with goggles and a mask...wash the pot thoroughly when you're done. Keep this bait out of reach of all people and pets.

◆ Combine equal parts of baking soda and confectioners' (powdered) sugar, and sprinkle the mixture wherever roaches hide and walk. The sugar will attract them and the baking soda will kill them (in a way that's too gruesome to explain).

Combating Roaches

The measurements for this popular roach-exterminating recipe seem flexible (no 2 sources agree), and since none of the roaches have lived to complain, it must work. *Here's our version...*

Roach Bait

¼ cup cooking oil or bacon drippings
¼ cup sugar
8 ounces boric acid powder
½ cup flour
½ cup onion, chopped

Combine the oil and sugar in a pot. Mix in the boric acid powder, flour and onion. The idea is to form soft dough. You may need to add a little more oil.

Shape the soft dough into small, marble-size balls and place them in open plastic sandwich bags (the bags help keep them moist longer). Distribute them around your home, in the corner seams of your windows and doors, tiny floor or wall cracks or wherever roaches enter, as well as their favorite hangouts—kitchen cabinets, drawers, under the sink and other dark, damp areas.

When the dough get hard as a rock, whip up a fresh batch of bait balls...unless, of course, the first batch wiped out the problem completely.

 CAUTION: Boric acid is toxic. Use extreme caution when you're preparing this bait...wear rubber gloves and protect your eyes, nose and mouth with goggles and a mask...and be sure to wash the pot thoroughly when you're done. Keep this bait out of reach of all people and pets.

 NOTE: You can also prepare a non-toxic version of this recipe with baking soda instead of boric acid powder.

◆ Combine 2 tablespoons of flour with 4 tablespoons of borax powder (available at most supermarkets) and 1 tablespoon of cocoa powder. Spoon it out on plastic lids and leave this lethal blend in cabinets...under the sink ...on a kitchen counter...or wherever you've seen the cockroaches crawling.

◆ Use the recipe at left—and please be aware of the caution.

OUTSIDE THE HOME

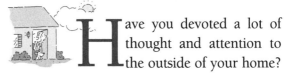 **H**ave you devoted a lot of thought and attention to the outside of your home? Well, now may be the time to start—or improve on what you've already done. Make the great outdoors safer in cold weather and more pleasant in warm weather. *Here are some ideas on what you can do...*

De-Icing the Sidewalk, Steps, Driveway, Patio

◆ If the sidewalk or patio that needs de-icing is near your garden, DO NOT use rock salt. The salt will leach into the soil and poison it. Instead, use natural clay kitty litter, sand or granular fertilizer (dry, tiny pellets that are natural or synthetic...available at garden-supply stores).

◆ Distribute a dusting of baking soda. It will melt the ice and help prevent slipping. And you don't have to worry about it eating away at the outdoor ground covering, or the soles of your shoes. (And if it gets tracked into the house, it may even help clean the floor.)

◆ When your wooden deck is iced over, get out the cornmeal. A sprinkling of it will provide traction without damaging the wood or harming your garden.

Safer Concrete Steps

Mix ½ cup of clean sand into a can of paint, and paint the concrete steps with it. The sand in the paint will offer some traction when the steps are icy or wet.

If you are going to paint the steps, consider painting them white so they're easier to see on dark nights, especially if your outside light burns out.

Snow Shoveling Made Easier

◆ Right now—no matter what the weather is in your part of the country—put a coat of floor wax on your snow shovel. It will help prevent a metal shovel from rusting, and when it comes time to use it, the snow will glide on and slide off.

◆ If you've neglected to do the floor-wax coating, and you have to use the shovel now, spray it with nonstick vegetable spray. Once it dries completely, get out there and start shoveling.

Removing Moss

If you have a brick or stone walkway, this remedy should get rid of any moss overgrowth. In a spray bottle, combine 2 tablespoons of rubbing alcohol and 1 pint of water. Spray the moss with the solution, then rinse it away with a hose.

Removing Stains on Concrete

If any of the concrete on your property has grease stains, drench it with liquid dishwashing detergent. Let it stay that way for about 1 hour. Then pour just-boiled water on it. If the stain isn't completely gone (and it probably won't be), repeat the process once or twice more.

Removing Storm Windows And Doors

Spray metal window and door frames with nonstick vegetable spray to make this putting-up and taking-down seasonal chore much less of a *pane in the glass*.

Unlocking Door Locks

If your key doesn't go in and out of the lock smoothly, any of the following should help…

◆ Spray the key with nonstick vegetable spray and, before it dries, insert it into the keyhole a few times.

◆ Dip a powder puff or a cotton ball in talcum powder and smack it on the keyhole. The idea is to have a bit of powder coat the inside of the keyhole.

◆ Rub the serrated side and the underside of a key using a soft lead pencil. (It's not actually *lead*, it's *graphite*.) Then transfer the pencil's graphite from the key into the keyhole by putting the key in the lock and moving it back and forth until the key comes out clean.

Unsticking Outdoor Bulbs

Moisture, pollen, dust, dirt and pollution all conspire to make it practically impossible to remove an outdoor lightbulb from the socket shell. If you lightly coat the threaded base of the bulb with petroleum jelly *before* you screw it in, when it comes time to remove and replace the bulb, unscrewing it will not be a problem.

Ladder Safety

If a household chore has you mounting a ladder on soft earth, make it safer by putting each leg of the ladder in an empty coffee can, which will help stabilize the ladder, making it safer.

If possible, have someone hold the sides of the ladder steady while you climb up. (To be even safer, hire an insured contractor to do the chore for you.)

Cleaning a Plastic Kiddie Pool

Dissolve 4 cups of baking soda in 2 gallons of hot water. When the water is still warm (but not hot enough to melt plastic), pour the solution into the plastic pool. Swish it around with a clean sponge, then pour out the solution and rinse the kiddie pool with clear water.

Create an Outdoor Dolly

Buy an old skateboard at a yard sale, thrift shop or from a teenage neighbor, and use it to cart around heavy or awkward things, such as moving your full garbage can to the curb or relocating big potted plants.

Make sure the skateboard is stable before you move anything, especially on an incline.

Cleaning a Swimming Pool

You'll have a cleaner pool if you keep a tennis ball floating in the water. The ball *serves* to absorb body oils. Don'tcha just *love* it?

Cleaning Plastic Patio Furniture

◆ Spray the plastic furniture with foam shaving cream and let it stay that way for 5 minutes. Use a soft brush or a coarse sponge to wipe the dirt away. Then hose it down.

◆ After wiping the dust and dirt off plastic, wood, or metal furniture frames—not chair seats or any other parts that come in contact with people's skin—buff the frames with liquid car wax. It will protect your furniture from pollution, bird droppings and anything else that may cause erosion.

◆ Protect and clean your white resin patio furniture when there's a big storm brewing. (A small detail we didn't mention yet—you need to have a swimming pool for this tip.)

Put the furniture in the pool and it won't blow away. When the storm is over and you take out the furniture, each piece will be sparkling clean, thanks to the chlorine in the water.

Cleaning Patio Umbrellas

While you're at the auto-supply store buying liquid car wax, pick up some cleaner for a convertible car top. It will go a long way in cleaning and giving your sun-beaten patio umbrella a revitalized look.

Using an Outdoor Grill

◆ Before you fire up the grill, lightly coat the racks with vegetable oil or a nonstick spray. Meats and vegetables will slide off easily.

◆ Toss some fresh herbs on the coals—rosemary, basil, sage or a few bay leaves work well. As the coals get hotter, the scent of the herbs will subtly flavor the food. The herbs will also permeate the air with the promise of good eats.

Grilling Safety!
Keep antibacterial wipes close by to clean your hands after handling raw meat.

◆ When you're finished barbecuing and the grill is still warm, sprinkle baking soda on it. Let it stay that way overnight. The next morning, wipe it clean, then rinse and dry.

Handling a Garbage Can

◆ Sprinkle about ½ cup of borax powder (available at supermarkets and drugstores) on the bottom of the garbage can to help prevent mold from growing.

◆ If you have a severe fly problem around your garbage can, line the bottom of the can with a light coating of powdered dishwasher detergent. The smell of the soap will repel the flies. And when you want to clean out the can, just add water and rinse.

◆ To keep the flies away, dip a sponge in oil of lavender (available at health-food stores), and wipe the inside of the can and lid with it. Do this after every garbage pick-up.

◆ If neighborhood dogs or cats insist on dining out at your garbage can, sprinkle black pepper around the can. They should stop coming over for take-out.

Tie Up Loose Lids
You can prevent the lid of the garbage can from flying away on a windy day—just get some rope or wire and tie the lid to the garbage can handle.

Dealing with Outdoor Pests

In addition to the millions of insects crawling around, there are pigeons in just about every city in America. Their droppings deface and hasten the deterioration of statues, buildings and walkways...mar windowsills and terraces...and make fire escapes dangerous. Pigeons' nests, along with their droppings, can clog drain pipes and air vents. Pigeons are also known to carry or transmit disease.

Then there are rodents. We have several good suggestions for getting rid of these vermin, but we can't bear to write about them. If you want to learn more, visit *www.kness.com/rodents.html* for insights into ridding your home of mice, rats and squirrels.

Meanwhile, here are a few bearable ways to solve your outdoor-pest problems...

Ants

Place the legs of your picnic table in paper cups that are filled halfway with water. Ants can't swim! If they crawl up the sides of the cup, they will fall into the water—and it will be no picnic for those ants.

Bees, Yellow Jackets and Wasps

◆ Put your yellow jacket away to keep yellow jackets away. These flying stingers are attracted to bright, warm colors, such as yellows, oranges and reds. Instead, use a pale pastel color scheme at your next outdoor shindig—perhaps a soft blue or green for the plates, napkins and tablecloth—and wear an outfit to match.

◆ Set your table with several fabric-softener sheets. They will keep away bees and yellow jackets as well as ants.

◆ Sculpt a sandwich-size brown paper bag into the shape of a beehive, and hang it somewhere along the air path outside your home where bees and wasps travel. The bag should mislead the flying pests into thinking there is already a hive on your property.

The theory is that bees and wasps avoid hives that are not their own. They do not want to be confrontational because it would turn into war.

If the bag needs help keeping its shape, fill it with polystyrene packing peanuts, or blow up a balloon and put it in the bag.

Cats

You can prevent cats from using a children's sandbox as their outdoor litter box—just pour distilled white vinegar around the box every month or so.

Flies

What's good for the sandbox (*see* "Cats," above) is also good for the pool. Pour distilled white vinegar around the sides of your pool, and it should help keep flies from hanging around. The smell of vinegar will disappear in no time.

Mosquitoes

A popular mosquito repellent is the mosquito coil. The coiled, clay-like material sits on a stand and is burned. It releases a pleasant odor that is very repellent to flying pests. Each coil burns for about 2 hours.

But many of them contain a potent lung carcinogen. Studies show that burning 1 coil could be the equivalent of smoking more than 100 cigarettes. Not good!

You may be better off with a couple of harmless mosquito bites…or, you may want to try the following suggestions to deal with those little buggers.

◆ Drink 2 teaspoons of apple cider vinegar in a glass of water. The smell of vinegar, emitted in your normal perspiration, will repel the mosquitoes, whose sense of smell is about 10,000 times better than ours.

◆ Dab 1 or 2 drops of lavender oil (available at health-food stores) on pulse points—including the inside of your wrists, inside your elbows, behind your ears and in back of your knees—when you know you're going to be in a wet, marshy or mosquito-infested area. The oil is a great repellent—and it also makes a lovely perfume.

FYI: The Problem with Citronella
First used in 1882, oil of citronella is the classic mosquito repellent. Most popular in candle form, the citronella creates fumes that will repel mosquitoes—but only if they fly within the fumed air space.

Because the candles' smoke emissions are not evenly spread out, some of the mosquitoes are bound to get through.

◆ Since mosquitoes enjoy taking up residence on top of tall weeds and grass, give your lawn and yard a crew cut—keep it trimmed down, especially during mosquito season.

◆ Mosquitoes lay eggs in standing water, such as in open-ended rain barrels, wheelbarrows, bird baths and kiddie pools. To prevent mosquitoes from breeding, put 2 tablespoons of olive oil in the water.

Avoid attracting mosquitoes by dumping any standing water—especially in overturned garbage can lids.

Pest-free Picnic

When you're having a picnic, barbecue or any other kind of outdoor gathering, put portable, battery-powered fans around the area (at least 2). Place 1 facing the center of the party, and 1 aimed at the food table.

The fans will keep flying insects (such as mosquitoes, bees, wasps, flies and gnats) away while keeping your guests cool.

Pigeons

Glop up the pigeons' landing strip—the railing or ledge of your terrace, balcony or patio—with petroleum jelly or powdered chalk. Those substances should make it uncomfortable for them and, with any luck, they will fly away...never to return.

Rodents

◆ Use steel wool to plug up every big and small hole that leads into your home (or any structure on your property). Stuff steel wool in all the cracks around gas and water pipes and around electrical outlets...even in the hole for your TV cable lines. Rodents do not like to chew through steel wool.

◆ Mice hate the smell of peppermint. Put a few drops of oil of peppermint (available at health-food stores) on cotton balls, and place them wherever you think the critters may visit—the garage, a workshop, a storage shed, a porch, etc. This is also a good reason to have mint plants planted in and around your home.

◆ If you have a cat, put some of his/her used cat litter in plastic containers. Put the containers wherever you suspect the mice will play when the cat's away. The cat's urine scent should make the mice run for their lives.

◆ Another use for baking soda...rodent repellent. Sprinkle baking soda liberally around your property and garage.

 NOTE: Although baking soda is generally safe, it's better to keep kids and pets away from the area you sprinkled.

 Humane Rodent Trap

Forgive us, but we can't bear researching and writing about trapping and killing rodents. While the thought of having them around is absolutely revolting to us, the thought of killing them is even worse.

If you have a rodent problem, and you do not want to use the popular commercial killing products on the market, contact Arbico Organics. This Tucson, Arizona, company offers humane traps. Visit their Web site at *www.arbico-organics.com* or call 800-827-2847 to ask questions or request a catalog.

◆ If you have greenery that's attracting mice, here's a solution that will repel them—in a 1-gallon jug of water that's almost full, add ½ cup of non-detergent soap powder and 1 tablespoon of Tabasco sauce. Mix it well, then pour some of the solution into a spray bottle.

Generously spray the tops and undersides of the leaves that are a magnet for mice, and the problem should disappear...along with the mice. ■

■ Products ■

Gorilla Glue

The company bills this product as "The Toughest Glue on Planet Earth." You'll get no argument from us. This product bonds wood, stone, brick, concrete, ceramic, metal, plastic laminate and more...lots more. It is 100% waterproof and not affected by sun, rain, snow and extreme hot or cold temperatures...it can also be sanded, stained and painted.

Gorilla Tape

The company bills this as "The Toughest Tape on Planet Earth"—notice a pattern here? This incredibly strong tape bonds to things ordinary tapes cannot, including brick, stucco, wood and more.

Source: The Gorilla Glue Company, 800-966-3458, *www. gorillaglue.com*.*

* Visit the company's user-friendly site for creative product uses and project ideas.

Gripping Stuff!

Here's a whole family of incredibly useful products. They are removable, reusable, repositionable, nontoxic and they eliminate the need for pushpins, tape and messy putty. They are fun to use...practically addictive.

This Gripping Stuff! is polyester felt with a special adhesive that allows you to press it on practically anywhere and peel it off—repeatedly. It comes in many sizes, several colors and makes an instant bulletin board.

Poster Pads let you hang up posters without tacks or nails. You can also snip off a little piece of the *stuff* and use it to turn any piece of paper into an adhesive note.

The *Memo Strip* is good for putting notes around your computer monitor.

Put *Gripping Stuff! For Cards* around your doorframe, and display your birthday or holiday cards on it.

There's also a *Dry-Erase Board and Pen* that wipes off with a cloth.

You can find these products at stationery, crafts and hardware stores as well as most supermarkets nationwide. Ask for it by name...or if you can't remember the name, just ask, "Do you have any of that gripping stuff?"

Source: Gripping Stuff USA, 919-462-6446, *www. gripping-stuff.com.*

CHAPTER 6

Great Greenery Solutions

M any people can appreciate the magnificence of a garden, but have you ever thought of the real value of creating and/or tending your own? Mike Steven, a researcher and lecturer in landscape studies at Australia's University of Western Sydney, worked on a project titled "The Congruent Garden: An Investigation into the Role of the Domestic Garden in Satisfying Fundamental Human Needs."

After interviewing gardeners on the importance of gardening in their everyday lives, Mr. Steven concluded that gardens have the potential to satisfy 9 basic human needs—leisure, subsistence, protection, affection, understanding, participation, creation, identity and freedom—along with 4 existential states—being, having, doing and interacting.

While satisfying the gardener's personal needs, the garden also increases property value. And that's not all. According to the US Department of Energy, properly placed shade trees can help lower your annual utility bills by shading windows and walls in the summer, and acting as windbreakers in the winter. Indoor gardens—or even just a single houseplant—can improve the quality of the air and nurture the soul by bringing nature as living sculpture into our homes.

If plants are living sculpture, then consider yourself the artist-in-residence who will care for your indoor and/or outdoor garden. In this section, we provide tips to help you develop a green thumb simply, safely and economically.

In the words of the innovative landscape architect Thomas D. Church—"When your garden is finished, I hope it will be more beautiful than you anticipated, require less care than you expected and have cost only a little more than you had planned."

TOOLS

G arden tools date back thousands of years. We heard it through the grapevine that the first woody plant—which actually *was* a grapevine in Armenia—was pruned by man around 6000 BC. (We can only imagine the crude pruning shears used then!) Spades made of bronze were used in China in 1100 BC, and the ancient Romans used iron spades and shovels.

Fast-forward to the middle of the 14th century when, thanks to iron-smelting technology, tools were made lighter in weight and more shapely. Then take another leap forward to the mid-17th century when gardens became the rage, and gardeners wanted to be well-equipped to both plant and prune. The industrial revolution had begun, and steel and alloys were used to make tools lighter, more precisely shaped and more durable.

Enterprising manufacturers met the needs of gardeners with a wide range of tools—including pruning and hedge shears, cultivating forks and trowels...just about every nonmechanical gardening tool that is still used today.

We bet you never thought that your gardening tools had their *roots* in the 14th or 17th centuries. Also, we bet you can find some helpful tips on organizing and caring for those tools if you'll just keep reading.

Organizing Tools

◆ Make room on your garage or shed wall to hang a clear-plastic shoe bag—the kind that has 12 or 16 or more shoe compartments. It's a great way to keep your gardening tools and gloves in 1 convenient place.

◆ Tired of misplacing your tools while you work in the garden? Get some bright, fluorescent (meaning, day-glo colors) spray paint or tape, and put some on the handles of your garden tools.

If you tend to garden after sundown, add strips of glow-in-the-dark tape (available at hardware stores and most crafts stores) to the tools' handles. The time you've saved looking for the implements will be extra time spent gardening.

NOTE: If you take a portable phone outside with you to the garden, add a piece of day-glo tape to the receiver so you can find it quickly.

◆ Use an old golf bag to store rakes, spades and hoes. You can get an inexpensive bag at a yard sale or a second-hand sporting goods store. When you decide to use your garden tools, is there any better way to drag them around than in a golf bag? Well, yes...have your *caddy* drag them around.

Tools Rule!

When planting and harvesting, a ruler often comes in handy—to calculate distances when planting seeds or bulbs...or to measure how deep seeds should be planted...or at what height they should be harvested.

So, turn the handles of your tall tools into rulers. Account for the number of inches from the tip of the tool to the start of the handle and, at the start of the handle, mark off and number each inch with a waterproof pen. Measure each of your small tools as well, and assign it a number for its length in inches.

Use colorful poker chips to mark the measured spots where you plan to plant.

Caring for Rusty Tools

◆ Pour some dry sand into a big bucket until it's about ¾ full. Then pour motor oil...or machine oil...or mineral oil...or even used cooking oil...evenly over the top. For every gallon of sand, use about 1 pint of oil.

To clean a rusty tool, stick it in the sand several times, then wipe it with a soft cloth or paper towel. The sand cleans the tool...the oil coats it and prevents moisture from rusting the metal.

You may want to store your tools in the bucket just for the night, but you can even keep 'em there for the winter.

◆ If you keep your garden tools in a toolbox, toss in moisture absorbers, such as some loose rice...or activated charcoal...or pieces of chalk ...or mothballs. Doing so will help prevent your tools from developing rust. Also, make sure that your tools are clean and not caked with soil before storing them.

Tool Case and Seat, All in 1

Put a large plastic bag in a big (5-gallon) plastic bucket. Then fill the bag (and the bucket) with your tools, gloves, bulbs, seeds, bottle of drinking water and cell phone, and take the bucket to the garden.

Once you've reached the patch of garden you plan on tending, empty the contents of the plastic bag onto the ground. Then turn the bucket over, have a seat and get to work.

Sanitizing Tools

◆ If you've had sick plants, your garden tools may be infected with the plants' disease. Kill the problematic bacteria by thoroughly washing the tools with soap and warm water. Wear rubber gloves while doing this task.

 NOTE: Don't forget to wash your gloves, gardening shoes and any other clothes that may have had contact with the ailing plants.

◆ If you want to use something stronger than soap and water to sanitize your tools, soak them in 1 gallon of water mixed with ¾ cup of bleach. Rinse the tools thoroughly with plain water before using them again.

 Make Your Own Scooper

Take an empty plastic detergent bottle...or a bleach bottle...or spring water bottle—the size depends on how big or small you want the scooper to be—and thoroughly wash it out with plain soap and water.

Then, with the handle in your left hand, use regular kitchen scissors to cut from the bottom of the right side of the bottle. Cut in a diagonal to the left side about 1" under the handle and go around to the other side, and then diagonally down to the bottom. (Cut in the opposite direction if you're left-handed.)

It may sound complicated, but when you follow these instructions, you'll see exactly how easy it is to create a terrific scooper that can be used to scoop seeds, fertilizer, mulch...and whatever else needs scooping.

Caring for Hoses

◆ Do not store a hose where the sun will shine down on it. The sun's heat will dry it out. Also, keep a hose away from any kind of heating source, like a furnace or outdoor barbecue.

◆ If the hose has sprung a little leak, instead of using glue or tape to repair it, try this fix— heat up the tip of an ice pick or Phillips-head screwdriver, and gently touch the rubber around the hole in the hose with the hot tip of the tool. It should seal the hole closed.

 Used Hose Uses

If your garden hose has sprung several leaks and is beyond repair, you can recycle it by poking more holes into it and turning it into a sprinkler (also called a "soaker hose") for your lawn or garden.

You can also cut up an old hose and use it to brace newly planted trees—it will protect their bark.

GLOVELESS GARDENING

 Gloves will help protect your hands from getting cuts, splinters and blisters. They will also help keep your nails clean.

Even though it's a good idea to wear gloves when gardening, many gardeners prefer to remain bare-handed while they commune with nature. *Here are a few suggestions for you gloveless gardeners, so that you don't get too "down and dirty"...*

Ensuring Clean Nails

Right before you start to garden, scratch a wet bar of soap with your nails. Make sure that a bit of soap gets under each fingernail. Doing so will prevent soil from getting under your nails.

Soil under the nails is hard to clean, whereas soap can be easily washed and nail-brushed away as soon as you've finished gardening.

Blister Prevention

Moist hands blister easily. When your hands get sweaty from working with a shovel or hoe, rub your palms with some soil to help keep them dry and blister-free.

Infection Prevention

It's not unusual for a person working in the garden to get a scrape…a scratch…a nick…a gash… or an insect bite. However, you don't have to run into your house to tend to every little abrasion.

The answer is to take a small spray bottle of full-strength distilled white vinegar outside with you whenever you garden.

Spritz the minor wound with the vinegar—which will help prevent it from becoming a major infection—then cover the boo-boo with a bandage until you go indoors and can clean and dress it properly.

Sweeter Soap Secret

After gardening, add 1 teaspoon of sugar to your soapy lather, and wash your hands with it. The sugar acts as an abrasive to clean away grass and garden stains.

Garden Lime Neutralizer

Garden lime—which is used to raise the *pH level* (the measurement of acid/alkaline) of soil, and to add calcium or break up heavy clay soil—can dry out your hands and make them look like alligator skin.

Whenever your hands have been exposed to lime—even a little of it—pour some distilled white vinegar on them. After 1 to 2 minutes— once the vinegar has had a chance to neutralize

the lime—rinse your hands with plain water. (And next time, you might want to wear gloves when you work with lime.)

Easy Knee Protection

Knee pads will add to your gardening endurance. To make an affordable pair, take your most comfortable work pants and sew on knee patches, leaving the top side of each patch open—as though you've sewn a pocket on each knee. (For proper placement of the patches, be sure to get into "gardening position" to determine exactly where the pants bend at the knee. Kneeling on something damp will help "mark the spot.")

In each knee-pocket, place a sponge…or a substantial shoulder pad…or a piece of foam rubber. If you have a couple of extra computer mouse pads, you can use them as knee cushions, too.

You can also put on an old pair of pantyhose and line up foam rubber pads (or thick sanitary napkins) at the knees. If you're uncomfortable being seen in this getup, put on a pair of work pants over the pantyhose.

SOIL

Soil is a mixture of organic material plus very small mineral and rock particles. It plays a vital role in the way plants grow because of its relationship to the roots. The roots gather moisture and fertility, and use soil as a storehouse for food elements and water. Roots also make use of soil to anchor plants and hold them in place. The bottom line is—the healthier the soil, the healthier your garden.

The soil of a famous French vineyard is so prized that the vineyard workers must scrape it off their shoes before they leave work each night.

Here are some ways you may be able to improve the quality of your soil and make it shoe-scraping good…

Testing Your Soil's pH

The pH level is the measurement of acid or alkaline. Many plants need acidic soil to thrive. Some types of acid-loving plants and bushes are roses, azaleas, gardenias, rhododendrons, English holly and camellias. Other plants need alkaline soil to thrive. Some alkaline-loving plants and bushes are lilacs, mimosas, bougainvilleas, common garden petunias and bird of paradise flowers.

To learn about your soil, perform 1 or both of these simple tests, and take the results into consideration when planning your garden...

◆ Take 1 tablespoon of wet garden soil and sprinkle a pinch of baking soda on it. If it fizzes, gurgles or effervesces, the soil is *acidic* and its pH is under 5. To raise it, add lime.

◆ If nothing happened, test 1 tablespoon of wet garden soil with ½ teaspoon of distilled white vinegar. If there's fizzing, gurgling or effervescing, then the soil is *alkaline*. The more excited the fizzing, the higher the soil's pH level. To lower it, add sulfur.

Supplementing Your Soil

Some gardeners will not sow their crops until they've enriched the soil with Epsom salt. It is said to help grow stalks stronger, leaves greener and blossoms more substantial. It also makes plants less vulnerable to disease.

Sprinkle about 1 cup of Epsom salt over every 100 square feet (or 10' x 10' patch) of garden. Of course, use a smaller amount if your garden is smaller.

SEEDS

The word "magic" aptly describes a seed. Seeds can be planted many ways. For example, gravity causes heavy seeds to simply fall off the plant and onto the soil. Very fine seeds just blow away on the wind. Some seeds are covered with hooks that catch on the fur of animals passing by and are eventually rubbed off on the ground. Some pods burst and toss their seeds out over a wide area. And, of course, there's the gardener who lovingly plants seeds with his/her own hope and hard work.

Here are some suggestions to make planting those seeds a more fruitful mission...

Fertility Test for Large Seeds

In order to weed out any seeds that may be infertile, fill a bowl with tepid water and empty the seeds into it. The fertile seeds will sink to the bottom of the bowl...the duds will float. Just strain them out and discard.

Dump the Clump

Tiny seeds have a tendency to clump together, which is not a good way to plant them. Prevent them from clumping by mixing the seeds with sand (bags are available at nurseries, pet shops and most hardware stores). Make sure the sand is moist.

Put the clump-free mixture of seeds-and-sand (4 parts sand to each part seeds) in a large salt shaker and sprinkle it over the soil. The even distribution of seeds will produce plants that grow better and stronger.

Create Your Own Seed Tape

You will need seeds, waxed paper, transparent tape and a landscaping plan. Once you decide which seeds are going to go where, then you're ready to prepare seed tapes that will help carry out your landscaping vision.

On a piece of waxed paper, put the seeds in a straight line that's as wide as the tape you're going to use. Then place the sticky side of the tape over the seeds, picking them up off the waxed paper.

After finishing the first row, put it aside, and continue the process until all of the seeds are on lengths of tape that you then can arrange according to the way you want them planted. Then plant them—tape and all!

Storing Leftover Seeds

The next time you finish a jar of vitamins, keep that little, moisture-absorbing silica gel packet that came in it. They are good to use when storing seeds.

Put any leftover seeds in a jar along with the silica gel, close it tightly and keep it refrigerated until next year. It's best to keep the jar in the fridge—a cool, bug-free environment. Most seeds will stay viable for 2 or 3 years.

Or you can store leftover seeds in empty, airtight, light-free 35mm film canisters.

 NOTE: Be sure to label the jar clearly so you know which seeds are which.

Caring for Seedlings

◆ To start seedlings, use plastic pots—they will retain moisture better and longer than clay pots. Of course, that doesn't mean that you have to go out and buy them. Recycle empty (and clean) margarine tubs, cherry-tomato or berry containers, or nursery cell packs. Any wide, flat plastic container will do.

◆ Gently brush your hand over seedlings several times a day to get them used to air movement, which will help them grow strong and hardy. Sound a little far-fetched? Tell that to the commercial growers who do this in their own greenhouses.

WATERING

 Water, which makes up approximately 90% of most plants, is used to carry nutrients from the roots to all parts of the plant. Water also provides elements used in making plant food.

Watering incorrectly is the #1 killer of plants. So, even though there are no hard-and-fast rules for correct watering—a lot depends on air temperature, soil conditions, the types of plants and their stages of development—these suggestions may help you get it right.

Watering Your Lawn And/or Garden

◆ Do your plants and lawn a big favor and water them early in the morning. That way, the moisture is absorbed before the hot afternoon sun has a chance to evaporate it.

As for watering at night...don't do it! Leaving leaves and grass wet overnight makes them vulnerable to fungal diseases.

★ **Protect Your Plantings**
Water plants, shrubs and flowers around the base—not over the leaves. Wet leaves can get burned by strong sunlight.

◆ Watering often, but a little at a time, can weaken plant or grass roots and causes them to grow upward instead of downward. A better idea is to water more thoroughly and less frequently, as evenly as possible, and never faster than the soil can absorb.

◆ The grass will tell you when it's thirsty by starting to wilt. Look for a change in color—from bright green to a drab blue-green.

◆ If you do not trust your eye for color, then ignore the "Keep Off" sign and step on the grass. If the imprint of your foot stays in the grass longer than a few seconds, get out the hose and start watering.

◆ It's also a good idea to water the grass thoroughly after fertilizing, so that the nourishment gets down to the roots—instead of sticking to the lawnmower blades.

FERTILIZING

Just as humans require vitamins and minerals, plants do as well. Fertilizer is plant food, helping plants and lawns meet their nutritional needs. Nitrogen, phosphorus and potassium are the 3 most needed nutrients, which are often referred to as *macronutrients*. There are other nutrients that plants need in small amounts, and they are often referred to as *micronutrients*.

Here are ways to help feed your plants all the nutrients they need…

Using Natural Fertilizers

◆ Pelletized horse feed (available at farm-supply stores or wherever horse-care products are sold) is an inexpensive organic fertilizer.

The pellets of crushed grains and molasses will supply your plants with much-needed NPK—the chemical symbols for *nitrogen*, *phosphorus* and *potassium*. Lightly sprinkle the pellets over the soil, or put some in your planting holes.

◆ If you do not have cats, consider this Native American method of fertilizing—gather unused fish parts (heads, tails, innards, etc.) and keep them in the freezer until you're ready to do your planting.

When it's time, defrost the fish parts, then dig holes deeper than you need for planting and bury the fish. Cover the parts with soil, and then plant as usual. The fish dissolve easily, and the plants will absorb the many nutrients they offer—such as calcium, phosphorus, sodium, potassium and iron.

For some other fertilizing suggestions, *see* "Popular Garden Plants A to Z" on pages 128–136.

 CAUTION: Do not let fertilizer come into direct contact with seeds or plants. Feed the soil *around* the plant, not the plant itself.

LAWNS

If you want your lawn to look as nice as your neighbor's, just wait until it snows. *But seriously, folks…if snow is not in the forecast, here are some ways to take good care of your lawn and make it look its best…*

Mowing the Grass

◆ Mow often—a couple of inches at a time and no more than ⅓ the total blade length—rather than waiting until the grass is as high as an elephant's eye. It's less stressful for the grass. Besides, the short, unseen, leftover clippings do not have to be bagged, and they will eventually decompose and return valuable nutrients to the soil.

How High the Grass?

It's beneficial for grass to be at least 3" high. It shades the soil and helps prevent it from drying out. It also shields weeds and crabgrass from the sunlight, so they have less of a chance to grow.

◆ For the cleanest cut, it's best to mow when it's cool and the lawn is at its driest—typically, in the late afternoon or early evening.

◆ Do not mow the lawn when it's wet. Mowing with wet-grass conditions—such as morning dew—will spread turfgrass disease pathogens, which already exist on your lawn.

Aeration—What, Why, When and How

As time goes by, the soil under your lawn becomes compacted. This is not a good thing. Soil compaction reduces the absorption of water and makes it hard for the grass roots to grow.

Aeration, which is loosening or puncturing the compacted soil, does the lawn a world of good. It increases the availability of water and nutrients, and enhances oxygen levels. It helps produce new shoots and roots that fill up the holes in the lawn, and makes the grass fuller, more dense and better looking. It reduces water runoff, increases the lawn's drought tolerance and improves its overall health.

If you have cool-season grass such as Kentucky bluegrass, aerate in the fall. If your lawn has a warm-season grass, such as carpetgrass, aerate in the late spring or summer when these types are actively growing.

No matter what kind of grass you have or when you aerate, choose a mild day when the soil is moderately moist and does not stick to your shoes. If the soil is too wet and messy, aerating may further compact the soil, which is exactly the opposite of what you want it to do.

Aerate your lawn as often as necessary. One way to test it is to stick a screwdriver in the soil when it's moist. If the screwdriver meets with little or no resistance, you probably don't need to aerate the lawn. If the screwdriver has a hard time making its way into the soil, chances are you need to aerate.

There are many kinds of aerating gadgets available at garden-supply stores and on the Internet, but you may not need any of them if you have spiked golf shoes or soccer cleats. Put them on and start walking on your lawn, especially when you mow. It's good exercise for you and great for your grass.

◆ Each time you mow the lawn, start at a different place. That way, you won't keep rolling over the exact same lanes, which means you won't be making permanent tire ruts in your lawn.

◆ To prevent grass from sticking to the mower's blades, spray the blades with nonstick cooking spray before you begin.

⏲ Best Time to Rake
Do not rake right after it rains. Wait until the leaves are dry and weigh half as much as when they're wet.

WEEDS

Have you ever heard the expression "One year's weed ...seven years' seed?" Well, it seems to be true. There's your garden without weeds. No weeds. No weeds. You cultivate the soil, make conditions right for the seeds to germinate—and then suddenly you have weeds! That's because weed seeds may remain viable for at least 7 years.

You could do 1 of 2 things—either you learn to love 'em. Some weeds (such as morning glories) have beautiful flowers...and some are edible, such as dandelions, purslane and chickweed. Plus, most weeds offer shelter to beneficial insects. Or, if you can't love 'em, you can get rid of 'em. *Here's how...*

Eliminating Garden Weeds

The following solutions are all safe, environmentally friendly weed killers...

◆ In a spray bottle, combine 1 quart of water and either 1 ounce of distilled white vinegar or 1 ounce of gin, plus 1 capful of baby shampoo. Spray the weeds until they're soaking wet. After a day or so, the weeds will turn brown, shrivel up and then die.

◆ Give weeds a killer shower with 5 tablespoons of liquid dishwashing detergent mixed in 1 quart of water.

◆ Prepare a mixture of 1 tablespoon of rubbing alcohol for each cup of water, and put the solution in a spray bottle. Take aim and drench the unwanted plants.

◆ This pet-safe formula consists of 2 quarts of distilled white vinegar, 1 teaspoon of liquid soap and ½ cup of orange oil (available at some health-food stores or garden-supply stores). Put the mixture in a spray bottle and drench the weeds with it.

 CAUTION: When using weed killers, be certain to spray *only* the weeds, not any of the plants you want to keep.

 Spray in the Box

Use this tried-and-true gardener's trick to kill *only* the weeds you want to get rid of and not your prized petunias.

Take an appropriate-sized box, carton or foam cooler (something with a top that opens), and cut off the bottom. Place the box over the weed, open the top, spray, then close the top for a few seconds. Doing this will keep the weed-killing spray from reaching surrounding plants.

If you have more weeds than desirable plants, cover the desirables with boxes to protect them, and just spray the exposed weeds.

Pulling Garden Weeds

If you want to do away with the weeds in your garden, get out there right after it rains. That's when you'll have the easiest time yanking the weeds out of the ground. Of course, if you don't want to wait until it rains, you can wet the soil yourself with a garden hose.

Low-Tech Weed Eaters

If you're a weed hater and an animal lover, consider getting a goat to do your weeding for you. Better yet, there are *weeder geese* that eat grass and young weeds, but stay away from certain cultivated plants. All you need are 2 to 4 geese per acre of row plantings. (Check your town's by-laws before buying geese.)

In addition to the geese being weeders, they are also manure spreaders and cultivators, continually adding fertilizer and organic matter to the soil. And their work ethic is unequaled. Geese work from daylight to dark, 7 days a week, feasting on grass and weeds as soon as new growth appears. Now you'll understand the bumper sticker that says— "Honk if you believe in *geeses*."

If you want more information about these weeders, contact the world's largest rare-breed hatchery, Murray McMurray Hatchery in Webster City, Iowa. Visit their Web site at *www.mcmurrayhatchery.com* or call 800-456-3280 or (in Iowa) 515-832-3280.

 Working on the Rim

If you're weeding, trimming or planting along the rim of a paved surface (such as your driveway), take the strain off your legs and back by sitting on a skateboard. This will make it easier to gradually roll along.

Eliminating Patio or Sidewalk Weeds

Personally, we think it's charming to see a feisty plant pop up through sidewalk cracks or in between patio stones. Then again, we don't have a patio, and any greenery seen on the sidewalks of New York City is generally appreciated. *But if you're not charmed by pavement weeds and want to get rid of them, these solutions may help...*

◆ Pour distilled white vinegar on the weeds—enough to get them good and wet—but don't hose it off. Let it stay there, and in a couple of days the weeds will be dead. Vinegar will also get rid of patio moss.

◆ For immediate results, boil ½ cup of table salt in 1 quart of water, and then pour the *hot-hot-hot* liquid onto the weeds. This will also work on patio moss.

 Make Weeds Stay Away
To prevent weeds from growing in the first place, sprinkle table salt or baking soda into the patio/sidewalk cracks.

PLANT & GARDEN PESTS A TO Z

 Garden pests? Oh, you can bombard them with pesticides—chemicals that the pests may not have developed tolerances to—but they generally smell bad, are unhealthy for you (and other living creatures), and they tend to be expensive.

Our goal is to protect your plants from pests with inexpensive remedies that will do the job, but will not harm you, any other beneficial garden organisms or the environment. So what are you waiting for? Bug off!

✳ **Plant Ugly Flowers**
There are flowers and vegetables that are not attractive to bees. If you want a bee-free garden, consider planting chrysanthemums, forsythia, daffodils, tulips and/or lilacs.
The bees will also stay away from certain vegetables that are generally harvested before they flower—such as carrots, Jerusalem artichokes, beets, cabbages and lettuce.

Ants

While most ants are harmless, nobody wants them crawling all over plants. *This "smear campaign" is an efficient, nontoxic deterrent…*

For an indoor plant, smear petroleum jelly on the base of the plant's pot. Petroleum jelly smeared on the stems of outdoor plants will keep ants and most other insects from crawling up.

Bees and Wasps

Chances are, if you refrain from shooing those flying insects away with your hand (which presents a threat to them), they will refrain from stinging you.

It's just hard to trust that fact and to ignore your instincts when they're buzzing around you. *Try using these deterrents instead…*

◆ One of the most popular bee, hornet or wasp zappers is hairspray…super-hold works best. Just point and shoot.

◆ Our cousin keeps her screenless windows open in summer, and when an occasional bee flies in, she kills it by spritzing it with Windex.

◆ We heard from a man who uses a spray can of WD-40 lubricant to zap any stinging bugs that get in his workshop.

◆ A spray bottle filled with vodka can also be an effective exterminator.

 NOTE: If it's a matter of *spray* or *be stung*, then *spray*. But please keep in mind that ⅓ of the foods you eat—either directly or indirectly—depends on pollination by bees. And wasps are an important part of the ecosystem and help control garden pests. So, you may want to think twice about ending their productive little lives.

Birds in the Garden— Pro or Con?

Birds are beautiful and fun to watch. They do the gardener a big favor by eating unwanted insects. However, they may also eat just-planted seeds, or pick at ripening tomatoes.

One school of thought is that if there is a birdbath and a birdhouse in the yard, then birds won't bother with the plants. Another school of thought is that you should attract the birds with a birdhouse and birdbath in the winter, but take them away during the spring/summer growing season. That way, the birds won't come around and eat plants growing in your garden.

Birds or no birds? You decide.

The best way to prevent birds from getting into your garden is to cover plants with netting (available at garden-supply stores). You can also program your sprinkler system to go off at set intervals—a sudden burst of water should scare off the birds.

But if you love having these fabulous feathered creatures flying around, give them the creature comforts—a birdbath regularly filled with fresh water and a birdhouse or feeder. *Here are some catering suggestions...*

◆ Stock the birdhouse with uncooked oats. Birds love 'em.

◆ Freshly popped, plain popcorn—without butter or salt—is a real treat for birds.

◆ Mix 1 part peanut butter with 5 parts cornmeal, then divide it and shape it into fat hockey pucks. Place each puck into a mesh (onion) bag. Tie the bags closed and hang them outside...wherever you want birds to come and feed.

◆ Save the seeds from summer melons, such as honeydew or cantaloupe, and let them dry out. Birds love to feast on them, so put them out in a bird feeder...or wherever birds can snack safely.

◆ Robins and bluebirds will flock to wherever you lay out a tray of raisins.

◆ Some of the many red- and orange-shaded flowers that will attract hummingbirds include columbine, coral bells, flag iris, lily, petunia, scarlet sage, trumpet honeysuckle and verbena.

 Keep Bees Away
◆ Wear neutral-colored clothes to keep bees away from you. Orange? Green? Red? Purple? **No!** Beige? Gray? **Yes!**

◆ Wearing perfume or scented hairspray is another no-no.

Birds

If the birds are feeding on your newly planted seeds or ripening fruit, and you want to get rid of them, tie flashy Mylar or tinsel-type strips (available at crafts stores) on posts and stakes throughout the garden. The shiny, flailing tinsel will frighten away most feathered pests.

Cats

◆ To deter cats from wandering around your garden, mince a few garlic bulbs and scatter the little pieces everywhere. (Pieces of citrus peel and eucalyptus oil also work.)

◆ If the garlic smell is too pungent for you, mix up a cat-repellent solution—use 2 tablespoons of mustard powder, 1 tablespoon of cayenne pepper, 2 tablespoons of flour and 2 cups of water. Pour the mixture into a spray bottle and spritz it around vegetable patches, flowerbeds and the border of your yard.

◆ If a cat has his eye on your birdbath, get out the distilled white vinegar and spray it on the birdbath's base. The smell of the vinegar should repel the cat and neutralize the cat's urine, which he uses to mark his territory.

◆ To keep your cat(s) from snacking on your indoor houseplants, place small pieces of citrus rind—lemon, lime, grapefruit or orange—on the soil.

◆ A non-odoriferous method of keeping your cat from turning your indoor plants into a playground is to place pine cones…or pebbles…or aluminum foil…or seashells…or marbles… around the plants. The rule to follow is—without harming the plants, cover up the soil and the cats will not want to dig in.

Deer and Other Animals

◆ At the risk of grossing you out, go to your local beauty salon and ask for a bag of human hair. Then cut the legs off a few pairs of old pantyhose, stuff the hair into each foot and knot them closed. Attach them to the trees and bushes near where the deer have been feeding.

When deer, rabbits or any other neighborhood animals pick up the scent of the human hair, they should be frightened off. Wouldn't you be?

You will have to replace the hair after it rains, but hopefully by then, the animals will no longer come around…and you will no longer need the hair to chase them away. (Human urine is also an effective repellent.)

◆ Wrap aluminum foil around young tree trunks, and keep the foil in place with rope or heavy cord. That should stop deer from taking a bite out of the tree's bark.

◆ Hang scented car air fresheners on trellises, trees, shrubs, bushes and fence posts—anywhere the deer and the antelope play on your property. The smell—especially mint—will chase them away.

◆ Hang deodorant soap (not the perfumed bars) in trees and on bushes. Drill a hole in the middle of each bar of soap, and use an "S" hook on a wire to attach each bar (almost like you're hanging Christmas ornaments). Put the soap about 4' off the ground. Use a few in each tree or bush.

 NOTE: To prevent the soap from bubbling up your garden and disappearing when it rains, you may want to use a wax-coated paper cup for each bar of soap.

Poke a hole in the bottom of the cup, and thread the wire through it so that the upside-down cup covers the soap. Then hang it that way in the tree.

◆ Deer and most other animals will not walk on bubble wrap. Place sheets of it around your garden, holding the corners in place with rocks, big flowerpots or stakes that you put in the ground.

◆ If you have old CDs that you can't use anymore, tie a string through the center hole of each, and attach them to bushes and trees. The shiny glint and constant movement from the CDs will scare off most animal trespassers.

◆ The smell of mothballs will repel many unwanted animals (including dogs, cats, squirrels and snakes) from munching on your garden greenery. Spread mothballs around plants and shrubs.

◆ If you find the mothball smell too offensive, scatter some cayenne pepper on the soil, or sprinkle a little directly on the plants.

Dogs

As you may already know, when dogs frequently urinate on the lawn, it can cause yellow burn marks. To bring back the grass to the way it should be, mix 1 cup of baking soda into 1 gallon of water, then saturate the peed-on area with this solution every 3 days.

The baking soda neutralizes the urine's acidity, which restores the grass back to normal—it also deodorizes the area so that the dog will not recognize it and mark the same spot again. (Is that why "Spot" is such a popular name for dogs?)

Insects

Certain critters can be the pestiest of pests. *Aphids* are plant lice—soft-bodied, pear-shaped insects that are less than ⅛" long and are most commonly green, yellow or black. *Whiteflies* (insects that look more like tiny moths than flies) are found on citrus fruit and just about any plant. And *red spiders* (also known as spider mites) are the bane of bonsai and ornamental plant growers.

These effective suggestions should help you to squash them…

◆ Aphids and whiteflies are attracted to the color yellow. So get a few yellow index cards, smear them with petroleum jelly and place them on the soil near where there is an aphid or whitefly infestation.

The idea is that the bugs will land on the cards and get stuck in the jelly. Later, when the cards are full, put on gloves and carefully discard them.

◆ A yellow pan filled with soapy water will attract most flying pests and then drown them.

◆ If you see aphids on your plants, mix ½ cup of powdered milk with 1 quart of warm water and put the solution in a spray bottle.

Spray the plants' leaves thoroughly. As they dry, the aphids will die.

◆ This potent formula should get rid of spider mites, whiteflies and aphids…in a blender, purée 3 cloves of garlic and 2 teaspoons of Tabasco sauce. Add 1 pint of plain water and 2 tablespoons of liquid dish detergent. Strain the mixture into a spray bottle and spritz the infected plant's leaves.

◆ If the plants in your garden suffer a plague of insects, plant garlic and/or onion throughout your patches. You can also stick a peeled clove of garlic in the soil of each plant that seems to attract bugs. Don't be surprised, though, if you end up with a crop of garlic!

◆ Most insects, including aphids, despise the smell of mint. If you don't grow mint, then get some mint leaves at the grocery store and spread them around your garden.

 CAUTION: If you plant mint, be warned that it grows without mercy! To prevent it from overtaking your garden, plant it in its own container. And be sure to keep it trimmed back—live mint will often root wherever it touches the ground.

Moles

Most gardening experts believe that a commercial mole trap is the best way to rid your garden and lawn of these burrowing little critters. We're sure that is so, but the thought of then having to dispose of the trapped animal is enough to have us try something that will just chase the pest away. This remedy is a *chaser* that takes advantage of the moles' intense dislike of noise.

To discover the mole's run, imagine a line between 2 molehills. Dig down at a spot along this imaginary line until you locate the run. See if you can get a portable radio to blare down there. If not, drop in the little mechanical movement from a musical greeting card. (They seem to go on playing forever.)

If this doesn't work, there's always the trap. Check your local garden-supply store, or search the Internet for "wildlife control supplies."

Rabbits

◆ Having a "bad hare day"? Stop rabbits from enjoying a salad in your garden. Wet down the leaves of your vegetable plants and sprinkle ground cayenne pepper on them.

◆ Hare today and seedlings gone tomorrow? Protect your seedlings by sprinkling baby powder on them. Rabbits hate the smell of baby talc. Other deterrents include used kitty litter, mothballs and human hair.

Raccoons, Woodchucks And Gophers

◆ If you're really desperate to get rid of any raccoons—especially when your vegetables (such as corn) are almost ripe—invest in 2 or 3 portable radios. Set them on different talk-radio stations, put them in plastic bags to protect them from the elements and leave them in your garden. The surround-sound effect will scare the raccoons away.

Remember, it must be *talk* radio only—*music* might actually encourage those masked bandits to stay for dinner and dancing.

◆ Nobody wants gopher or woodchuck holes in his/her garden or lawn. In a blender, put all the cloves from 3 bulbs of garlic, a few chili peppers and 3 cups of water. Blend thoroughly and transfer the mix to a jar.

Pour some of the solution into each hole…then, put a hose down the hole and let the water push the strong mixture deeper into the hole. This formula will help you get rid of gophers or woodchucks for good.

Slugs and Snails

Collect any clean and empty tuna cans and use them to set traps for beer-loving critters (we're referring to slugs and snails, of course!). Since you don't want the slugs in your garden, scatter the cans around your garden. Dig shallow holes, or carefully press the cans—open side up—into the soil so that the rim is level with the ground. In the early evening, fill ⅔ of each can with beer. The next morning, you will be able to dispose of cans of slugs that died happy.

Squash Bugs

If you grow squash, cucumbers or pumpkins, keep squash bugs away by placing strips of heavy aluminum foil under the vines. The foil will help keep the soil moist and block sunlight, which will keep weeds from growing. It may also speed up the crop-ripening time.

Squirrels

If you have a *bird* feeder and don't want it turned into a *squirrel* feeder, then try coating the metal feeder pole with petroleum jelly. (Suddenly, the old Simon & Garfunkel song came to mind—"Slip Sliding Away.")

PLANT & GARDEN FRIENDS

Almost 90% of all the world's plants rely on insects (such as bees) to spread their pollen and perpetuate the plant species. *So, before you pick up that fly swatter, you may want to know about a few helpful garden insects…*

Beneficial Bugs

◆ Praying mantids gobble up aphids, mites and scale insects. Pray that you have these critters in your garden.

◆ Ladybugs—also known as lady beetles or ladybirds—are attractive assets in your garden. They devour aphids, scale insects and other plant-eating pests. During the average ladybug's lifetime, it destroys 5,400 aphids. Let's hear it for the ladybugs!

Buy Your Bugs

If there are no garden ladybugs in your area, they are available on-line. A package of 1,000 costs about $20. Check out *www.ladybuglady. com/ladybugs.htm.*

Butterflies

Who wouldn't want butterflies in their garden? These *flying flowers* are especially drawn to red, scarlet, purple and blue blossoms.

If you want to extend a butterfly invitation, plant any or all of the following flowers and herbs—cornflower, aster, dill, morning glory, verbena, mint, globe thistle, goldenrod, lilac, pansy, parsley, shasta daisy, sweet marjoram, zinnia, sage and (wouldn't you know?) butterfly bush.

POPULAR GARDEN PLANTS A TO Z

alk about popular! Tomatoes are by far the most popular garden plant, with almost 90% of all home gardeners growing this delectable red fruit. According to a survey reported by Heirloom Seeds (*www.heirloomseeds.com*), the next 9 most popular home-grown vegetables in the US and Canada are (in order of their popularity)—peppers, cucumbers, onions, beans, lettuce, carrots, sweet corn, radishes and cabbage.

No matter which plants are your favorites, and whether or not they're among the top 10, here are some ways to add to the life and beauty of all of your plants.

African Violets

Grow bigger and heartier plants by feeding them an iron supplement—simply stick a few nails in the soil around them, and enjoy the lovely results.

Azaleas

These acid-loving plants will love you if you give them an occasional bracer. Once a month, fill your watering can with 2 tablespoons of distilled white vinegar in 1 quart of water to promote bloom growth and color.

The same mixture is also great for rhododendrons and gardenias.

NOTE: In case you are wondering, of all the colors the plant comes in, white azaleas stay in bloom the longest.

Beans

See "Legumes (Beans and Peas)" on page 131.

Bulbs

◆ Before planting bulbs, protect them from burrowing insects and rodents by dusting them with medicated baby powder.

◆ After you dig up your cold-vulnerable bulbs, apply medicated baby powder all over them to prevent rot and fungal problems when you put them into winter storage.

Cabbage

◆ Keep animals from snacking on cabbage by sprinkling a little cayenne pepper on the plants as they grow. Remember to resprinkle with more pepper after it rains.

◆ You can also trickle a little milk mixed with water on the cabbages to protect them from cabbage worms.

◆ After cutting off the first mature head of cabbage, leave the rest of the plant as is. Chances are, a few more small heads will grow in the same place.

Cacti and Other Succulents

In addition to keeping moths away, mothballs or camphor flakes added to your potting mix will help prevent mealybug problems in the roots of cacti and other succulents.

Be sure to plant the mothballs only in clay pots—they may ruin plastic pots.

Carrots

Mix your carrot seeds with some coffee grounds. The seeds will have more substance and be easier to work with. Another plus is that coffee grounds will add nitrogen and other nutrients to the soil as they break down.

Also, the coffee grounds will be a deterrent to root maggots that might otherwise eat some of your carrot crop.

Climbing Plants

Give climbing plants something creative to hang on to. Simply take a large, no-longer-used umbrella and remove the fabric from it, then drive the handle into the ground and open the umbrella so the spokes are extended.

At the base of the umbrella, plant clematis or wisteria (in a sunny location)...or honeysuckle or morning glory (in partial shade)...or any other climbing plant you like. Then watch the blooms turn the bumbershoot frame into an unusual trellis.

Corn

When it comes to harvesting corn at its prime, the window of opportunity is limited to a few days. Start testing the ears about 2 weeks after the corn silk can be seen, to make sure that you don't miss those few days.

To test for ripeness, peel back the husk enough to see about 2 inches of kernels. Press a kernel with your fingernail until you split the skin and juice comes out. If the juice is milky, the corn is ripe—so start picking. If the juice is watery, put the husk back in place and give the corn a few more days. If the juice is gooey, the corn is getting too starchy. Of course, that won't happen to you—the ripeness test is the *ear*mark of a good corn grower.

Corn tastes best when picked, cooked and eaten all on the same day. Writer and humorist Mark Twain once said—not entirely in jest—that folks should just set up kettles in their cornfields, build a fire under them and shuck the ears of corn directly into the boiling water. Really, that's not a bad idea if you want the tastiest corn!

In general, the best time of day to pick corn is late in the afternoon, when the sugar content is at its highest.

Cucumbers

Coddle those cucumber seedlings by giving them the warmth they love. If you don't mind the look, place an old rubber tire around each plant. The tire keeps in heat during the day and releases it at night.

Harvesting Popcorn

Popcorn seeds are completely different than the regular corn-on-the-cob (sweet corn) seeds. Do not plant any variety of popcorn in the same garden as your sweet corn. The quality of the sweet corn will be diminished once it is cross-pollinated by popcorn.

If you do grow your own popcorn, be sure to let the kernels dry in the garden as long as possible. Don't harvest them until the kernels are hard and the husks are completely dry.

After harvesting them, remove the husks, put the ears in mesh bags, then hang them in a warm, dry, well-ventilated place. When you've tested a few kernels by popping them—and they taste good—then it is time to remove all of the kernels from the ears.

The easiest way to do it without using and bruising your thumbs is to hold 1 ear in each hand and rub them against each other. The kernels will knock each other off the cobs. Then store the kernels in jars with tight-fitting lids—this will keep moisture in and bugs out.

One of the most popular products that's in Paul Newman's philanthropic line of all-natural foods is *Newman's Own OldStyle Picture Show Microwave Popcorn.* Newman's experience is that *small* kernels yield tastier popcorn—the bigger the corn pops, the more dissipated the taste.

Eggplants

If you would rather have 4 big, impressive eggplants per plant instead of lots of little unimpressive ones, then read on…

As soon as you see 4 fruits starting to plump up, pinch off all the other flowers as well as the buds. In doing so, the eggplants that may come along later will not have enough time to amount to anything before the season ends, and most of the plant's energy will go into producing the 4 beauties.

To help nourish this fruit-bearing plant, occasionally treat it to a magnesium and sulfur drink—1 tablespoon of Epsom salt (available at supermarkets and drugstores) dissolved in 1 gallon of warm water.

Ferns

For a fantastic fern fertilizer, finely chop 3 to 5 raw oysters and work the pieces into the soil. Your ferns will love it!

Forsythia

Once a forsythia bush blooms, it should be pruned. To revitalize mature forsythias, remove ¼ to ⅓ of the oldest (largest) branches at ground level. Do this every other year. New shoots will come up from the ground and bloom in subsequent years.

Geraniums

Geraniums are thirsty plants that require lots of water (but make sure the roots don't sit in water). After preparing your morning coffee, rinse off the coffee grounds, and put them on top of the soil surrounding the geraniums. The grounds become a marvelous mulch that helps keep in moisture.

Herbs

Fresh herbs are most flavorful when harvested right before their flowers open.

Hollyhocks

When you've finished drinking your beer, add a little water to the can, bottle or glass, swish it around and water your hollyhocks with it.

The yeast in the beer will help the plant rise to new heights—in addition to its usual watering, of course.

Hydrangeas

Pink or blue, it's up to you. Grow a particular variety of hydrangea bush in acid soil, and the flowers will be blue…grow another type in alkaline soil, and you'll have pink flowers.

So, to enhance the pink, add *dolomitic lime* (available at garden-supply stores) to your plants several times a year to help raise the soil's pH to about 6.0 to 6.2.

For blue hydrangeas, lower the soil's pH to 5.2 to 5.5. You can do this by adding a solution made from 1 tablespoon of *aluminum sulfate* (available at garden-supply stores) per gallon of water, and use it to water the plants (make sure the plants are at least 2 years old) throughout the growing season.

 CAUTION: Water the plants thoroughly before applying this aluminum solution, and be warned that too much can burn the plants' roots. Talk to a knowledgeable salesperson at the garden store to get more information.

Kale

If you're new at gardening and don't want to run the risk of crop failure, plant fail-safe kale seeds. The vegetables are beautiful, healthy and very easy to grow in just about any kind of soil.

Legumes (Beans and Peas)

Right after you pick the first crop of legumes, use a hand mower to mow the plants down to about 3" from the soil.

That way, you will have another crop to harvest before the end of the season.

 CAUTION: Do not plant members of the *allium* family—such as garlic or onions—in or around a pea patch. They may inhibit the growth of peas.

Lettuce

Grow lettuce in a shady patch of your garden. If you keep the lettuce cool as a cucumber, it will mature without any bitterness…but then again, wouldn't we all?

Lilac

After a lilac bush blooms, it should be pruned. To revitalize an older bush, remove entire dead branches at ground level and all weak or broken branches. Cut back the healthy stems to 1' or 2'.

Then start taking care of the bushes by watering and fertilizing them regularly. The lilacs may take 1 or 2 years to rebloom, but they're worth the effort!

Melons

Put melons on a pedestal while they're growing, and they'll happily ripen early. To do so, place each melon on an empty coffee can that has been turned upside down and pressed into the soil. The metal attracts and holds on to heat from the sun, which is a ripening agent.

Onions

Before you plant onions, save up several days' worth of used coffee grounds and let them dry out. When it's time to plant, spread a layer of the coffee grounds on the bottom of each row of onions. Doing so will help prevent worms from getting at your onions.

Perennials

Perennials are meant to grow back year after year. But a premature thaw, followed by a deep freeze, can be the end of your perennials.

If you put a layer of hay, shredded leaves or grass clippings on the ground over your perennials, it will keep the ground frozen and

Good Advice for Allergy Sufferers

According to Clifford Bassett, MD, an allergist at Long Island College Hospital in Brooklyn, New York, seasonal allergy sufferers should avoid planting chrysanthemums, privet, palm and mulberry trees, juniper and cypress, as well as Bermuda, fescue and perennial rye grasses.

Allergy-prone gardeners will do better planting hydrangeas, viburnum, begonias, bulbs like tulip and iris, dogwood trees, azaleas, boxwood, daisies, geraniums, pansies, petunias, sunflowers and zinnias.

It's best to garden on low pollen–count days, and also when it's damp or rainy...and in the evening, if possible. Also, be sure to eliminate all weeds from your garden.

And the last bit of advice to help you keep allergic reactions at bay—before entering your house, always remove all of your gardening clothes...dust off your shoes...and don't forget to clean your glasses.

prevent a premature thaw. Do this after the first frost, but before it gets *really* cold. And then you'll be able to enjoy these bloomin' plants for many seasons to come.

Petunias

If you smoke, scrub up like a surgeon before working with petunias. These sensitive plants are extremely susceptible to the *tobacco mosaic virus*, a disease that can be spread by cigarette, cigar or pipe smoke.

Poinsettias

These traditional winter holiday plants can be enjoyed all year 'round if you give them plenty of sun in the winter, and nondirect sunlight in the summer. Poinsettias like sun but not heat. They need moderately moist soil...water thoroughly whenever the soil feels dry to the touch.

Potatoes

If you're going to plant potatoes, start eating lots of canned soup, and save the cans. Turn them into protective cylinders by taking off their lids and bottoms.

Then press each soup-can cylinder into the soil around each young potato plant. Not only will the can shelter the young plants from the wind, it will also protect them from cutworms, grubs and other pests.

Pumpkins

If you want a pumpkin to grow really big, cut off all of the blossoms except 2. Then all of the pumpkin's energy will go into pumping up its size, rather than nourishing lots of blossoms.

Radishes

To invigorate your radish plants, serve them a monthly tonic made from 1 tablespoon of apple cider vinegar in 1 gallon of water. They'll thrive on the trace minerals that the apple cider vinegar has to offer.

Raspberries

The best time to pick ripe raspberries is after the morning dew is gone, simply because dry fruit is less perishable.

Gather the raspberry harvest in wide, shallow containers so that these delicate berries aren't piled up on each other. Piling up means *mush* on the bottom.

Roses

- Every rose grower should know the secret to a healthy and beautiful rose crop—banana peels! The peels are rich in calcium, magnesium, phosphorus, potash, sulfur, sodium and silica…so they make a great fertilizer.

  Save the banana peels or air-dry them until they're crispyish and crumblyish. Figure on using about 3 peels per rosebush—cut the peels into small pieces and bury them around each bush, a few inches deep into the soil.

- Nourishing your rosebushes using Epsom salt (available at supermarkets and drugstores) will help strengthen the color of the flowers. During the first and third weeks of May and during the first and third weeks of June, feed your up-and-coming bushes according to their height—1 teaspoon of Epsom salt per foot—worked into the soil around the stems.

  For a mature rose bush, sprinkle ½ cup of Epsom salt on the soil around it. You may also notice that the plants blossom faster due to the magnesium in the Epsom salt, which helps boost their rate of growth.

- As the day progresses, rose stems stock up on food manufactured by the leaves. By the time evening rolls around, the stems are at their most hale and hardy. That's the best time to cut the flowers—they, too, will be hale and hardy. If you cut roses in the morning, before the stems have had a chance to bulk up, they will not have as much staying power.

- The best way to cut roses is to look for the uppermost 5-leaflet branch and cut the stem above it. By doing this, you can be sure of the abundant regrowth of more roses. Cut below that branch and the new shoot may be flowerless.

- Thorns help the rose plant drink water. If, in the process of removing the thorns, you tear, peel or damage the bark, you will impede the amount of water that makes its way up to the flower. A damaged stem will shorten the life of the rose.

  If the thorns on the rose are a thorn in your side, buy a de-thorning tool (available at garden-supply stores) and follow the instructions. You may wound a few flowers until you become a proficient de-thorner, but stick with it.

- When you're pruning roses or any thorny plant, use kitchen tongs to hold the branches out of your way—this will prevent the thorns from pricking your fingers and/or scratching your arms.

 Sun- or Shade-Loving Produce

- If a section of your garden is bathed in sunlight, consider growing corn, melons, peppers and/or tomatoes. They thrive in the sun.

- If a section of your garden doesn't get much sun, consider growing lettuce, pumpkins and/or spinach. They thrive in the shade.

Tomatoes

- Protect your seedlings from the cold air by planting them during the afternoon—the warmest part of the day. (And protect yourself from the sun with a hat, sunglasses and sunscreen.)

◆ Consider including carrots, lettuce, nasturtiums, chives, onions and parsley in the tomato patch. Any or all of them can help prevent disease, stimulate growth and enhance the flavor of the tomatoes.

◆ Another beneficial addition to the patch is dill. It will keep away pests, such as hornworms. French marigolds will ward off whiteflies and rabbits. Sagebrush will stimulate tomatoes to produce a pest-repelling chemical. Asparagus will help deter any *nematodes* (including pinworms, hookworms and roundworms), while tomatoes will help repel the asparagus beetle.

 Protect Your Tomatoes!

Do not grow cabbage, fennel, kohlrabi or potatoes near your tomato patch. *The Moosewood Restaurant Kitchen Garden* (Ten Speed Press) suggests that you won't be doing any of the plants a favor—they will attract pests that will attack tomatoes.

◆ Lower the acidity of the tomatoes, and they'll taste sweeter. To do that, sprinkle baking soda around the plants and work it into the soil.

◆ To prevent blossom-end rot, mix a packet of powdered milk with water (follow package directions), and feed it to your plants. Or use crushed oyster and crab shells (available at garden-supply stores)—follow the directions on the package and sprinkle the powder around the plants.

The milk and shells both contain calcium, which will keep the plants healthier and help produce juicier tomatoes.

◆ According to Cornell University researchers, gently petting tomato seedlings every now and then produces short, stocky plants that are more desirable for transplanting. Start stroking the plants when they are 2½" tall, and continue until you're ready to transplant them.

◆ If you smoke cigarettes, find the strength to stop…at least while you're in the garden. Tomato plants are susceptible to the *tobacco mosaic virus*, a disease that can be spread by cigar, pipe and cigarette smoke. (It's always a good idea to wash your hands before you start to garden.)

◆ It can happen! You can save tomatoes from a frost. The first thing to do is to pick them—no matter how green they are. Wrap each tomato in 3 layers of newspaper and they will eventually ripen.

If you can't pick them, cover the plants with a clean, empty milk jug—cut the top off and place it over them. It will make an effective shield.

◆ Instead of throwing out that shabby old bra, use it to support *zaftig* tomatoes. Brace the tomato plant by tying it to 2 wooden stakes. Then attach each end of the bra to each stake, making sure the cups are positioned under 2 large tomatoes.

The bra will give the plant the extra support it needs, and prevent it from collapsing under the weight of the plant's oversized love apples.

 Black or White?

If you have a choice as to which color bra to use, black will attract more sun and should be used *before* the tomatoes ripen…a white bra should be used for ripe tomatoes, during the last days before picking.

◆ When you're cleaning your garden in autumn and you come across unripe tomatoes, pull out the plants—roots and all. Then shake off the dirt and hang the plants upside down in your basement or garage. Believe it or not, the tomatoes will ripen on the vine. Think of it, fresh tomatoes at Thanksgiving!

◆ You have 2 options when it comes to planting tomatoes. You can help them grow either by getting *over* them or getting *under* them.

Over: If you're concerned about providing moisture and warmth to the plants, spread black plastic over the soil. Then cut out holes in the plastic and plant the plants through them.

Under: Wad up some newspaper and set it on the bottom of each planting hole. The paper will absorb water as it trickles through the soil, and the roots can make use of it throughout the hot, dry summer.

Another "Under": Sprinkle 1 teaspoon of Epsom salt on top of the newspaper in the planting hole. The magnesium sulfate in the Epsom salt will help the plant grow more and bigger tomatoes.

Tulips

Protect bulbs from rodents by planting them in metal cylinders. Gather large cans—such as those from fruit or vegetable juice—and use 1 can for each bulb.

Remove the contents and the top and bottom lids of each can, and wash inside the empty can. Press each clean cylinder into the soil until the rim is ground level. Take out ⅔ of the soil, place the bulb inside and replace the soil around the bulb up to the rim.

This can system is an *uncanny* way of keeping animals away from the bulbs while allowing rain to reach them.

Safe Way to Handle Poison Ivy

If you discover poison ivy on your property, **DO NOT** burn it. You don't want the plant's oil to get into the air that you breathe. Instead, put 1 ounce of vodka and 2 cups of water into a spray bottle, then saturate the poison ivy plants with it. Oddly enough, even though you're spraying it with a liquid mixture, the alcohol in the vodka helps to dehydrate and kill the plants.

If you don't want to waste your good vodka on the misery-causing greenery, put on gloves and uproot the plants, then leave them on the ground to dry out in the sun.

As soon as you've done the deed, clean all your tools thoroughly in a solution made from ¾ pound of table salt mixed with warm, soapy water. When you take off your gloves, turn them inside out and dispose of them. Be careful and make sure that the gloves or oils do not touch your skin.

You should also *carefully* remove any clothes that came in contact with the poison ivy. If you do not want to throw away the clothes you were wearing, then you can wash them in the washing machine—but separately from other clothes.

Be sure to wear disposable rubber gloves when handling the clothes. And use 1 ounce of liquid dish detergent rather than laundry detergent—it's better at breaking up *urushiol*, the poison ivy oil. Run the washing machine's rinse cycle twice after you take out the clothes.

 CAUTION: Urushiol oil is sticky and can stay on clothes and cause new rashes—even years later.

Also, while wearing the disposable rubber gloves, scrub your boots or shoes with warm, soapy water (use 1 capful of liquid dish detergent in 1 gallon of water). Leave the footwear in the sun to dry.

Vegetables

◆ While *pantyhose on plants* doesn't sound very practical, it does seem to provide protection to the vegetables that tend to attract harmful bugs. (We hope by now that you know to NEVER throw away old pantyhose!)

Snip off the feet of the pantyhose and cover each growing vegetable with a foot. Use a rubber band or string to secure it in place. The nylon fabric will let the sun and air get in and will keep the bugs out. Also, as the veggie grows, the hose will stretch.

◆ If you find it hard to plant your veggies in straight rows, use 2 wooden stakes and a ball of string to lead the way.

Insert 1 stake in the ground where you want the row to start, and put 1 stake where you want the row to end. Tie the string on 1 stake, then stretch it across to the other stake. The string is your straight line. Follow it as you distribute your seeds.

TREES

Trees are the longest living organisms on Earth. You may have heard that you can calculate a tree's age by its rings. Ahh, but do you know that those rings also provide precise information about environmental events, such as volcanic eruptions…and that the study of these rings is called *dendrochronology*?

If you plan on planting a tree—or if you already have a few trees on your property—you may find some suggestions here that will help them live long and grow tall.

Planting Trees

Over the life of a tree, its roots can be far-reaching. With that in mind, plant the tree so that its roots will not come in contact with (and do damage to) your house's foundation—no matter how old the tree gets or how big it grows. Make sure any tree is planted well away from sidewalks and sewer pipes and/or septic tanks.

Once you find the right spot for the tree, project into the future. Envision the tree mature and all grown up. Is it shading your driveway so that your car stays cool in the summer? Or is the sap from the tree messing up your car? Is the tree blocking the sunlight from your garden? Are the tree's fruits falling off and possibly attracting hungry critters?

Think about it before you plant the tree so that you won't have any regrets down the road. (Hey, perhaps *that's* where you should plant the tree!) As a general guideline, most trees should be planted 7–15 feet away from your home.

When you finally find the perfect place to plant a tree, be sure the drainage is good. Test the drainage by digging a hole in the exact spot you plan to plant the tree, and fill it with water. Check on the hole about 10 hours later. If the water has completely drained out, that means drainage is good and you can start planting.

 Line the Tree Hole

Any young tree that you're going to plant will need all the help it can get. Start by lining the hole that's been dug for the tree with baking potatoes. They will help provide moisture for the young plant.

As the potatoes decompose, the tree will benefit from their nutrients. *This spud's for yew!*

Apple Trees

◆ Before it's apple-blossom time, collect empty gallon jugs (like from milk or spring water). You'll need 1 jug for each apple tree. You'll also need 1 quart of distilled white vinegar, 1 quart of water, 1 cup of sugar and 1 banana peel for each tree.

Combine all of the ingredients in each jug *in the order they're listed.* Then hang a filled jug in the middle of each tree (and be sure to leave off the cap). Put the jugs in place *before* the apple blossoms open, and this will ensure worm-free blossoms.

◆ There are 2 ways to check if apples are ripe enough to harvest. First, take an apple off the tree with a clockwise twist. If it comes off easily, the apple is ripe.

If you have to keep twisting until it finally lets go of the tree, give the rest of the apples more time to ripen.

Another way to check for ripeness is by the color of the apple's seed. If it's dark brown, then the apple is ripe...if it's pale tan or white, the apple is not quite ripe.

Other Fruit Trees

◆ If your fruit trees have been barren, the soil may need boron, a nutrient found in borax. Sprinkle about 1 cup of borax powder (available at supermarkets and drugstores) around the base of each tree right before you give it a thorough watering.

◆ Or you may just need to smack your trees around...*really.* To do this, take a rolled-up newspaper and hit the tree with it, up and down the trunk.

The idea is to loosen the vessels that carry sap to the leaves and buds. According to the wisdom of folklore, it's best to whip fruit trees in early spring, by moonlight.

HOUSEPLANTS

A nice addition to any room is a splash of color—courtesy of plants and indoor flowers. These decorative accents can lend a feeling of hominess to your living space. Here are some ideas that will help you make your household greenery thrive. *But first, an important warning...*

> **CAUTION:** We would be very remiss—especially if there are children and/or pets in the home—if we didn't make readers aware of the fact that several common house and garden plants are poisonous (and potentially lethal) when ingested. *Read on...*

All parts of philodendrons, rhododendron, azaleas, laurels, dieffenbachia, elephant ears and buttercups are toxic...as are the seeds and pods of wisteria...the leaves and flowers of lily-of-the-valley...the bulbs of autumn crocus, hyacinths, narcissus and daffodils...the leaves of foxgloves, the berries of jasmine and mistletoe...and the leaves and branches of oleander.

In fact, the beautiful oleander bush that's grown indoors and outdoors throughout the country is so potent that ingesting a *single leaf* can kill a child. Even using oleander twigs to spear meat that's roasted over a campfire can (and has) proven fatal. While this sounds like material for a fictional murder mystery, it shouldn't be taken lightly in real life.

If you want to check out a plant that you would like to bring into your home—or a plant that's already there, visit *www.yardener.com/AvoidingPoisonousPlants.html.*

Or call the US National Poison Hotline at 800-222-1222. When you dial this number, you will automatically be linked to the poison center in your local area. The operator will look up the plant in question in a comprehensive database and tell you all that you need to know about its toxicity. This service is free, and it's available 24 hours a day, 7 days a week.

New Plants

A gardener at The New York Botanical Garden told us that April is generally the best month to bring home new houseplants. The reasoning is that the light becomes stronger and the days become longer in the springtime, which means better conditions and fewer problems for plants.

Cuttings

If a friend offers you cuttings of plants that you admire, ask him/her for a raw potato along with the cuttings. Cut off a chunk from one end of the potato, and make holes in it with a chopstick or ballpoint-pen cap. Gently insert the cuttings into the holes. Then put the potato with the cuttings in a bag or box, and they should stay safe and moist during your trip home.

Once the cuttings are home, you should mist them with a solution of ¼ teaspoon of 3% hydrogen peroxide to 2 cups of water. This will serve to help prevent them from getting a fungal spore infection.

Live-Long-and-Prosper Plants

If you haven't had much luck with plants due to your unintentional neglect, start over with those that require very little care. Select from Devil's ivy, snake plants, corn plants, Chinese evergreens or begonias. And, this time, don't forget to water them!

 Clean Means Sunny

Up to twice as much beneficial sunlight will stream into your home through windows that are clean as opposed to windows that are dirty.

See Chapter 5, "All-Around-the-House Hints," pages 95–96, for easy and effective ways to clean windows.

Sun-Loving Plants

If you have a particularly sunny room, plants such as jade, coleus, cacti and *orchids* should all thrive there.

 NOTE: The secret of growing orchids successfully is to keep them in a room that's heated to between 75°F and 85°F during the day and 60°F and 65°F at night.

Many orchids will remain bloomless unless they live with the temperature variation of 15°F to 20°F between day and night.

Shade Plants

You can grow healthy plants in a room without sunlight streaming in the window—and even without a window—as long as you have the right types of plants. Pothos, ferns, peace lilies and prayer plants do not require a sunbath to be hale and hardy. Just be sure to keep them watered properly or placed in a shady and humid area (such as the bathroom).

Potting

◆ Have you ever dissected a disposable diaper? Well, now's your chance. Cut open a diaper (any brand/absorbency will do), remove the polymer flakes and mix them into the potting soil. Since the flakes absorb 300 times their weight in liquid, they will keep plant soil nice and moist. The polymer also stores nutrients, which will gradually feed the plant.

◆ When it comes to pots for flowering plants, bigger is *not* better. For the health of the plant, use a pot that will keep the roots close together rather than spread out.

Pot Liners

◆ Instead of lining the bottom of your pots with rocks or pebbles, use polystyrene packing peanuts. They are good at retaining moisture—so you may not have to water plants as often—and they weigh next to nothing. That can make a big difference when you have to lug around a large potted plant.

It's an especially good idea to use the packing peanuts in hanging plants because of how weightless and absorbent they are.

◆ Line the inside of the pot with a coffee filter or with the leg piece from an old pair of pantyhose. Then add the soil and the plant. The drainage hole will let the water out, and the pantyhose acts as a filter to keep the soil in.

Enhancing the Sun

◆ Plants that need lots of light—but do not get enough—usually look weak, gangly and yellowish. If you have sun-worshipping plants like geraniums, jade plants, ficus and cacti, line the windowsill near them with aluminum foil. The foil will enhance the reflection of the sun.

◆ Get a cardboard box big enough to house your plant(s). Cut off the top of the box and 1 of the sides. Then line the inside of the box with aluminum foil—shiny side out. Put the plant(s) inside the box and then place it near the window.

 NOTE: The foil-lined box is better than the foil-lined windowsill because the plants in the box will be surrounded by reflected sunlight and will grow straight up—while the plants near the windowsill will be leaning toward the source of light—the window. If the cardboard box appears unsightly, cover the outside with attractive contact paper (self-adhesive vinyl).

Use Plants to Clear the Air

In 1989, the National Aeronautics and Space Administration (NASA) conducted extensive (and expensive) research during a 2-year study. The scientists found a list of common, attractive and easy-to-grow houseplants that can dramatically reduce toxic chemical levels in the home. One plant will generally remove up to 87% of the toxic organic pollutants in a 100-square-foot area—increase the air-cleaning with even more plants.

Putting plants in each room may go a long way in eliminating problems like sore throats, stuffy noses, headaches, nausea, teary eyes and even acne—all of which may be caused by indoor contaminants that come from drapes, carpets, insulation, paint, household cleaning products, paper towels, tissues, plastics…really, almost everything. *Take this list with you when you shop for air-cleaning plants…*

◆ Golden pothos
◆ Peace lily
◆ Spider plant
◆ Chinese evergreen
◆ Boston fern
◆ Rubber plant
◆ English ivy
◆ Bamboo palm
◆ Weeping fig (*Ficus benjamina*)

 CAUTION: The ficus tree or shrub is sensitive to gas leaks. If all of the leaves suddenly fall off your ficus plant, open your windows, then call the gas company to test your gas lines. Do not ignore what may be a warning that could save lives.

Misting

Plants should be misted several times a week to make up for the low humidity level in most homes. This is especially important during dry winter months.

Brush the Fuzzies

Do not mist plants that have fuzzy-surfaced leaves, including cacti. Clean the *fuzzies* with a soft brush instead. A clean, new makeup brush or a baby's hairbrush both work well.

Watering Houseplants

◆ Overwatering is the leading killer of houseplants. Know when to water a plant by sticking your finger about 1" into the soil. If the soil feels dry, then it's time to quench the plant's thirst.

◆ Water your plants in the morning, when they begin to wake up. It's when they will best absorb water.

◆ Watering often, but a little at a time, can weaken the roots. Instead, water plants thoroughly once every week—or whenever the soil feels dry to the touch.

◆ Plants prefer lukewarm or room-temperature water because it's easier for them to absorb. But ice-cold or boiling-hot water—NEVER!

Enriching Elixirs

◆ Gelatin is a great source of nitrogen. Dissolve 1 envelope of unflavored gelatin in 1 cup of just-boiled water. Then add 3 cups of tap water and—when it cools to room temperature—use the mixture to give your plants an energy boost once a month.

◆ Water from boiled pasta or potatoes has a high starch content and makes an excellent plant fertilizer. Let the water cool to room temperature before using it.

◆ After you hard-boil an egg, douse your plants with the protein-enriched water. Wait until the water is lukewarm before you use it.

◆ Whenever you steam or cook vegetables, save the excess water as a vitamin-filled treat for your plants. Let the water cool to room temperature before using it.

◆ If your plants aren't doing well, they may be sensitive to the chlorine gas in your city or town's water system. Instead, let tap water sit in the watering can overnight (which will allow most of the gas to escape), then use it to water your plants.

Also, when it snows, gather a few handfuls of fresh powder in a bucket, let it melt and warm up to room temperature, then water your plants with the gas-free water.

◆ If you maintain a fish aquarium, save the old water every time you change it, and feed the nutrient-rich water to your plants. They will thank you by thriving.

◆ Alkaline-loving houseplants, especially African violets, always appreciate a dairy boost. Instead of throwing away an empty milk carton, fill it halfway with tap water and water your plants with it.

◆ Dissolve 2 tablespoons of Epsom salt (available at supermarkets and drugstores) in 1 gallon of warm water to quench your plant's thirst. Epsom salt (magnesium sulfate) provides the plant with magnesium.

Do this once a month, and you'll see your plant revive and thrive, and it will become more resistant to disease.

◆ Used coffee grounds enrich the soil with nitrogen. In addition to being a good chemical-free fertilizer, the grounds will also make the plant undesirable to any cats you have roaming around.

Once a week, scatter 1 tablespoon of the moist, used coffee grounds onto the potted plant's soil.

Flowering Plants

◆ To make a young plant grow into a full-bodied plant (instead of a tall, scrawny plant), pinch off the growing tips of the stems. This will wake up the lower-down dormant buds.

 NOTE: You can do the same tip-pinching with vines, but never pinch a palm or any other 1-point-of-growth plant.

◆ When a flowering plant starts to wither, gently remove the dead flowers so that the plant doesn't waste its energy on them.

Luminous Leaves

◆ Water your plant with sodium-free seltzer water or club soda that has gone flat. Make sure the fizzy stuff is at room temperature. This drink will help brighten the color of your plants' leaves.

◆ To make the leaves of a plant appear their greenest, gently massage each leaf with castor oil or mineral oil.

◆ Use a soft cloth and wipe plant leaves with Cool Whip or milk (make sure it's at room temperature). *Sodium caseinate*, the natural protein in dairy, is said to be an effective cleaner for plant-cell walls.

◆ Mix ⅛ cup of baking soda into 1 quart of lukewarm water, and then use it to wash 1 leaf at a time.

◆ Add a few drops of liquid dish detergent to 1 quart of lukewarm water, then wash each leaf. Not only will the plant be clean, it will also repel bugs.

◆ If the leaves of your plant are yellowish and yucky instead of bright and beautiful, try giving them an iron boost. Soak a steel-wool pad or some metal nails in a tin can filled with water overnight. Then you can use the heavy-metal water to supplement the plant's iron deficiency.

 The Sound of Music
Research suggests that playing music for your plants can help them flourish. Not all music, though…according to some experiments, *rock* music killed the plants, and *classical* music helped them thrive.

Hanging Plants

◆ Do not water hanging plants by putting ice cubes in them. It may be easier that way, but your plants will hate you for it. They prefer lukewarm or room-temperature water.

◆ If you place a potted plant inside a hanging basket, put a pair of baby or adult diapers (such as Huggies or Depends) under the pot to absorb the excess water that can leak from the drainage hole.

   Once the pot is in the basket, it will look fine, but forget this suggestion if you have a hanging pot *without* the decorative basket—nobody wants to see a plant wearing a diaper.

◆ To prevent floors and carpets from getting wet each time you water a hanging plant, forget the silly superstition about opening an umbrella indoors…just turn the open umbrella upside down, and place it on the floor under the pot you want to water.

   Let it stay there during and after the watering, until all of the excess water has dripped out of the pot's drainage hole. Then you can empty and rinse out the umbrella, or move it along to the next hanging plant you want to water.

◆ Put a shower cap or plastic bowl cover on the bottom of the pot or basket to catch the excess water. Secure it in place with a tight, thick rubber band around the cap or cover.

FIRST AID FOR PLANTS

All sorts of plants and green growing things can get weak, sick or injured. If you ever thought about taking a class to learn CPR—*Caring Plant Resuscitation*—you may want to start here with some useful treatments.

"Planti-Aging" Cure

If you have a frail, old plant that needs a boost, try this solution—twice a week for 3 months, before you water the plant, give it about ⅛ cup of Geritol (available at drugstores).

Within a month, you should see healthy, new leaves sprouting up. Of course, if your plant seems worse, suspend the treatment.

Infections

When you *know* your plant has a viral or fungal infection, and you want to treat it yourself, these remedies are worth a try…

◆ Combine 1 gallon of warm water with 1 cup of molasses. Once the molasses completely dissolves, transfer it to a trigger-spray bottle and spray the infected plant. The plant will be nourished by the sugar, while the sulfur that is in the molasses should help destroy the fungi.

◆ If your plant is ailing and you suspect that it has some kind of leaf infection, combine 1 tablespoon of baking soda, 1 tablespoon of dishwashing liquid and 1 gallon of water.

Put the mixture in a trigger-spray bottle and spray the infected plant, including the underside of the leaves.

Mealybugs

If you see little white cottony masses on your plant's leaves and stems, those are mealybugs. Soak a washcloth in soapy water and wipe off the mealybugs. Or get them with a cotton swab that has been dipped in rubbing alcohol.

Once the plant is clear of the bugs you can see, check the plant pot carefully—including the underside—for mealybug egg masses. (You'll know the whiteish, gooey clump of eggs when you see it.) Get rid of the eggs the same way you got rid of the bugs—with a warm, soapy washcloth or rubbing alcohol.

> **Create a Basic Pesticide**
> If you see insects in the plant's soil, add a few drops of liquid dishwashing detergent to warm water, and use it to water the plant. It will put an end to anything in the pot that crawls.

WHILE YOU'RE AWAY…

If you're traveling for vacation or a business trip, you don't want to worry—or even think about—your plants withering away at home. *Here are a few ways to keep them alive and well while you're out of town (for up to about 2 weeks)…*

◆ Place plastic trash bags on the floor of your bathtub. Put big towels on top of the bags and pour water on the towels until they're completely wet. Check each plant to make sure it has a drainage hole at the bottom of its pot, and bring it into the bathroom—then set it on top of the towel.

Right before you leave the house, give the plants a thorough watering, kiss them good-bye and *bon voyage*!

◆ For a clever method of letting gravity help water your plants, you'll need a stool or a chair, a bucket of water, a plastic drop cloth and several long strips of ½" cotton rope or unwaxed cotton wicking (available at craft stores)—1 strip for each plant—and ample space in your living room (or wherever you keep your plants).

Put the plastic drop cloth on the floor and set your plants on top of it. Place the stool or chair close to the plants, and then put the bucket of water on the chair. Take a strip of wicking or rope, drench it and bury 1 end of it deep in the soil next to the plant. Place the other end of the strip in the water bucket. Do this with each strip and each plant.

> **NOTE:** If you have delicate, rare, exotic plants that need special care, you should probably not rely on any of these methods.
>
> Instead, ask a neighbor who has a green thumb to stop by and tend to those unique plants while you're away.

CUT FLOWERS

There is an old Lithuanian saying—"The seed is hope; the flower is joy." What a sweet sentiment. With that in mind, here are some ways to cut and keep your flowers—and in doing so, prolong your joy.

Cutting Live Flowers

◆ Take a bucket of lukewarm water with you to the garden, along with a pair of garden or pruning scissors, or a sharp knife. (A dull scissors or knife can pinch the flower's stem closed.) Always cut flowers on a slant. Then, as soon as you cut each flower, put it into the water bucket.

◆ Venture out into your garden to cut flowers during the coolest parts of the day—early morning or late evening. The flowers will stay fresh longer.

◆ Tightly closed buds may never open in a vase, and fully bloomed flowers will not last long. So pick the buds that are about to open or have just opened.

◆ As soon as you bring the flowers indoors, cut each stem again on a slant while keeping it under water. That way, the flower will drink in water, not air.

◆ After you put your slant-cut flowers into a vase filled with lukewarm water, be sure to remove all of the leaves that are below water level. This will keep them from poisoning the water.

Life Extenders (General)

◆ Most tap water contains minerals that make it *alkaline*. And alkaline water has a hard time moving through cut flower stems. This means that the life of cut flowers in a vase will be shortened because the flowers do not get the hydration or nutrition they need to thrive…and survive.

To overcome this challenge, simply lower the pH of the water…or *acidify* it. You can do this by adding 1 part of non-diet lemon–lime soda (such as Sprite or 7UP) to 3 parts of water in your flower vase. The citric acid in the soda helps lower the pH, and the sugar in the soda gives the flowers an energy boost.

> **NOTE:** You can avoid the pH problem altogether by using distilled water (available at supermarkets and health-food stores) in your flower vase, instead of tap water.

◆ Protect flowers from harmful bacteria that cause stems to rot by adding ½ teaspoon of antiseptic mouthwash (such as Scope or Listerine) for every quart of water in the vase.

◆ For every quart of water in the vase, add 2 tablespoons of distilled white vinegar and also 2 tablespoons of sugar. The vinegar helps prevent the growth of bacteria and the sugar gives the flowers nourishment.

◆ Hydrogen peroxide is another preventive measure against stem-killing bacteria. Add 1 teaspoon each time you refresh the water.

◆ As soon as cut flowers start to wilt, reach for a can of aerosol hairspray. Hold the can about 1 foot away from the underside of the leaves and petals, and spray in an upward direction. The glycerin and the *acrylates* (a class of acrylic resins) found in commercial hairspray should help the flowers survive another few days.

◆ To revive wilting flowers, dissolve 1 or 2 regular adult aspirin (325 milligrams each) in ½ cup of warm water, then pour it into the vase.

◆ One last-ditch effort before you ditch the flowers—in warm water, cut the stems again on a slant.

◆ To freshen flowers, put the tired-looking flowers in a closet an hour or so before daytime guests are due to arrive. When you bring them out—and don't forget to bring them out—they will perk up when exposed to the light of day. (Obviously, don't try this at night!)

◆ Apples, pears and bananas emit ethylene gas that is harmful to most flowers. Do not place cut flowers near a bowl of fresh fruit. And do not refrigerate flowers if you have fruit in the refrigerator.

◆ For short-stemmed flowers…arrange them in a container with sand that's been saturated with lukewarm water. They will thrive.

Life Extenders (for Specific Cut Flowers)

Use these helpful suggestions as soon as you bring cut flowers inside the house from the florist or garden…

◆ **Carnations**—Add a capful of boric acid (available at drugstores) to the water, and then you should be able to enjoy having them around for a few extra days.

◆ **Chrysanthemums**—Prolong them by adding about 1 tablespoon of sugar to the water.

◆ **Daffodils**—Before you add daffodils to a floral arrangement, put them in a vase half-filled with lukewarm water. Within a couple of hours, after they've released their saplike fluid (which can be harmful to other flowers), empty the water out of the vase, rinse off the daffodil's stems with lukewarm water, and then they can be safely included in a vase with other flowers.

◆ **Gardenias**—Be very gentle with these sweet-scented blossoms. Their petals bruise easily. Floating in a bowl, gardenias make an elegant centerpiece.

◆ **Marigolds**—Add 1 teaspoon of sugar or empty a couple of activated charcoal capsules (available at health-food stores) to the water to help prevent these beautiful flowers from reeking.

◆ **Roses (and other woody-stemmed flowers)**—Place them in a vase with hot (not boiling) water. That way, the stems will expand, making it easier for water to zoom up to feed the buds and blooms.

    Also, roses seem to love salt. Add a pinch of table salt to their water, and they'll stay fresher longer.

◆ **Tulips**—These flowers will keep growing, even once they're cut. After 2 or 3 days, you may need to move them to a taller vase to keep the stems from falling over.

Or throw a few pennies into the vase. The copper seems to keep the blooms from opening too wide and drooping.

Daily Care

Out with the old, in with the new…water, that is. If your vase fits under the sink faucet, let lukewarm water run until the new water replaces the old.

If the vase is too big for the sink, use a turkey baster to suction out the old water before replacing it with fresh lukewarm water. Also, be sure to keep the water level just below the rim of the vase.

As the days go by, keep removing any flowers and leaves that have wilted.

Hue Knew?

If you have white or very light-colored flowers, add food coloring to the water they're in. As they absorb the colored water, the flowers will become a muted version of that new color.

Flower Arranging

◆ When a flower has a long, thin stem that can't stand up straight, help it by sticking the stem in a plastic drinking straw.

Magical Words

In the wonderful words of author and land-scape designer Barbara Damrosch—"I don't think we'll ever know all there is to know about gardening, and I'm just as glad there will always be some magic about it!"

◆ Put transparent tape across the mouth of the vase, crisscrossing it according to the size of the vase and the amount of flowers you intend to put in the arrangement.

The tape will make it easier to do the arranging because it will hold the flowers in place.

◆ To lengthen stems that are too short for a vase, stick each in a plastic drinking straw, and then cut them to the proper length for the vase.

◆ If the flower stems are too thick to fit into plastic drinking straws, then layer the bottom of the vase with marbles or a crumpled piece of aluminum foil.

◆ You know those mesh bags that onions come in? Wad up a bag and place it on the bottom of your vase, then arrange the cut flowers —just stick the stems through the holes in the mesh. ■

CHAPTER 7

Car & Travel Smarts

Americans love their cars! But before we get to the helpful stuff, we thought you might like to know some intriguing facts about your home-away-from-home. First of all, for those of you who think that cars are a guy-thing, think again—the next time it rains, say "thank you" to Mary Anderson, who patented windshield wipers in 1905. In fact, in 1923 alone, women patented more than 170 automobile-related inventions, including the carburetor, a clutch mechanism and an electric engine starter.

A woman is also responsible for helping to make safety belts and air bags mandatory equipment in all cars. That woman is Elizabeth Dole, who was US Secretary of Transportation from 1983 to 1987. Mrs. Dole was also the first person to propose installing a third rear brake light in all automobiles.

According to the National Insurance Crime Bureau (*www.nicb.org*), approximately 1.2 million vehicles in the US are stolen annually—that's 1 car almost every 30 seconds. And at least 21% of car owners do not lock their car doors, which makes thieves' jobs a lot easier. (Of course, you're part of the 79% who *do* lock their car doors, right?)

So buckle up, lock up and take the time to check out some information that will keep you safe and happy behind the wheel.

CAR SAFETY

Car manufacturers and the US government want you to be safe in your car. Sturdier construction, air bags, antilock brakes and stricter seat belt laws have all contributed to improved driver safety on the road. But the biggest contribution is up to you, the person behind the wheel—you are responsible for doing everything within your power to monitor the safety of the car you drive.

Please read through this section and consider ways you can use the information to keep yourself and your passengers as safe as possible.

Baby on Board

The safest place in a car is the center of the back seat. According to the American Academy of Pediatrics (*www.aap.org*), babies who weigh less than 20 pounds should ride facing backward in a car seat that has been properly secured in the middle of the back seat.

When you purchase a car seat, read the manufacturer's instructions and cautions *thoroughly* to be sure that you understand every word before using the product.

Once the baby weighs more than 20 pounds, the car seat and baby should ride facing forward, also in the middle of the back seat.

Pumping Gas— A Shocking Revelation

There have been stories about some gas station fires, involving mostly women. After starting the nozzle to fill the gas tank, a woman often gets back into the car to get her purse. When she slides out of the car, the fabric of her clothes rubs against the seat upholstery, creating static electricity. When the woman touches the gas pump's nozzle again, the static electricity sparks can ignite the free-floating gas fumes.

Whether or not this is an urban legend, here's how to prevent it—after sliding out of the car, discharge the static electricity from your body by touching something metal— your door handle, hubcap or the car itself— *before* you touch the gas nozzle. Or better yet, stay outside of the car to pump your gas.

Buckle Up *Everyone*

A study from the University of Tokyo concluded that, in an accident, the driver and any front-seat passengers (who are buckled up) are 5 times more likely to be seriously injured if back-seat passengers are not wearing their seatbelts.

Think about it. In a rear-end crash, the back-seat passengers tend to be flung forward with a great deal of force. According to the Japanese study, 80% of front-seat injuries could be avoided if back-seat passengers were strapped in.

For your own safety, as well as for the rest of the passengers, the car shouldn't start moving until everyone has his/her seatbelt buckled.

Steering

If you took driver's education classes as a teenager, you were probably taught to hold the steering wheel at the 9 o'clock and 3 o'clock position or the 10 o'clock and 2 o'clock position—both of these combinations allow you to have control to turn the wheel more freely.

Eileen Beetar, an instructor with the AAA Driver Improvement Program, suggests holding it at 8 o'clock and 4 o'clock. You may have slightly less control of the wheel, but this position keeps your arms out of the way of the airbag in the event of a collision.

 CAUTION: Never hold your arms *across* the steering wheel, such as at the 1 o'clock and 3 o'clock position. It's bad form for steering control, and the airbag could potentially break your arm(s) during a collision.

Driving in Fog

Since it's difficult to see oncoming cars when you're driving in a thick fog, keep your window open. Chances are, you'll *hear* the cars coming toward you before you can *see* them.

COLD WEATHER CURES

Prepare for winter weather before it arrives. Go to your local service station and make sure that your car is in good working order. *Here's a basic checklist...*

- Antifreeze
- Battery
- Brake fluid
- Brakes
- Defroster
- Emergency flashers
- Exhaust system
- Fuel
- Heater
- Ignition
- Oil
- Radiator
- Tires (air pressure and wear)
- Windshield wiper fluid (wintertime mixture)

Once your car is in tip-top shape for the cold months, you will have prepared yourself to *weather* whatever hazardous road conditions may come your way.

The following hints should pull you through the little nitty-gritty challenges that come with the cold…

Stuck in Snow

Carry around 4 strips of old carpet, measuring about 1' x 4'. If you get your car stuck in the snow, take the strips out of your trunk and place a strip under each tire for traction.

What? You don't have carpet strips in your trunk? If desperation sets in, use the floor mats from inside the car, and put them under your tires to provide traction. Or keep a bag of clay kitty litter in your trunk—putting some under the tires will provide traction in the snow.

Frosty Windshield Prevention

- When you park your car outdoors overnight, spread a large plastic trash bag or sheet of plastic over the front windshield. Secure it under the windshield wipers and/or by shutting the doors on the edges of the bag(s). If you don't have plastic bags, you can also use brown paper bags, which will be held in place by the windshield wipers.

  The next morning, when you remove the bag(s), there will not be any frost or ice on the windshield.

  Put little plastic or paper bags over your side mirrors to keep them frost-free, too.

- Before leaving your car outside overnight, combine 6 cups of distilled white vinegar with 2 cups of water, and drench a cloth with the solution. Then use the cloth to give the windshield and other windows a good once-over. (You can also pour the solution into a trigger-spray bottle and spritz it all over the glass.) The next morning…come out to find frost- and ice-free windows.

  Use the solution on your side mirrors so that they, too, will be frost-free.

- If snow is coming, and your car is going to be out on the street all night, pull up your windshield wipers and coat the windshield with sulfuric compounds.

  Does that sound extreme? In other words, cut an onion in half and rub the glass with the onion's cut surface. The coating will prevent the formation of ice on your windshield. Don't forget to onion-up your side mirrors.

Defrosting the Windshield

- If you did not prevent your windshield from frosting with our tips (above) and you don't have a proper ice scraper, use a plastic dustpan—it will do the scraping job without scratching the windshield.

◆ If you don't have a plastic dustpan to use as a scraper, pour some cola on a cloth and rub off the icy buildup.

> **CAUTION:** If cola splashes on the car, wipe it off quickly. You don't want it eating through the paint.

Frozen Door-Lock Prevention

◆ Don't let the frost get in. Cover the door locks with magnets…thin, flat ones are best (available at hardware or crafts stores). You may not want to tempt the neighborhood kids by using the big, novelty magnets from your refrigerator—although they would work, too.

◆ One of the most popular of the more than 2,000 uses for the lubricant WD-40 (available at hardware stores) is to spray it in the car door or trunk lock *before* it gets cold—this will prevent the locks from freezing. But you can also spray the locks after they've frozen to defrost them.

◆ Coat the rubber gaskets around the doors with vegetable oil or petroleum jelly to prevent cold weather from freezing them shut.

　　You can also use a bit of vegetable oil or petroleum jelly to prevent your trunk from becoming frozen shut.

Opening Frozen Door Locks

◆ If your locks are already frozen, light a match and carefully stick your car key in the flame. Keep it there long enough to get hot but not long enough to burn your fingers. Then quickly put the key in the lock and turn.

◆ Do they say you're full of hot air? Prove it. Take a plastic drinking straw and put it over the lock, then blow through it and into the lock. After a few minutes, the lock should be warm enough to open.

FUEL ECONOMY

Everyone wants to save money on fuel. The US Department of Energy has a Web site (*www.fueleconomy.gov*) that may help you learn what would be the most fuel-efficient vehicle to meet your needs. *Meanwhile, here are some suggestions that may show you how to save some money with the vehicle you have…*

Keep Windows and Sunroof Closed

Driving with all the windows and/or sunroof open—especially when you're zooming down the highway—causes wind drag, which slows down the car and decreases fuel efficiency by about 10%.

Keep Tires Properly Inflated

You can improve your vehicle's gas mileage by about 3% by keeping the tires properly inflated. Using the recommended tire pressure (specified in your vehicle's owner's manual) will also allow the car to handle better and will help prevent flats.

> **DID YOU KNOW?**
>
> **U**nderinflated tires wear out faster. So that is another reason to check your tires' air pressure regularly—at least once a month. Be sure to check your spare tire, too.

Penny for Your Tires

Learn when it's time to replace your tires by putting Honest Abe to work. While holding a penny on the words *In God We Trust*, insert it into the tire's tread. If the top of Lincoln's head cannot be seen, that tire is fine. However, if Lincoln's hair is sticking out, your tire is worn down and probably needs to be replaced.

Less Is More Cost-Efficient

◆ Except for a spare tire and other emergency equipment, don't use your trunk as a storage bin. Driving around with extra weight decreases your car's fuel efficiency.

◆ While you're at it, take off the roof rack when it's not being used. The added weight adds drag on the engine, causing it to use more fuel.

Cruising Speed

Since most gas is consumed when you hit the pedal to accelerate, it's best to select a speed and maintain it.

Keep in mind that every 5 miles per hour (mph) you drive over 60, you add approximately 21 cents to the cost of a gallon of gas (depending on current prices). More important, slower speeds can also help keep you safe.

> **NOTE:** It's also important to not accelerate and brake suddenly. Try to use even, gentle pressure to accelerate and slow the car—especially in stop-and-go traffic—which will improve your fuel efficiency.

Cheapest Gas Prices

Not all, but many gas stations raise their prices from Friday to Sunday when the demand is greatest. Instead, gas up on Tuesday, Wednesday or Thursday to avoid the jacked-up prices over the weekend.

 Get More Gas for Your Buck!

◆ Fill up your tank in the early morning or late at night. Gasoline expands with heat, so if the outside air temperature and the car's gas tank are cooler, you end up getting more for the same price.

◆ Visit the Web site *www.gasbuddy.com* and enter your ZIP code or the ZIP code of the area to which you're traveling. You'll be given a list of local gas stations, along with their current gas prices.

Car Battery

The main job of a car battery is to start the engine. If the battery is in bad shape, chances are the car won't move. But a well-maintained battery should last anywhere from 2 to 5 years.

Here are some suggestions that will help you maintain your battery...so that it stays in good working order for more like 5 years than 2.

Battery Corrosion

◆ Slowly add plain tap water to 1 cup of baking soda until it becomes a paste. Then, using a small paintbrush, apply the paste to the car battery posts (also called terminals) to help neutralize corrosion (also known as rust). Leave the paste on for 1 hour, then clean it off with a damp cloth.

◆ Fizz away the corrosion by pouring a can of cola over the terminals. Since the phosphoric acid in cola can dissolve a nail in about 4 days, it should be able to bubble away dirt and rust in no time. After it's done bubbling, wipe the terminals clean with a fresh, moist rag, and towel dry.

> **CAUTION:** If cola splashes on the car, wipe it off quickly. You don't want it eating through the paint.

Prevent Battery Corrosion

◆ Smear petroleum jelly on the battery terminals before attaching battery cables. This will help prevent corrosion.

◆ Using regular transparent tape, attach a copper penny to the top of your battery. The penny may corrode, but the electrodes should remain clean.

Battery Recharge, Then Recycle

According to television actor Richard Karn—the knowledgeable sidekick on the television show *Home Improvement*…and author of *Handy at Home* (St. Martin's)—many batteries can be recharged up to 1,000 times. Once a battery cannot be revived anymore, it should not be thrown in the trash. The battery can explode if the trash is incinerated.

Karn suggests that you recycle it at 1 of the more than 30,000 recycling centers throughout the country. To find the center nearest you, visit *www.rbrc.org*, or call the toll-free number, 800-8-BATTERY or 877-2-RECYCLE. Don't be surprised when you hear Richard Karn's voice at the other end of the phone.

 NOTE: For those of you who are brave enough to tinker, we suggest that you visit *www.icarumba.com*.

This site offers a Reference Library that deals with everything you ever wanted to know about car repair, including testing the battery, recharging it, what to look for when buying a new battery and installation.

Caring for a Fan Belt

The fan belt is the traditional term for what is known now as the *drive belt*. There are 2 kinds of drive belt—V-belts and serpentine belts. Their job is to provide power to engine-mounted accessories like the air-conditioning compressor, the power-steering pump and air-injection pump.

The chances of a drive-belt problem rise dramatically after the car has been driven for 3 years or 36,000 miles for a V-belt…and 50,000 miles for a serpentine belt.

Have your drive belt checked every time the oil is changed, to make sure that it is properly tightened and in good shape.

Belt Moisturizer

If your car's engine has a dry fan belt, smear a bit of petroleum jelly on the inside edges of the belt, then start the car and let the engine idle for 2 or 3 minutes. The jelly will recondition the belt, help grip the pulleys better than commercial lubricants, and do away with squeals and slippage.

Buying a Used Car?

Get the car's *vehicle identification number* (VIN) —it's stamped onto a small metal plate and is attached to the driver's side of the dash where it meets the window—and then invest about $25 to $30 in a CARFAX Vehicle History Report —go to *www.carfax.com*.

As they say on their Web page "…[this is] the first step to protecting yourself against buying used cars with costly hidden problems."

Some car dealers may offer this information for free. Be aware that repair/accident information that was never officially reported may not appear in the CARFAX summary.

CAR COMFORT

 Fine-tune your driving experience with ways to make it more comfortable to get and be behind the wheel. *These suggestions may help…*

Shade Against a Hot Seat

When you park your car in the sun on a hot day, open an umbrella and leave it on the seat. When you return to the car and sit behind the wheel without burning your backside, you'll be glad you did that umbrella thing.

Smoother Antenna

If your car's radio antenna doesn't slide up and down easily, you can gently rub it with a piece of waxed paper.

Sun Visor Trapper Keeper

Clamp a few big clothespins to the sun visor on the driver's side of the car. If you don't have clothespins, you can also put a thick rubber band around each side of the visor.

Then when you have directions...or a map...or toll tickets...or parking stubs...or a pen and paper...or your shopping list...or your Weight Watchers Points–system page...or anything else you may want to reach for while in the car, clamp it to the visor with the clothespin or slide it under the rubber band.

CAR CLEANING

I n 1913, Richard Spikes invented the automatic car washer (and, in that same year, Spikes also invented automobile directional signals). In 1955, Dan Hanna, known as "The Father of the Modern Carwash," convinced his mother to mortgage the family home to finance what was to become Hanna Enterprises, a famous, innovative car wash manufacturing company.

Thanks to Spikes and Hanna, you can use your appropriate directional signal and drive into a car wash to have your car cleaned. *And*

thanks to our suggestions, you can learn to keep your car cleaner and spiffier in several ways...

Bugs Off

◆ Before a long car trip, spray vegetable cooking oil on the car's clean bumper, grille and hood. The bugs you pick up along the way will wash off easily, and the spray won't damage the car's finish.

◆ If you forget to spray and the car gets covered in bugs, scrunch up a mesh onion bag or shower sponge, pour on some baking soda and wipe off the splattered bugs. Clean up with a damp cloth.

✱ Pantyhose Power!

Instead of using rags and sponges, dip an old pair of clean pantyhose in warm sudsy water. Use the hose to wash away any dirt and dead bugs on the car's exterior.

Cleaning Windshields

◆ If you get bugs splattered on your windshield, mix 1 tablespoon of liquid dish detergent with 1 pint of water, and pour it on the windshield. Then use a mesh onion bag or shower sponge to scrub off the bugs. Finish the job by wiping the windshield with a clean cloth.

◆ Prepare your own windshield cleaner in an empty gallon-sized spring water or milk jug. Add 2 tablespoons of liquid dish detergent, 3 cups of rubbing alcohol and fill the rest with water. Pour 1 or 2 tablespoons on a clean cloth and wash the windshield with it. Rinse clean with plain water.

◆ To remove haze from the windshield (inside or out), dip a clean cloth in distilled white vinegar and wash the windshield. Rinse off the vinegar with plain water, then wipe dry. The windshield will be haze-free and showroom clean.

◆ Use a blackboard eraser (available at art-supply and stationery stores) to clean steamed-up windows. It's easy, fast and does the job without leaving streaks.

◆ Wipe the insides of your car's windshield (and windows) with a little gel shaving cream to help prevent them from fogging up. Apply, let dry and then rub off with a clean cloth.

Cleaning Wipers

◆ If your windshield wipers have caked-on gunk, clean the blades with rubbing alcohol. The alcohol will clean the blades and also prevent ice from forming on them.

◆ You can also use a piece of extra-fine sandpaper to clean gunk off windshield wipers. Bend the sandpaper in half, and run it along the edge of the wiper. (This also helps keep the wiper blades fresh under normal circumstances.)

Fixing Nicks, Chips And Scratches

◆ If your windshield gets a little nick, a tiny hole or a small scratch, you can patch it up with a few dabs of colorless nail polish.

   Be sure to let the polish patch dry thoroughly before using the windshield wipers.

◆ Buy a box of Crayola® Crayons that contains the same color crayon as your car. Carefully work the crayon into the scratch to fix it.

◆ If you don't intend to get a matching-color crayon or have a scratch professionally touched up...then, as soon as you see the scratch, apply clear nail polish. This will prevent the nick, chip or scratch from rusting and getting worse.

Cleaning Tree Sap

◆ Don't let sticky sap cake on—clean it off your car as soon as possible. Slather the sap with mayonnaise and let it sink in for a few minutes. Then rub the mayo and sap off with a soft, clean cloth. Finish the job by washing the car.

◆ You can also pour a bit of rubbing alcohol or even WD-40 on a soft, clean cloth and gently work at cleaning off the tree sap.

Cleaning Bird Droppings

Bird droppings contain harsh acids that can burn through your car's paint. The secret to cleaning up—and saving your car's exterior—is to take action as soon as you spot the plop.

◆ Pour on some seltzer and let it bubble up. Once the bubbling stops, wipe the area clean with a microfiber (available at supermarkets and hardware stores) or cotton cloth.

◆ Since time is of the essence when it comes to cleaning off bird droppings, you might want to keep some special wipes in the car to deal with roadside cleanups (it's easier than taking a bottle of seltzer with you).

   One product that was recommended to us is a quick detailer. It's available in soft, paint-safe wipes. Travel Pack Speed Shine Wipes fit in your glove compartment and are perfect for cleaning those messy bird hits before they etch your paint.

   For more information on these helpful wipes, contact Griot's Garage (a catalog that offers car-specialty products) at 800-345-5789 or *www.griotsgarage.com.*

Howzabout Those Headlights?

Don't be that person who cleans the car but forgets about the all-important (and often grimy) headlights. Mix 1 cup of distilled white vinegar in 1 quart of water and, as a mild abrasive, add 1 tablespoon of cornstarch. Use a sponge to wash the headlights with the solution, then rinse with plain water. You'll see the light!

Bye-Bye Tar

◆ Spritz your car's tar stain with laundry pre-wash spray, and let it sink in for 1 to 2 minutes. Then wipe it clean with a soft cloth.

◆ If you don't have any prewash spray, you can dab on a dollop of mayonnaise, keep it there for a couple of minutes, then wipe it clean with a soft cloth.

Grease Away

Had a tailgate party and got some of the barbecue grease on the car? Whether the mess is from food or grease your car picked up at the service station, wipe it off with a baby wipe. If it's gentle enough for a baby's skin, you can trust that it won't damage your car's paint job.

Amazing Trunk Extender

When you leave that yard sale and put your oversized purchase in the trunk, you may need to secure the trunk lid for the trip home. If you don't have rope, twine or a bungee cord—pantyhose to the rescue! Keep an old pair—as well as rope, twine or bungee cords—in the trunk to tie down the trunk lid.

Removing Decals and Bumper Stickers

◆ Time to remove the old campaign sticker? The college decal? The bumper sticker that once seemed so funny—but isn't anymore? Saturate a cloth with distilled white vinegar and cover the sticker with it.

Give the vinegar at least 30 minutes to soak through and dissolve the glue. Then peel off the sticker or gently scrape it off with an expired credit card. If some glue

When Your Car Needs Repair...

If your car needs a repair that isn't covered by the manufacturer's warranty, go to the dealership and ask to read the Technical Service Bulletin. This document describes the manufacturer's authorized repairs, and it may include a repair your car needs that was caused by other defects or problems your car model has had.

If you have a newer car, you can also save yourself a trip to the dealership by visiting *www.mycarstats.com/auto_tsbs/Auto_tsbs.asp*. This Web site has Technical Service Bulletins and Car Reports for 1990–2008 model cars.

still remains, you can rub it off with a bit of vegetable oil.

◆ If you have a portable hair dryer...or 1 with a long extension cord from your house to your car...or if you keep your car in a garage and there's an electric outlet, then you may want to use the hair dryer to loosen the sticker's glue.

Set the dryer on *high* heat and blow it over the sticker for a couple of minutes, until you're able to easily peel off the sticker. If some glue remains, rub it off with vegetable oil or WD-40.

Cleaning Vinyl or Cloth Upholstery

To clean vinyl or cloth upholstery, use unscented baby wipes. Dry the vinyl with paper towel, and let the cloth upholstery air-dry.

 NOTE: *This cleaning tip is NOT for leather upholstery.* Instead, use saddle soap (available at tack stores, where saddles and all other equine supplies are sold, as well as some shoe repair shops) on leather or leatherette upholstery.

GARAGE FLOOR & DRIVEWAY CLEANUP

Bet those oil and grease stains bother you every time you drive in or out of your garage or driveway. So why let them remain? *Now is the time to do something about them, and here's how…*

Wiping Out Oil or Grease Stains

◆ To start the cleaning process, turn 1 or 2 cups of standard clay kitty litter into powder. Pour the litter on a piece of cloth or a dish towel. Bring the 4 ends of the cloth together so that the kitty litter is enclosed and won't fall out, then hammer the cloth until the litter gets powdery.

Cover the oil stain with the powder, put a piece of cardboard on top and step on it. Make sure the kitty litter powder works its way into the stain—you may even want to brush it in with a scrub brush. Let the powder sit there for 1 to 2 hours. Then sweep up or vacuum up the powder.

◆ Pour cola on the stain and let it stay on overnight. The next day, mix ⅓ cup of liquid dish detergent with 3 cups of plain water, and rinse the stained area with the soapy water. Then hose it down with plain water.

◆ If you don't want to use cola, then drizzle liquid dish detergent on the stain. Let it sit there for about 10 minutes, then pour some boiling-hot water over it. When it cools, scour the area with a stiff scrub brush and hose it off.

◆ Sawdust (available at home improvement stores) also makes a great oil absorber.

Changing Oil

Check the owner's manual for your car's oil-changing schedule. It may be a lot less often than your mechanic suggests. For example, instead of every 3,000 miles, it may only be necessary every 5,000 miles or more.

Stain Prevention

Get the goop before it stains the garage floor. Place a piece of cardboard under the vulnerable areas, like where your car drips oil or where you park your lawn mower.

An even better idea should be obvious—get your leaky car fixed!

GARAGE PARKING

If you still park your car in your garage…then good for you for not taking up the space with clutter overflowing from your home. *To fully enjoy the luxury of this perfect place to house your car, here are a few suggestions…*

X Marks the Perfect Spot

Pull your car into the garage and park it just the way you like best. Then wrap some string around a tennis ball and hang it from the garage ceiling, positioning the ball against the windshield—the ball should be at your eye level when you're sitting in the driver's seat.

The next time you pull into the garage, the tennis ball will touch your windshield—and that's the signal that you've made it to the perfect spot.

Prevent Dings

If you need to pull in close to the garage wall, protect the front-end of your car from dings by hanging a couple of old tires on the wall or nailing carpet remnants to the wall.

This lining will help prevent dents and scratches if you misjudge the distance from your front bumper to the garage wall.

Finding Your Car

Make your car a standout in a crowded parking lot by tying a Day-Glo or any brightly colored ribbon to the radio antenna.

Cleaning Your Hands

The proclamation that was issued for Clean Hands Week (*www.cleanhandscoalition.org*) in September 2005 stated that the role of hand-washing in America has been overlooked and undervalued. *Well, we are doing our best to value clean hands, especially those made dirty from car care…*

◆ If you get grease or oil on your hands after working on your car, rub a little olive oil on the greasy/oily areas, then wipe your hands with a paper towel. Follow up by thoroughly washing with soap and water.

◆ If you are at a service station and your hands are dirty after pumping gas or from touching something greasy, clean your hands with a baby wipe. Yes, you should keep a box of baby wipes in the car.

CAR SMELLS

Everyone loves that new-car smell, but it doesn't last long —especially if you have smokers, children and pets as passengers. *Here are some ways to clear the air and keep your vehicle smelling fresh…*

Cigarette Smoke

Stick an unused citrus-scented fabric softener sheet under the driver's seat. It will help to eliminate smoke odors and replace them with a fresh, clean smell.

Also, the scent of citrus has been known to keep people more alert than usual. Replace the softener sheet every couple of weeks.

Bad-Smell Neutralizer

A pet has an accident in the car…a child gets sick…someone has too much to drink—you get the idea. There's a *baaaaaaad* smell in the car! Put a shallow bowl of distilled white vinegar on the car's floor, both in front and in back. Then close the windows and lock up the car for the night.

In the morning, the offensive smell should be gone. Remove the bowls, then open the doors and windows for a few minutes so that any lingering vinegar smell will also disappear.

Sweeten the Air

If there are ashtrays in your car that are not used—particularly those in back—fill them with some pleasant-smelling potpourri (available at crafts stores as well as herb and health-food shops).

You can also put unused dryer sheets under the seats, or place fragrant sachets in the seat corners.

CHECKLIST OF CAR SHOULD-HAVES

While it's true that driving around with extra weight decreases your car's fuel efficiency, it's also true that there are some things you should have with you at all times—for your safety and in case of an emergency. *Keep these items handy in your car and/or garage...*

- Cell phone and cell-phone car charger
- Carpet strips for traction
- Sand or kitty litter for traction
- WD-40 for frozen locks
- Plastic straw to unfreeze a lock
- Rope, twine, bungee cords and/or pantyhose to tie down the trunk
- Umbrella to prevent a hot seat or to keep you dry when it rains
- Blackboard eraser to clean fogged windows
- Unscented baby wipes to clean hands after pumping gas
- Pack of chewing gum in case there's a small leak or puncture that needs plugging up
- A few plastic trash bags with head and arm holes cut out to use as emergency raincoats for you and your passengers
- Funnel—store-bought or improvised by cutting a liquid laundry detergent bottle in half and removing the cap—necessary for an emergency infusion of motor oil, antifreeze or water
- Small container of motor oil
- Aerosol can of Fix-a-Flat
- Travel Pack Speed Shine Wipes for bird droppings
- Two roadside flares
- Safety matches

- Jumper cables to start a dead/low battery
- Flashlight and fresh batteries (or flashlight that doesn't require batteries)
- Thermal blanket(s)
- Bottled water—for yourself or an overheated radiator
- Packages of dried fruit, crackers, protein bars and/or nuts
- Small hand shovel
- Spare tire
- Jack
- Lug wrench
- Work gloves (in case you have to shovel or change a tire)
- Ice scraper and brush for your windshield and windows
- Small fire extinguisher
- Tire chains (depending on the weather in your area)
- Pen and paper
- Money (keep an emergency $20 in the glove compartment)
- Tissues/napkins/paper towels

CAR TRAVEL

Although driving may be a relaxing way to travel, it is definitely not a mindless activity. Stay alert and stay defensive—it will take you a long way in staying safe.

If you want to improve your skill as a driver, consider learning how to drive a race car. You will have the chance to practice accident-avoidance maneuvers and skid recovery in a controlled environment. Besides, it promises to be lots of fun.

One of the premier schools is Skip Barber Racing School LLC. It offers high-performance driving instruction, with classes in 5 locations nationwide. For more information, call 800-221-1131 or visit *www.skipbarber.com*.

Until you sign up for racing school, here are some suggestions that will help make the going easier and enhance your good time behind the wheel…

Packing Clothes

Keep your clothes on hangers, then put them in clothing bags, dry-cleaning bags or even large plastic trash bags. Spread out the bags in your trunk, placing them on top of any other luggage you've packed. The clothes will stay wrinkle-free, and unpacking will be a cinch.

Pillowcase Smarts

If you plan on taking a pillow for comfort in the car, put a few pillowcases on each pillow. When the top pillowcase gets dirty, you can take it off and use it as a laundry bag for dirty clothes. When the second pillowcase gets dirty, take it off and put it in the first pillowcase that has become a laundry bag.

Directions on Tape

Go over a map to plan out your trip or use an on-line map-and-directions service, such as *www.mapquest.com*. Once you have your route figured out, take some time to record the directions on a cassette recorder.

When you're on the road, pop the tape into your cassette deck and hit the *play* button when you're ready for the next direction. It may be easier than reading directions on paper while you drive.

If your car doesn't have a cassette deck, bring along the recorder you used to make the tape. Just make sure its batteries are in good working order before you leave home.

 NOTE: Always bring along a set of directions on paper (and copies of all necessary maps), just in case technology fails you.

Traveling with Pets

Pull into a rest area at least every 2 hours to let your pet take a potty break, have a drink of water (and maybe some food) and get some exercise outdoors—a walk for 10 minutes or more is ideal. The exercise will be good for *your* road-weary body, too.

Cleaning Pet Hair

When pet hair is all over the seats of your car, put on a rubber glove and rub the upholstery with it. The hair will cling to the glove. Take off the glove by turning it inside out, and discard it along with the pet hair.

TRAVEL FUN & GAMES

Here are some ways to distract the young and the restless from asking those inevitable questions, "Are we there yet?" and "How much longer?" Incidentally, these games are also fun for the not-so-young-but-still restless.

Create a Trip Travelogue

All it takes is a cassette recorder (the same recorder you may be bringing to play the directions that you recorded) and a few blank audio tapes.

Let each passenger take a turn talking about his/her experience of the trip…the things that he's seeing out the window...a description of the place you stopped for a meal...funny incidents that happen along the way. The tape will be a real vacation keepsake.

 "Award-Winning" Vacation Videos
A video recorder is even more fun to bring on a trip. Have family members pretend that they are filmmakers doing a documentary or newscasters reporting on an important event.

Geography—A Classic Game

One person names a place—city, state or country. The last letter of that place is what the next person has to use as the first letter of another place.

Example: Cincinnati (ends with an "i"), then Indiana (begins with an "i" and ends with an "a"), then Armonk. The next person has to name a city/state/country that starts with a "k."

When a player is stumped, he/she drops out. Continue the game until only 1 player is left...or just quit playing when you're all geographied out.

A Game of Questions

Start with 2 players. One asks a question. Every question has to be answered with a question.

When 1 of the players messes up by not asking a question, he/she is out and is replaced by the next player, who starts a new conversation by asking a question. The winner is the player who is still asking questions after everyone else has been eliminated.

Example:

Player #1: "Are you going on vacation?"

Player #2: "Would you like to come with me?"

Player #1: "Would you mind if I go with you?"

Player #2: "Would I ask you if I minded?"

Player #1: "Can you please tell me where you're going?"

Player #2: "Wouldn't you rather be surprised?"

Player #1: "Don't you remember that I dislike surprises?"

Essence—A Game Of Perception

One person pretends to be someone that everyone in the car knows either personally (like a relative or friend) or knows of (like a famous celebrity). The player who is "it" tells whether the person he's pretending to be is male or female, living or dead.

The other players take turns asking a question that will establish the essence of the person. *Sample questions...*

◆ If you were a flower, what kind of flower would you be?

◆ If you were a magazine, what magazine would you be?

◆ What color would you be?

◆ Which American city would you be?

◆ What article of clothing would you be?

◆ What kind of car would you be?

◆ What snack would you be?

The game ends when someone correctly guesses the identity of the "it" player. Then the correct guesser gets to be "it."

Watch What You Say— A Gotcha! Game

Come up with any 2 common words, such as "how" and "that," or "it" and "yes." Player #1 starts a conversation by making a statement about any subject...the trip he/she is taking... the weather...a favorite television show—anything. Player #2 must carry on the conversation without using the 2 no-no words.

Players get eliminated when they say either of the 2 words—the more players, the more fun. The winner is the last player remaining.

Story Time—A Game Of Imagination

You may want to turn on the cassette recorder for this game—1 person starts telling a story and stops a few sentences into it. The next person picks up where the first player left off. Keep the story going as long as possible.

If the story is any good, transcribe the tape and get a literary agent to represent it!

GENERAL TRAVEL

Whether you're traveling for business, pleasure or both…if you're going by plane, train, bus, boat, camel, camper or car…if you're staying at a motel, hotel, hostel, lodge, chalet, castle or camping grounds…off season or in season…alone, with a tour group or with family or friends—there's valuable information that can help make your trip the best it can be.

Travel Planning

"Without leaps of imagination, or dreaming, we lose the excitement of possibilities," said feminist journalist Gloria Steinem. "Dreaming, after all, is a form of planning."

Many people consider the planning stage of a trip to be as much fun as the trip itself. So we hope these suggestions help you plan the most exciting trip possible.

Airfare Prices

Generally, most major airlines offer bargain prices on Tuesdays and Wednesdays as well as Saturday mornings. Fares tend to be highest on Mondays and Fridays. Discounted rates are most often given on midday and late-night flights, but hardly ever during morning and evening business-commuting hours.

Hotels—Bargain Prices

Several hotel chains offer low-low prices on rooms that would otherwise go unoccupied. It's very last minute, and you'll find these bargains only on the Internet.

If *short notice* is not your way of planning a trip, there are also lots of bargains on the Internet for advance reservations. But always read the fine print and confirm the deal with the hotel directly. *When you're ready to start looking, check out these sites…*

- **Priceline**—*www.priceline.com*
- **Radisson**—*www.radisson.com*
- **Quikbook**—*www.quikbook.com*
- **hoteldiscount!com**—*www.hoteldiscount.com*
- **TravelWeb**—a site created by Hilton, Hyatt, Marriott and Starwood—*www.travelweb.com*

Before the Trip…

Travel light! When in doubt, leave it out! You don't want to lug around unused or unwashed clothing. Nor do you want to have to be dependent on porters, cab drivers or other travelers for lifting and carrying your overstuffed luggage. Give lots of thought to what you *really* need to take, keeping in mind that packing light can add to an enjoyable time.

Packing Styles

There are several different packing options to consider when it comes to proper packing. Read through our suggestions—keeping in mind the kind of clothes and accessories you will be taking with you when you travel—and decide which packing style will work best for you.

No matter how you decide to pack, be sure to button buttons, zip zippers, tie ties, snap snaps and buckle buckles before putting your clothes into the suitcase.

◆ This packing order should keep the creasing down to a minimum—first, lay out jackets…then shirts/blouses and pants/skirts… followed by jeans—all folded in half across the length of the suitcase. Shoes go in the corners.

◆ Instead of folding clothes, roll them. It doesn't take up any more room in a suitcase, and your clothes will be less creased when you unpack. If you have clothes on hangers, put plastic dry-cleaner bags over them and, yes, roll them up.

◆ If having wrinkle-free slacks is your priority, fold them in half and stretch out the top half in the bottom of your suitcase, and let the bottom half (the legs) hang over the side of the suitcase. Then pack the rest of your clothes on top of the slacks in your suitcase. (It's starting to sound very confusing, but if you do a dry run as you read these instructions, it will make sense.)

Once your clothes are packed on top of the slacks, cover the clothes with the legs of the slacks that have been draped over the side of the suitcase.

This method of packing will eliminate the creases in pants that are packed after being folded in half at the knees.

◆ For an overnight stop at a hotel, you may want to have your nightgown handy, and for that morning swim, you may want your bathing suit easy to reach. It would be nice to not have to search for those garments, messing up the other clothes you packed so neatly.

The solution is to pack your clothes in the order in which you will need them, with the ones you will need first on top in your suitcase.

◆ An editor at Fodor's Travel Publishing suggests folding shirts, pants and skirts in half lengthwise, and then stacking or rolling them from the bottom up.

Pack to the Proper Capacity

A suitcase that's *appropriately* full—rather than emptyish or overstuffed—will help minimize the creasing of clothing.

Packing Suggestions

Before you begin to pack, think about what you'll need on your trip and write out a packing list. Then, as you pack, check off each item as it goes into the suitcase.

Once you've finished packing, pack the list in the suitcase so that you can recheck everything when you pack to go home.

◆ If you don't have a toothbrush holder, find an empty plastic pill bottle—you know, those little amber containers that you keep because you think they just might come in handy someday. Well, today's the day!

You'll want a pill bottle that has a childproof cap—a soft-plastic cap inside the hard-plastic cap. Pluck out the soft-plastic cap. Then, using a knife or box cutter, carefully cut about a ¾" slit in the cap. Push the handle of the toothbrush through the slit and put the head of the toothbrush into the pill bottle. Move the cap down, closing the pill bottle with the toothbrush inside its new, clean, covered holder.

◆ Put your underwear in thin plastic bags, and stuff your shoes with them. It will use suitcase space wisely and help your shoes keep their shape. You can also stuff your shoes with socks. *Or you can...*

◆ Put socks *over* your leather shoes (just make sure they're clean first). Doing this will prevent them from getting scratched inside a super-stuffed suitcase.

◆ All expert packers seem to agree that belts should not be rolled up. They should line the perimeter of the suitcase.

◆ If you're into necklaces, you know how easily the chains tangle. Open the clasp and thread 1 end of the chain through a plastic straw, then bring the 2 ends together. Close the clasp the way you would if the chain was around your neck. *Ta-da!*

 Pack Bring-Alongs
Pack a couple of large plastic garbage bags in your suitcase. You'll find many uses for them, including as a waterproof layer in your suitcase, a laundry bag for dirty clothes or as an impromptu raincoat.

If there's room, take a few different-sized bags. Chances are, you will use them in ways you may not be able to anticipate. They come in handy for carrying leftover food from a restaurant, for leaky bottles or for wet shoes and bathing suits.

You may also want to take a lightweight, fold-up bag that opens to become an extra piece of luggage, especially if you like to shop for clothes and souvenirs when you travel.

Preparing Medication

◆ Buy a thermal-insulated lunch bag in which to keep your medication cool, especially if you're traveling when the weather is hot.

◆ Bring an extra supply of necessary medication—about 3 days' worth—before traveling.

And get a note (and duplicate prescriptions) from your doctor for all medications and health gear, such as syringes, glucometers, lancets, blood pressure monitors and inhalers.

 Fly Through Airport Security
Be sure to have a doctor's note for anything that might delay you in getting through airport security, such as metal plates or pins, artificial limbs, a pacemaker, etc.

Copy Credit Cards and Personal Documents

Photocopy 2 sets of all your important identification and travel documents—such as your passport, driver's license, travel tickets, credit cards and traveler's checks—and anything regarding your health and medication.

Make sure that credit card cancellation instructions and phone numbers are included. Keep a set filed away at home and carry a set with you in a safe place.

 And Just to Be Safe...
When copying your identification and documents, you may want to copy a third set and leave it with a hometown contact person.

In general, it's a good idea to give your travel itinerary (with flight numbers, hotel contact information, etc.) to someone at home, just in case of an emergency.

Preparing Snail Mail

If you plan to send "wish you were here" postcards to all your friends and family, write or type their names and addresses on self-stick labels to take with you. And if you're traveling within the US, don't forget to bring postcard stamps.

Power Outage Protection

The following tip doesn't prevent a power outage, but it lets you know if something happened while you were away...

Before you leave on your trip, put a few ice cubes in a resealable plastic freezer bag and leave it in the freezer. When you get back home, check to see if the ice cubes are still shaped like cubes and not a frozen puddle.

If it's a solid puddle, it means there was a power outage and the food in your freezer thawed and refroze. And if that's the case, you should throw away that food.

Prevent a Musty Home

A house can smell musty if it's been closed up for a while. Before you go away on a trip, place small bowls of distilled white vinegar in each room. The vinegar will keep the air fresh, so you'll breathe easier when you get home.

Prevent Bathroom Mildew

Buy a big bag (it's not expensive) of clay kitty litter. Pour it into a big, flat box. The top of a cardboard storage box (about 25" x 15") is perfect. Place the box top in your bathtub and pour some kitty litter into it. It will absorb moisture and prevent mildew while you're away.

First-Night-Back Bliss

Before you leave home, plan for your return! You'll have traveled all day and you'll be tired—the last thing you'll want to do is to change the linens on your bed. Here's what to do—before you leave on your trip, place an unused fabric-softener sheet between the flat and fitted sheets of your bed.

The porous material of the dryer sheet absorbs moisture, keeping the linens nice and crisp. The scent from the dryer sheet will also leave your bed sheets smelling fresh and clean. All of this should ensure that you settle easily into slumber upon your return.

Light Up the Place

Light timers (inexpensive and available at hardware and discount stores) installed near the front and back windows of your house will give the impression that there is life and activity inside a home (especially if you keep the curtains drawn).

Noise can further enhance the illusion of people at home. You can use the same light timers to turn on radios and/or television sets.

Luggage—Ship Ahead

There are companies that will pick up your luggage, golf clubs, skis, gifts for the grandkids (and whatever else you want to take on your vacation) and deliver it all to your destination—just about anywhere in the world.

This service will save you the hassle of dragging stuff through airport check-in and security lines. Before you get excited about this, though, keep in mind that luggage-shipping services are *expensive*.

But if you're still interested, check out these companies…

- **Luggage Express**—866-744-7224 or *www.usxpluggageexpress.com*
- **Sports Express**—800-357-4174 or *www.sportsexpress.com*
- **Skycap International**—877-775-9227 or *www.skycapinternational.com*

You can also use Federal Express, UPS, DHL or even the US Postal Service to send the luggage, but you would have to box or shrink-wrap everything you send yourself. The ship-ahead services handle all of that.

Plants

Don't forget to plan for your plants! *See* "While You're Away" on pages 142–143 of Chapter 6, "Great Greenery Solutions."

During the Trip...

In the earlier section on packing (*see* pages 161–162), we advised you to pack light...so you definitely don't want to take this book with you! Instead, read through our suggestions, take notes or commit the information to memory, and then be on your way—knowing when to take your medication...how to keep track of your finances...how much to tip...and finding your hotel.

Taking Medication

If you will be crossing time zones, you may wonder exactly when you should take your medication. Most drugs that are meant to be taken once a day build to steady levels in the body, so discrepancies of a few hours shouldn't matter. But if you take medication(s) several times a day, consult with the prescribing physician and get specific instructions before your trip.

Credit Card Expenditures

Write down everything you buy as you buy it. Include a description of the item, the date/time, the price, the credit card used, the store name—all the details.

We know you're on vacation and you don't want to have to do clerical work, but this running tally can give you an overall picture of your finances, help prevent you from going over your budget (and perhaps your credit limit) and keep you from being charged for items you did not purchase. Be sure to keep the list with you in a secure place.

High-Tech Gear

Place a sticker with contact information—the name and number of a relative or friend, or the address and number of your travel destination, hotel or office—on a cell phone, laptop, iPod, BlackBerry, digital or video camera...or any other high-tech equipment you are traveling with.

If you lose it or leave it somewhere, a person with a conscience and a kind heart can return it to you. (You may also want to add the word "Reward" to the sticker.)

Tipping

Based on advice from several travel experts, we came up with a few tipping guidelines. These ranges are generally accepted, with the exception of an unusual circumstance that requires someone doing something above and beyond his/her job description—for example, a cab driver brings your luggage into the hotel...a waiter packs your leftover food in a doggie bag...a maid gives you extra towels or soap. In that situation, show your gratitude by tipping an amount that would make you happy if you were the person being tipped.

Here are tipping ranges for some common travel services...

◆ **Airport porter or skycap**—$1 to $2 (or the equivalent in foreign currency) per bag.

◆ **Taxi, limo, shuttle or van driver**—15% of the total fare.

◆ **Valet parking attendant**—$1 to $2.

◆ **Driver of a courtesy shuttle**—$1 to $2 (or the equivalent in foreign currency) per bag if he/she helps with the bags.

◆ **Hotel doorman**—Opening the door, nothing.

   ◆ If the doorman brings your luggage into the hotel, $1 to $2 (or the equivalent in foreign currency) per bag.

   ◆ If the doorman hails you a cab, $1 to $2 (or the equivalent in foreign currency).

- **Bellman**—Taking your bags to your room, $1 to $2 (or the equivalent in foreign currency) per bag.

- **Hotel maid**—$2 to $5 (or the equivalent in foreign currency) per night. Tip daily because maids often rotate. Put the money in an envelope marked "Housekeeping" and leave it on your pillow.

- **Tour guides**—Check with the tour company to see if the tip is already included. If not, give 10% to 15% of the tour price.

- **Restaurant tipping**—Food server, 15% to 20% of the food bill (before tax)...coat check, $1 (or the equivalent in foreign currency)...cocktail service, 15% to 20%...maître d', nothing unless he seats you when the restaurant is full and you didn't have a reservation—then give him at least $10 (or the equivalent in foreign currency)...wine steward, 10% of the wine bill (before tax)...restroom attendant, $1 (or the equivalent in foreign currency).

     Be aware that in many European and Asian countries, the tip is included in the lunch and/or dinner bill.

 Invaluable Tipping Tip!
When tipping, be prepared. Have lots of singles (or the equivalent in foreign currency) handy. Giving the exact tip amount is easier than asking someone to make change.

Hotels

As soon as you arrive at your hotel, take a matchbook...or a piece of hotel stationery...or a pen that has the hotel's address and telephone number on it, and throw the item in your pocket or purse.

     Once you leave the hotel, if you need to contact the front desk for any reason, you can just look at the matchbook, stationery or pen and get assistance.

TRAVEL SAFETY

Knowledge is power! Before you leave home, contact the US Department of Transportation (*www.dot.gov/citizen_services/index.html* or 202-366-4000), a government agency that provides travel warnings and safety alerts for domestic and international travel. You can also contact another agency, the National Transportation Safety Board (*www.ntsb.gov* or 202-314-6000), to find out if there have been any accident reports or travel delays issued for your flight, train, highway route or cruise.

     If you are traveling outside of the United States, research the areas you plan to visit (and *see* pages 168–170 for detailed safety information). There are tourist guidebooks available for just about every place on Earth, and there are Web sites that have all the information you will need to have a safe journey.

     So don't be lazy—do your homework before you walk out the door. And ALWAYS put safety first. *In the meantime, here are some other ways to stay safe...*

Money Smarts

If you're in the habit of keeping your wallet in your pants pocket—don't! It's much safer to carry your wallet or billfold in a jacket's breast pocket. (This is a good idea even if you don't travel outside of your hometown.)

Prevent Hotel Break-ins

Pack a small rubber doorstop in your bag. Once you're in your hotel room for the night, lock the door and wedge the doorstop under your room door from the inside. It may give you peace of mind and a better night's sleep.

Safer Water Bottle

When on vacation, touring and sightseeing, it's common for people to take along a bottle of drinking water, especially during hot weather. Fine—good idea.

What's *not* a good idea is to keep refilling the same water bottle. In fact, it's a terrible idea! According to the International Bottled Water Association (*www.bottledwater.org*) most plastic water bottles are not intended for multiple uses. The necks of the bottles are too small for soap and water to thoroughly clean them. Bacteria thrive in these made-to-be-disposed-of bottles.

Also, these bottles are not designed to stand up to commercial dishwashing. The heat, and even the detergents, used to wash the bottles can degrade the plastic and cause chemicals to leach out into the water you drink. Some of those chemicals may be carcinogenic.

It's important to start every day with a new bottle of water, keep it away from direct sunlight and discard it at the end of the day. Or, you can get a sturdy, *high-density polyethylene* (HDPE) bottle, the kind you can buy at a sporting goods or outdoor store (Nalgene is a good brand).

These bottles are meant to be reused, they can be easily washed, and they are not affected by the sun's heat nor by hot water and detergents.

Let There Be Light

If you wake up in the middle of the night to go to the bathroom, it can be confusing or just plain scary to be in a strange room in the dark. Before you leave home, pack a nightlight and/or a flashlight. Plug in the nightlight before you go to bed, and keep the flashlight on the night table next to the bed.

 You *Can* Take It with You!
If you're traveling abroad, remember to take all the equipment—batteries, adapter, transformer or converter—needed for your electrical items. Most foreign countries use different types of currents.

Common Sense

◆ When traveling abroad or in touristy sightseeing areas, keep a low profile. Do not wear expensive or ostentatious clothes and jewelry, and don't flash around a stuffed billfold.

◆ Before you venture out, talk to the hotel concierge about the city, and ask him/her which areas are unsafe for tourists.

AIRLINE TRAVEL

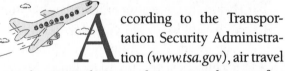

According to the Transportation Security Administration (*www.tsa.gov*), air travel in the United States has never been safer. Besides continually bolstering security at the nation's airports, the TSA is always looking for ways to refine processes that improve customer service at checkpoints.

Visit the TSA on-line for up-to-date rules and information about items that are allowed and those that are prohibited on board aircraft. Their site also has details about transporting special items and other travel considerations. *But first read the rest of this section to help you prepare for your flight...*

Luggage Allowances

Regulations regarding allowable luggage size and weight may vary with each airline. Most carriers allow only 2 carry-on bags, and they may charge extra for oversized luggage (generally, anything weighing more than 50 pounds).

Always contact the airline (or check its Web site) before your trip to confirm its specific luggage guidelines.

Better Packing

◆ Do not wrap gifts before you leave. Chances are, the packages will be torn open when your bags go through airport security.

Instead, measure, cut and pack wrapping paper and ribbon, along with a roll of transparent tape. Or buy those items at your destination.

◆ If you're traveling by plane, leave some room at the top of each bottle (of lotion, tonic, cough syrup, shampoo, etc.) you pack. Changes in air pressure may make contents expand, causing a leak in a bottle that is filled to the brim.

◆ Be sure to pack in your carry-on bag all medications, an extra pair of glasses, a change of clothes and anything else you might need for health or emergency reasons.

 Share a Suitcase
If you're traveling with your mate, family or friend(s), pack a change of clothes in someone else's suitcase and pack an outfit of theirs in your suitcase. That way, if one of your suitcases gets lost, you'll each still have something to wear.

Luggage Identification

◆ Make your luggage easy to spot. Tie a stand-out ribbon (a loud plaid or a Disney print) or a piece of brightly colored, braided wool around the handle.

Or, wrap glow-in-the-dark electrical tape around the handle. Not only will it be easy for you to identify your luggage, but if someone takes it by mistake, he/she should see the ribbon, wool or tape and realize that it's not his.

◆ Name tags on the outside of luggage can fall off. Airline personnel know to check inside lost luggage for identification information. For that reason, put an index card with your name, address and home and cell phone numbers in a small plastic bag and pack it in your suitcase. You may also want to include the contact information at your destination.

You may also want to include the name and number of a relative or friend who is not traveling with you—it should be someone who can be contacted in case your luggage is found and you can't be reached. You know, the "hometown contact" we mentioned in "Copy Credit Cards and Personal Documents" (*see* page 162)…the person who also has your personal information and travel itinerary. (Of course, check with him/her first to make sure it's OK to put personal information in your luggage.)

More Comfortable Airplane Travel

◆ Request seats over the wing, and you will enjoy the least bumpy ride on the plane. Also, the exit seats located over the wing have extra legroom. To sit in exit-row seats, you must meet Federal Aviation Administration (FAA) criteria—be over the age of 15, able-bodied and able to lift at least 50 pounds, so that you can assist passengers and crew in the event of an emergency.

 NOTE: For comfort, avoid seats that are in front of exit rows—for safety reasons, they do not recline.

Seats located behind *bulkheads* (the partitions that divide the plane into compartments)

also offer plenty of legroom. The downside is that on some planes, these seats are often close to the food/drink station and restrooms, which can be busy, crowded and/or noisy.

The safest seat? According to a study by the aircraft manufacturer Boeing, there is no evidence that any single part of an aircraft is safer than another.

To get the seats you want, check the airline's seating chart before making your reservation. Select and request specific seat numbers. When placing the reservation, check and recheck to make sure you are asking for the exact seat(s) you want. It often helps to book your reservation as early as possible, before the seat(s) are taken. Also, a great on-line source for seating details is *www.seatguru.com*.

◆ If you are traveling with a baby, during take-off and landing, feed him/her a bottle of his favorite drink. The constant swallowing can help equalize ear pressure, making the baby more comfortable...which will make you more comfortable...and make everyone around you more comfortable.

◆ Ladies, save the high heels for dinner parties, night clubs or the office—not for airplane travel. Chances are that you will never have to exit via the emergency slide, but if you do, high heels can be a real impediment.

Heels can also be impractical when going through airport security checkpoints or if you have to make a quick connection between flights. Wear flat-soled, slip-on shoes to get around quicker and easier.

Water on Airplanes

The US Environmental Protection Agency (EPA), which is responsible for water quality, conducted tests on airline drinking water. According to their findings, water on airplanes may be contaminated with harmful bacteria.

The agency said that it would take steps to improve the situation, but until it does, it's important to avoid anything dangerous that you may potentially be exposed to on planes. *And be aware of these suggestions...*

◆ Bring your own water with you in a clean, *high-density polyethylene* (HDPE) bottle—the kind sold at sporting goods or outdoor stores (Nalgene is a good brand).

◆ If you don't bring your own water onboard, ask the flight attendants if they have commercially bottled water. If that's not available, ask for sparkling water, seltzer or club soda.

 Quench Your Thirst

It is said that the air in the cabin of an airplane is drier than any of the world's deserts. That being the case, it's extremely important to keep hydrating yourself...wisely.

A sensible guideline is to drink an 8-ounce cup of water for each hour of air travel.

◆ Avoid airline drinks that must be made with water, such as coffee, tea and lemonade. And, for the drink that you do choose, ask whether the airline makes its own ice cubes onboard. (Many airlines get ice elsewhere...from safe sources—but it's important to ask.)

FOREIGN TRAVEL

 You are about to embark on an adventure, leaving your home soil. *With that in mind, here are some profound thoughts and advice from fellow international travelers...*

◆ **James Michener** (American author)—"If you reject the food, ignore the customs, fear the religion and avoid the people, you might better stay home."

◆ **Seneca** (ancient Roman philosopher, dramatist and statesman)—"Travel and change of place impart new vigor to the mind."

◆ **St. Augustine** (1st-century bishop)—"The world is a book, and those who do not travel read only a page."

◆ **William Least Heat-Moon** (Native American author)—"When you're traveling, you are what you are right there and then. People don't have your past to hold against you. No yesterdays on the road."

We wish you a safe, happy and memorable trip and hope that the following information helps you every step of the way…

International Travel Warnings

◆ Before you travel abroad, check the Web site of the US Department of State, the Bureau of Consular Affairs, at *http://travel.state.gov*. It lists conditions abroad that might affect your safety and security.

The Web site also offers several links to requirements for Americans traveling overseas, including information on passports, visas, immunizations and other medical information.

If you don't have access to the Internet, you can call American Citizen Services at 888-407-4747 to obtain more information.

◆ The Association for Safe International Road Travel (ASIRT) is a nonprofit, humanitarian organization that provides travelers with reports on road safety and driving conditions in more than 150 foreign countries.

Take advantage of this incredible service by calling ASIRT at 301-983-5252, or visiting their Web site, *www.asirt.org*.

US Representatives

When you arrive in a foreign city, find out the location and telephone number of the closest US embassy (*www.americanembassy.com*), consulate or mission. Contact the American Embassy for the names and numbers of English-speaking doctors and of the best local hospitals. Keep the information handy in case of emergency.

Electrical Appliances

Most foreign countries use a different type of electricity. So, when you're traveling outside the US and you're taking along electrical appliances, you will probably need some or all of the following…

◆ Plug adapters
◆ Transformer
◆ Converter
◆ Batteries
◆ Rechargeable batteries
◆ Battery charger

Chances are, a good guidebook for the country you plan to visit has specific information. But double-check with the country's official visitors' site, your travel agent or an electrical-supply store.

Money

◆ Before you leave home, exchange some of your cash for the currency of the foreign country you're going to visit. But do not use an international airport's bank or currency exchange window if you don't have to. They are hangouts for thieves who are watching and waiting for tourists to exchange big bucks.

Thomas Cook, authorized dealers in foreign currency exchange, has more than 50 locations throughout the world. Chances are, no matter what your foreign exchange need is, you'll find help at a Thomas Cook location. For more information, visit *www. thomascook.com*.

◆ Exchange rates fluctuate. The only way to know if you are getting the best exchange rate is to know what the *current* currency rate is. You can do that by visiting the Universal Currency Converter at *www.xe.com/ucc/*—it has up-to-date rates and information.

◆ If you are going to travel to several countries and encounter more than 1 foreign currency, pack a few resealable plastic bags in your handbag or travel kit. Assign a plastic bag to each currency so that the currency of 1 country doesn't get mixed in with the currency of another country. By keeping each currency separate, you will eliminate the chances of currency confusion.

Water and Food Precautions

Contaminated drinking water is the leading cause of health problems for travelers. Bacteria, such as *E. coli*, *cholera* and *salmonella*, are most often responsible for water-borne illnesses, and they can cause anything from a mild upset stomach to a serious (even fatal) bacterial disease.

Therefore, DO NOT take any chances. Instead, take every precaution possible. When you're traveling outside of the US, drink only bottled beverages. If you have a stove or hot plate, drink water after it has been boiled for 3 to 5 minutes. Remember that ice cubes made with local tap water can also be contaminated. Play it safe and do not drink anything that contains ice cubes.

While you're at it, eat only fruits that you yourself peel, and order only well-cooked foods.

Pack Washcloths

If you are traveling outside of the US, bring along a package of disposable cloths (like Handy Wipes) just in case your hotel, motel, bed-and-breakfast or castle doesn't provide washcloths. You may be surprised to find that many places don't offer this amenity—simply because it's not part of their culture.

Also, be sure to bring along liquid hand sanitizers and/or sanitary wipes to keep hands clean while flying or sightseeing.

Contact Lens Caution

When traveling out of the country, be sure to bring your own sterile contact solution and eyedrops. You do not want your contact lenses anywhere near tap water—especially water that might be contaminated.

HOME AGAIN!

You've just come home after a wonderful vacation. You check your snail mail, your e-mail and your phone messages. You water your plants and then relax a little. After grabbing something to eat, you start to unpack. Once that's done, you're ready to put away the luggage. *Phew!*

All that for this tip—toss a fabric softener sheet into each piece of luggage before you store it away. This will leave a fresh, clean smell for the next time you use it.

So when's the next vacation? ■

■ Products ■

We found so many clever, magical products that make travel safer and more efficient than ever before that we almost want to jump on a plane ourselves!

We surveyed many products and found that, unlike our other chapters, we can recommend 1-stop catalog shopping. Magellan's offers a wide array of travel products—really, everything you can think of...and some you probably hadn't thought of. We especially suggest that you look at the variety of personal security pouches in which you can stash your valuables.

Here are some other favorite Magellan products that will help you travel well...

Ear Planes

Avoid that awful pain in the ear with these ear filters, tested by US Navy pilots. They relieve air-pressure discomfort and reduce harsh noise naturally, without drugs. They are safe, soft, made of hypoallergenic silicone and disposable.

Children suffer the most from ear pain caused by changes in cabin pressure. EarPlanes are available for children from 1 to 10 years of age, as well as for adults.

EarPlanes are also good for elevator rides in high-rise buildings!

No-Jet-Lag

This product gets great reviews. Our favorite comment—"No jet-lag. No kidding." This natural, homeopathic product has been proven effective for all the symptoms of jet lag, including sleeplessness.

It's safe for all ages, can be used with other medications and has no side effects. Each packet contains 32 pleasant-tasting chewable tablets—enough for about 450 hours of flying time.

Also available at some drugstores and on-line.

Ultra Soles

Ultrathin soles protect your feet from athlete's foot, fungi, mold and other bacteria, as well as from sharp objects. Use the soles anywhere you don't want to walk barefoot while traveling, like the cabin of an airplane or a hotel hallway.

They also help prevent potential slips in hotel showers, campground facilities or any other damp/moist surfaces.

SteriPEN

The money you will save on bottled water will pay for this product tenfold. SteriPEN is a portable water purifier that uses proven ultraviolet (UV) technology to kill viruses (such as *hepatitis* and *poliovirus*), protozoa and bacteria (including *E. coli* and *salmonella*). Purifies up to 16 ounces of water at a time. Easy to use and lightweight. Requires 4 AA batteries.

Source: Magellan's, 800-962-4943, *www.magellans.com*.

Door STOP Alarm

Wedge this anti-break-in device under almost any door. If the door opens, an ear-piercing, high-pitched alarm goes off—this sound alerts you and most likely scares off the intruder. It takes a 9-volt battery (not included).

This alarm is great for travellers who want to feel more secure in a hotel or motel room.

Source: Improvements, 800-634-9484, *www.improvementscatalog.com*.

CHAPTER 8

Care for Your Fuzzy Friends

 Your dog...he's your best friend, your partner, your defender. You are his life, his love, his leader. He will be yours—faithful and true—to the last beat of his heart, so you owe it to him to be worthy of such devotion.

Thousands of years ago, cats were worshipped as gods. And the cats seem to have never forgotten this. A wise man once said, "In order to keep a true perspective of one's importance, everyone should have a dog that will worship him and a cat that will ignore him." We say, "Whoever said you can't buy happiness never had a pet."

In the United States, humans are outnumbered by their domestic animals. According to the *2003–2004 National Pet Owners Survey,* which was conducted by the American Pet Products Manufacturers Association (APPMA), there are approximately 290 million people in the US, and 377.8 million pets.

Aside from freshwater fish (185 million), cats are the most popular pets (77.6 million), followed by dogs (65 million). Think about it —almost 78 million cats and 65 million dogs... that's a lot of kitty litter and poop scooping!

For more information on pet products or to learn more about the APPMA Pet Owners Survey, contact the organization at 800-452-1225 or *www.appma.org.*

Naming Pets

The most popular dog name in the United States is "Max." The second most popular name is "Jake," and then "Buddy." The most popular name for cats is "Tigger."

If you're in the market for a pet's name, stay away from those with only 1 syllable, which may sound like a command. For instance, "Sid" can sound like "sit," and "Joe" can sound like "no." Names like these may confuse a pet, especially when you train it to obey commands.

For pet-name suggestions, or if you want to know the meaning of your pet's name, visit Amy Lyden's informative Web site at *www.bowwow.com.au* for answers.

It has been estimated that American pet owners spent $34.3 billion on their companion animals in 2004 (the most recent year for statistics)—this includes veterinary care, food and treats, supplies and grooming services. The hints in this section may help you save some of that money, while still giving your pet the best care possible.

PET SAFETY

Although having a pet is generally a wonderful experience, it comes with many responsibilities, including keeping your pet safe. Much like children, pets sometimes have a way of getting into things that can be dangerous to them. *Here are some tips that should help keep your pet out of harm's way…*

No "Strings" Attached

We've all seen cartoons of cats frolicking with balls of yarn. But that's the only place it should happen. In real life, yarn, twine, ribbon and tinsel can choke a cat—either the cat can swallow it, or get tangled up in it during play.

Keep those stringy things out of kitty's reach, and invest instead in some safe toys for your furry friend.

Electrical Cords

If your pet wants to live dangerously by chewing on electrical cords or household wiring of any kind, rub the cords with a dry bar of soap. If the smell of the soap doesn't deter him/her, then the taste certainly will.

Ensure Your Pet's Safety

In America, a companion animal is lost, stolen or goes missing every 30 seconds. Collars and identification tags may not be enough to keep your pet safe. They can fall off—or be removed—and the animal can slip out of a collar. *But tattoos and microchips are forever…*

Tattoos

There are several companies that work with veterinarians to tattoo ID numbers on all pets. The number is then entered into a national database, along with the owner's name and contact information.

When a tattooed animal is found and brought to a humane society, municipal animal shelter, SPCA, breed club, police station or veterinarian, the person in charge will call the Tattoo-A-Pet's toll-free number.

A live 24/7 operator will put the tattoo number into the database. If the number is in the database, the animal owner's name and contact information will be retrieved, and he/she will be contacted—and soon reunited with his no-longer-lost pet.

If you want this kind of protection for your pet, find out more by visiting *http://tattoo-a-pet.com* or call 800-TATTOOS (828-8667).

Microchips

The microchip is the size and shape of a grain of rice. Your pet's veterinarian injects the chip through a needle between the animal's shoulder blades. (In birds, the chip is injected under the wing.)

This 10-second procedure causes the same amount of "Yelp!" as any other injection—well, maybe a bit more since a bigger needle is used. The numeric ID code stored on the chip corresponds to the owner's contact information in a database.

If you're interested in this kind of protection for your pet, find out more by visiting *www.avidid.com* or call 800-336-AVID (2843).

 NOTE: Implanted microchips may not be compatible with all scanners. Check with your pet's vet and the local animal shelter and/or animal control officer for the most compatible brand for your area.

Toxic Plants

We hate to tell you this, but there are more than 700 kinds of plants that may be poisonous to your pet. Chances are, you've never even *heard* of most of the plants, let alone have them in your home or on your property.

But there are some common plants that are toxic, which you may have in your garden...or sitting in your living room...or hanging overhead—such as hydrangea, Easter lilies, tiger lilies, daffodils, larkspur, foxglove, lily of the valley, philodendron, dieffenbachia, schefflera, asparagus fern, rhododendron and azaleas, as well as the leaves and stems from tomato plants.

Holiday greenery—such as holly, mistletoe, ivy and poinsettias—can also make your cat or dog sick. If you have any of them decorating your house, be sure they're in a place where your pet won't be able to nibble on them. And, as a rule, it's a good idea to keep pets out of all vegetable and flower gardens.

If you think that your pet has eaten a poisonous plant, look for symptoms—diarrhea, loss of appetite, vomiting, mouth swelling and excessive salivation—then take your pet to the veterinarian. Since treatment is based on the type and amount of the plant that was eaten, if possible, bring along a leaf from that plant.

Before bringing home a new plant, check the list of the most frequently encountered toxic plants. It's available on the ASPCA's Poison Control Center Web site at *www.apcc.aspca.org,* or call customer service at 888-426-4911.

If your pet has been exposed to a poisonous plant, you can call the ASPCA Hot Line at 888-426-4435 (there may be a charge for a consultation).

The Humane Society of the United States (HSUS) also has a list of plants that are toxic to cats and dogs on its Web site, *www.hsus.org.*

Accidental Falls

Accidental falls from high places kill or injure thousands of animals annually. The only time your pet should be allowed on a balcony or terrace unsupervised is if the area is screened in or the pet is on a leash (just make sure it's short enough so that he can't jump over the edge and hang himself).

Install tight-fitting screens on all open windows or make sure that any existing guard rails are secure.

Professional Pet Care

When you must travel and can't take your pet with you, wouldn't it be comforting to have a reliable pet-sitter? The National Association of Professional Pet Sitters (NAPPS) has a database of certified members available throughout the country. For more information, visit the NAPPS Web site at *http://petsitters.org.*

Fire

Stick several brightly colored "Pet Alert" decals (available at pet stores) on the doors or windows of your home.

If there's an emergency when you are away from home, the decals will let the firefighters know how many—and what type of—pets need saving. If possible, include the pets' names and a brief physical description of each.

Pools/Water

◆ It's important to be just as attentive with puppies around a swimming pool as you would be with a young child. Better yet, put up a fence to keep pets away from the pool or any body of water.

If a fence is not possible, and your dog is determined to stay poolside, teach him how to get out of the pool. Do this by getting in the pool with him and guiding him to the steps. Keep doing this until he can swim to the steps and get out of the pool by himself.

◆ Not all dogs are natural swimmers. If you're taking your dog out on the water, you may want to put a life vest (available at most pet stores) on him. Even if your dog can swim, a life vest can save his life in emergency boating mishaps.

The Kitchen

◆ Store or throw away food, including leftovers, as soon as possible—don't leave anything out on a kitchen counter where your pet can get to it. Meat bones can choke or damage a pet's throat or intestinal tract.

◆ You may mean well, but shoveling leftovers into your pet's bowl is not doing him any favors. If there's a little too much fat in the food scraps, it may affect the pet's digestive system in a very negative way.

Also, you may not realize that some food may contain ingredients (such as onions or chocolate) that can be harmful.

◆ Be sure that your garbage can is impenetrable. Just as you don't want your pet getting at food on the counter, you don't want him getting at the discarded food in the garbage.

◆ If your pet pokes his paws into places that may be dangerous for him, install child-safety locks on your kitchen cabinets—for example, the cabinets in which you keep household cleaning products.

The Bathroom

◆ Do not leave plugged-in appliances—such as a blow-dryer, curling iron, electric rollers or face steamer—unattended. A pet may pull it off a counter and burn himself (or accidentally start a fire). If you're lucky, your pet won't get hurt, but you may have to replace the broken appliance.

◆ Do not give your pet access to water unless it's in a bowl for him to drink. Keep toilet-seat covers down…keep sinks and the bathtub empty.

◆ All medications should be stored in a secure or locked cabinet. You don't want your pet showing you how easy it is for him to chew through a child-proof pill bottle.

Every Room in the House

◆ Examine venetian-blinds cords and drapery tiebacks to make sure that they won't accidentally turn into a noose when a playful pet has access to them.

◆ Think twice about having lit candles around if you have a dog or cat who may want to make a game of playing with or putting out the flame—or whose tail may be at the same height as the fire.

◆ Regular exposure to secondhand smoke can lead to allergies and other health challenges for your pet. (We won't even begin to get into the harm it can do to you.)

Birds' delicate respiratory systems are especially affected by smoke. Do not allow any visitors in your home to light up…for the sake of your pets.

The Garage and Driveway

You know the little dark syrupy puddles that pool under or near a car? Chances are, it's *ethylene glycol*, which is antifreeze. Sometimes the liquid is bluish-green or pink. Dogs and cats like to lick it because it tastes sweet.

But antifreeze is extremely toxic to pets— a few licks could be fatal—so be sure to check regularly for spills and thoroughly clean up any leaks. If you have a supply of toxic solutions stored in the garage (or basement), keep them in a secure place where pets cannot get access to them.

> ✍ **NOTE:** If you notice any antifreeze leaks, sprinkle some sawdust or kitty litter on the spill to absorb the liquid, then mop up any remains. And have your car checked because it shouldn't be leaking antifreeze!

MEDICINE FOR CATS & DOGS

Several pet owners we know have to sedate themselves before going through the ordeal of giving medicine to their pets. We found some ways to make the job more humane...maybe even easy. *Read through these suggestions, which may help you help your pet...*

Giving Your Cat Medicine

◆ It's not easy to get a cat to swallow a pill. You may need someone to help you keep the cat in place. Start by holding your cat firmly either on your lap or between your knees.

 To open his/her mouth, put pressure on each side of his jaw. Place the pill as far back on the tongue as possible and then close his mouth. Hold it closed until he swallows. You may have to gently massage his throat to make that happen.

◆ A gentler way of dealing with medicine in pill form is to mash it and combine it with enough milk or tuna juice to make a paste. Then spread the tasty paste on the cat's paw or nose, and he'll do what comes naturally... lick it up.

◆ It is easier to get a cat to lick liquid medicine than to pop a pill. Drip the liquid on his fur—on any area his tongue can reach.

Giving Your Dog Medicine

◆ If your dog won't take a pill, stick it in a clump of peanut butter, cheese or any yummy food that he would consider a rare treat.

◆ If your dog won't eat food that contains liquid medicine, add some plain yogurt to cover up the strange smell. If he balks at that, then you have no choice but to force the medicine down his throat.

 Prevent messy spills by putting your dog in the bathtub (make sure that there is a rubber mat or non-skid pads on the tub floor). It also helps to have an assistant who can hold your dog still.

 Pull out the corner of the dog's lower lip, forming a pocket. Dispense the medicine into that pocket a little at a time. Hold the dog's jaws closed until he swallows. You or your assistant should be able to get him to swallow by gently rubbing his throat.

> ✍ **NOTE:** When administering any supplement or medication, it's best to check with your pet's veterinarian to determine the appropriate dosage, based on the animal's weight. *The general weight classifications for dogs are...*
>
> ◆ **Miniature:** Less than 10 lbs.
> ◆ **Small:** 11 to 20 lbs.
> ◆ **Medium:** 21 to 50 lbs.
> ◆ **Large:** 51 to 80 lbs.
> ◆ **Extra-large:** More than 80 lbs.

Pet Prescriptions

When you buy medication directly from your veterinarian, chances are you pay top dollar. However, more than 600 veterinary drugs are approved for human use (such as certain anti-depressants and antibiotics), and are likely to be available at your local pharmacy.

This means that you can save money by buying the *generic* form of your pet's pre-scribed medicine at your local pharmacy. Ask your pet's veterinarian for a prescription and for appropriate dosage instructions.

White Cats and the Sun

White cats do not have protective pigment, so it's important to keep them inside on sunny days when there is snow on the ground. The sun reflects off the snow and increases the cat's risk of developing skin cancer.

WEATHER

 Humans are not the only creatures who suffer from extremes of heat or cold. You should be aware that weather conditions affect your pet. It's important to keep your pet comfortable and happy—so here are some safeguards to help protect him/her in all types of weather.

> **CAUTION:** Cats should not go outside when the temperature dips below 0°F. Their ears have very little protective fur, and frostbite can set in very easily. Dogs should not go outside when it's –10°F or below. Then again, neither should you.

Cold-Weather Insulation

If your pet goes outside during the cold months, feed him 10% to 20% more food and supplement his diet with healthy *essential fatty acids* (EFAs), such as flaxseed oil, black currant–seed oil, cod-liver oil (available at health-food stores) and olive oil. Dosage for a cat or a small dog is only about ⅛ teaspoon of oil daily. The EFAs along with the extra calories help pets build insulation against the cold.

Dogs Walking in Snow

Chemicals like rock salt, which is used to melt snow or make it less slippery, can irritate a dog's paws. And what does he do? He licks his sore paws, ingesting those nasty chemicals, and that can make him sick.

You can prevent that from happening by protecting your dog's paws *before* he goes outside. Put small plastic sandwich bags over his paws, keeping them in place with rubber bands. If they're too slippery (or if your dog simply won't wear them), cover his paws with baby socks, also kept in place with rubber bands.

Clean Your Dog's Unprotected Paws

If your dog went out in the snow without protection, as soon as you both get home, wash his paws with a mixture of 1 tablespoon of baking soda and 1 cup of warm water. It will soothe the burning caused by the rock salt.

Prevent Stuck Pads

When your dog is going out in clean, pure, out-in-the-country, unsalted snow, spray the bottom of his paws with nonstick vegetable spray so that the snow won't get packed between his pads.

Soothe Winter Paws

Dry winter air and walking on snow and ice can cause a dog's pads to become cracked and sore. Massage a little petroleum jelly into his pads and between the toes to soothe them.

The Calm During the Storm

If your dog or cat gets frightened during a thunderstorm, you can calm him down by pressing his *Tin Yang* acupressure point.

It's located in the center of the forehead, a little higher than the eyes and a little lower than where the animal's eyebrows would be—if he had eyebrows. Use your thumb to press that point for 2 minutes.

According to an acupressure practitioner, when an animal is frightened, his *chi* (life energy) becomes scattered. The *Tin Yang* point stimulation will distract him from his fear of the thunder by refocusing his life energy and replacing that fear with a wonderful sense of safety. This remedy may be used whenever your pet is in need of calming.

 NOTE: You can find a certified veterinarian-acupuncturist by visiting *www.ivas.org,* the Web site of the International Veterinary Acupuncture Society.

To learn more about the benefits of acupressure for your pet, for training programs or to locate an acupressure practitioner, visit *www.animalacupressure.com.*

Dog Days of Summer

During the summer, protect your dog from the sun's strong rays. Keep him indoors or in the shade between 10:00 a.m. and 4:00 p.m.

If you do take him out in the sun for a long stretch of time between those hours, then ask your pet's vet to recommend a nontoxic sunblock (SPF 15 or 30) to put on the tips of his ears, the top of his nose and around his mouth—any of the places where there's hardly any protective fur.

 CAUTION: If you have a molded-plastic pet carrier, DO NOT use it in hot weather. If you need to transport your pet in it, be aware that the heat inside can build up and present a real danger to your pet.

FOOD & DRINK

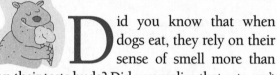 Did you know that when dogs eat, they rely on their sense of smell more than on their taste buds? Did you realize that cats can't taste sweets? And it's just as well since sweets are not good for cats and dogs. Here are some important details about food no-no's for pets and other ideas to make the most of mealtime.

Chocolate? Never!

Chocolate, especially baking chocolate, can be toxic to both cats and dogs. Don't leave a candy dish with Hershey's Kisses or other wrapped chocolates lying around. Your pet may be able to smell the chocolate and eat it with the foil.

In case you're wondering, it's the *theobromine,* an alkaloid in chocolate, that affects the animal's central nervous system and heart muscle. As little as 2 ounces of milk chocolate can be fatal to a puppy.

 CAUTION: If you discover that your dog has ingested chocolate, call your veterinarian immediately. You can also contact your local emergency vet clinic (check the *Yellow Pages*), animal hospital or poison control center for instructions.

Grapes, Currants and Raisins? Never!

It's been discovered that grapes, currants and raisins can cause kidney failure in dogs and possibly in cats as well. The toxic amount is 1 ounce for every 2.2 pounds of body weight.

The reason these fruits are poisonous is still unknown. So, if your pet swallows more than a few grapes, currants or raisins, call your vet immediately. Prompt treatment can often result in a full recovery.

Onions? Bad!

Onions are a no-no for dogs and cats because they can cause *anemia* (low blood iron) and possibly death. You may not remember the onions in your leftovers, which is another good reason not to feed your pet leftovers.

Symptoms to watch for include vomiting, diarrhea and poor appetite—contact your pet's vet if you think he consumed onions.

> **NOTE:** Garlic also can be toxic to dogs and to cats.

Yogurt for Gas Prevention

Twice a day, feed your pet some plain yogurt— 1 teaspoon for every 10 pounds of body weight. The yogurt's friendly bacteria, *Lactobacillus acidophilus*, helps break down food quickly in the intestines, improving digestion and preventing gas buildup.

To reduce excess flatulence, add ¼ teaspoon each of dill and fennel to the yogurt.

Dry Food vs. Canned Food

Many vets recommend dry food over canned food. Dry food is just that...dry. Canned food is

Beware of These Foods

Here is a list of foods (provided by the Humane Society of the United States, *www.hsus.org*) that are potentially poisonous to pets...

- Alcoholic beverages
- Apple seeds
- Apricot pits
- Avocados (toxic to birds, mice, rabbits, horses, cattle and dairy goats)
- Cherry pits
- Candy (particularly chocolate, which is toxic to dogs, cats and ferrets...and any candy containing the sweetener Xylitol)
- Coffee (grounds, beans, chocolate-covered espresso beans)
- Hops (used in home beer-brewing)
- Macadamia nuts
- Moldy foods
- Mushroom plants
- Mustard seeds
- Onions and onion powder
- Peach pits
- Potato leaves and stems (green parts)
- Raisins (excessive intake of red grapes should also be avoided)
- Rhubarb leaves
- Salt
- Tea (caffeine)
- Tomato leaves and stems (green parts)
- Walnuts
- Yeast dough

sticky and will stay on your pet's teeth, attracting odor-causing bacteria.

Dry food has an abrasive crunch that can help polish your pet's teeth. The best thing to do is mix a bit of water or oil into the dry food to soften it. Your pet will get all the teeth-cleaning benefits of dry food without the stinky breath that may result from canned food.

179

An equal mix of dry and canned food might be better for cats, who don't have a thirst mechanism and might not drink enough water.

Canned Food

If you feed your pet an entire can of wet food at a time, it's easier and more efficient to open each end of the can and push out the food with a lid, rather than to scoop out the food with a spoon. Just make sure no metal splinters get into the food.

Dry-Food Storage

If you store big economy-sized bags of dry food in your garage or basement, keep hungry 4-legged critters from getting into them—put the bags of food in big plastic garbage cans with secure lids.

Cat's Bowl

A deep, narrow bowl is a no-no for a cat because it's not roomy enough for his/her whiskers. As you may know, a cat's whiskers have sensitive nerve endings. A shallow bowl or saucer—the wider, the better—will allow him to enjoy his food and water in comfort.

Bowl Placement

Your pet will be more comfortable and secure if he faces the room when he eats and drinks. Place his food and water bowls 2 or 3 feet away from any wall so that there's enough room to position himself behind the bowls, facing out into the room.

When the bowls are placed against the wall, the pet has to eat with his back to the room. That may make him feel vulnerable and nervous, and he will scarf down his food as quickly as he can.

Place Mat

Put a place mat of some kind—an old bathtub mat, a frayed towel or a section of a no-longer-used runner—under your pet's bowls. The idea is to keep the bowls in place, and keep the floor clean and dry.

If the place mat doesn't work for you, glue a rubber jar ring to the bottom of the bowl to keep it in place while your pet eats.

Making Cat's Food Appetizing

If your cat is acting finicky about his food, trickle some oil or water from a can of tuna fish on whatever you're serving. This should whet his appetite.

Garden Water Dish

Create a permanent place for your pet's outdoor water dish. But instead of a dish, use a Bundt pan (most supermarkets sell them), which has a big hole in the middle. Hammer a stake into the ground where you want the dish to be, then place the pan around it.

> **NOTE:** As with any outdoor water dish, make certain that you thoroughly clean it every day. Birds, insects and bacteria can get into it, making it potentially harmful for the pet to drink the water.

Hydrate Outdoors

If you and your dog go outside on a sunny summer day, be sure to bring a bottle of water and a Frisbee. After playing catch, turn over the Frisbee and use it as a saucer for the water.

FLEAS

Despite any suggestions we offer on how to prevent flea infestations and how to get rid of them, the fact is this—the healthier your pet is, the fewer fleas (if any) he/she will attract. Fleas tend to prey on malnourished, weak and sick animals.

One of the most effective ways to improve the health of any animal (including us humans) is to improve the quality of its diet. And the best way to improve the diet is by including more wholesome, natural foods and fewer processed, commercial foods.

If you're willing to put in the time preparing food for your pet, rather than just opening a can or a bag, we suggest that you pick up a good book like *Dr. Pitcairn's New Complete Guide to Natural Health for Dogs and Cats* (Rodale Books) by Richard Pitcairn, DVM, PhD, and Susan Hubble Pitcairn, and let it guide you.

Meanwhile, here are some ways in which you can help your pet fight fleas and win....

Check for Fleas

Get your pet to stand on a large piece of white paper, then brush him. If he has fleas, you will see tiny black specks land on the paper. And they will probably be moving.

Lemon Chaser

Thinly slice 2 lemons and place the slices in a pot with a quart of water. Boil for 1 hour, then let it steep overnight.

In the morning, strain out the lemon and keep the liquid in a jar or spray bottle. Once a day, groom your pet with a flea comb, then spray or sponge his coat with the lemon water.

 CAUTION: Test a bit of the tonic on a small patch of your pet's skin first to make sure he's not allergic to citrus oil.

The smell of citrus repels fleas. The elixir may also help heal your pet's flea-bitten skin. And if that's not enough, the astringent properties in lemon will help to clean and brighten your pet's coat.

Fleas Hate Vinegar

Add distilled white vinegar to your pet's drinking water—1 teaspoon to each quart of water.

B-1 Without Fleas

Brewer's yeast (available at health-food stores) is rich in vitamin B-1 (thiamin) and—when added to your pet's diet—is said to build your pet's immune system and help repel fleas. The recommended dosage is 1 rounded tablespoon for each 50 pounds of pet.

The good news is that your pet may not be bothered by fleas...the bad news is that brewer's yeast may cause excess gas. To minimize the gas situation, feed the brewer's yeast to your pet in small amounts—in plain yogurt and other moist foods.

CAUTION: According to Alfred Plechner, author of *Pet Allergies* (Very Healthy Enterprises), brewer's yeast is among the most common allergens...along with beef, wheat, eggs and corn. If your pet has a history of food allergies, have his veterinarian test him before using brewer's yeast.

Cat Coat Shiner and Flea Repellent

Rub mayonnaise into your cat's skin and fur, then wipe him clean with a damp washcloth. It should give him a shiny coat while helping to keep fleas away.

Flea Collar

Many pets have had a bad experience with side effects from a commercial flea collar's overly powerful ingredients.

Instead, try this simple and safe herbal flea collar...soak a piece of heavy and smooth twine—long enough so it fits securely around your pet's neck—in pennyroyal oil (available at health-food stores) for 24 hours. Then hang it up in the bathtub until it stops dripping.

When it's dry, tie the twine around your pet's identification collar to repel fleas. Fleas hate pennyroyal!

 CAUTION: DO NOT use pennyroyal if you, your pet or *anyone* in your household is pregnant, including other pets.

Flea-Repellent Pillow

◆ Drive fleas away by attacking their keen sense of smell. Make a small pillow or sachet bag and fill it with cedar chips or shavings, or chamomile leaves—loose or in tea bags. Attach the sachet securely to your pet's collar, especially since fleas tend to work their way up to their victim's head.

◆ You can also use a small piece of an old pillowcase, and make a little pillow. Fill it with equal parts (about ½ cup each) of rosemary and oregano, and keep it in the doghouse or attach it to the pad on your pet's bed.

Getting Fleas Where They Live

Get rid of fleas on your pet by combing his coat thoroughly, especially around the neck and head. Check your pet-supply store for flea combs. These combs have closely set teeth and will dig out the fleas and flea eggs.

Dip the comb in a clean, empty 32-ounce jar filled with water, and add 1 tablespoon of liquid dish detergent. Then comb and dip, comb and dip until your pet is flea-free.

Old-Fashioned Soap and Water

Bathe your dog once a week with Dr. Bronner's Peppermint Soap (available at health-food stores) or any good, natural dog shampoo (a friend of ours recommends Green Ban). Doing this will go a long way in controlling fleas.

Salt Them Away

Fleas live and breed in carpeting and on furniture. If you have a serious infestation of fleas, you must vacuum (at least every week) all the areas where your pet hangs out.

Then sprinkle common table salt in all of those same places and, after 48 hours, vacuum again. Repeat the procedure—sprinkle salt, and 48 hours later, vacuum.

Hopefully by then, the vacuum will have sucked up all of the original fleas and those that hatched during the 4-day salting.

You may be surprised to know that fleas love salt so much that they will probably gorge themselves to death on it.

 NOTE: It's not necessary to change the vacuum bag in between each cleaning, since the fleas sucked into the vacuum are (or will be) dead.

But if the thought of them being in the vacuum bag bothers you (as it would us!), then by all means replace the bag.

Let Fleas Take a Powder

There are all kinds of flea powders available. Some contain harsh pesticides and potentially harmful chemicals.

If you use a flea product and you suspect that your dog is having an adverse reaction to it—signs to look for include thrashing and/or foaming at the mouth—immediately bathe the animal with mild soap and rinse him off with lots of water. If he does not seem to be getting any better, call your local emergency veterinary clinic and take him for treatment right away.

Once your pet is fine, be sure to report the incident to the manufacturer of the product as well as to the Environmental Protection Agency (*www.epa.gov*).

CLEANING & GROOMING

 According to author James Gorman, "Cats are the ultimate narcissists. You can tell this because of all the time they spend on personal grooming. Dogs aren't like this. A dog's idea of personal grooming is to roll in a dead fish." Of course, they look so adorable doing it, who could be mad? *To groom your pet properly, these hints should help…*

Dog Hair–Catcher

Before each bath, put a hair catcher (available at home improvement, bed/bath and hardware stores) over the drain to prevent hair clogs. The catchers generally come in 2 sizes. Measure the diameter of your drain before you go to the store.

Eye and Ear Protection

◆ Before giving your pet a bath, pop a drop of castor oil in each of your pet's eyes. This will protect the eyes from soap.

◆ To protect your pet's ears from water during a bath, gently place a cotton ball in each ear. Be sure not to push it in too deep!

✳ **Best Water Temperature**
Cats and dogs prefer lukewarm bath water… not too hot and not too cold.

Soft and Shiny Coat

To make your pet's coat extra-nice, put ¼ cup of baking soda in his bath water.

 CAUTION: Do not use this remedy if your pet is on a low-sodium diet. He/she might ingest or absorb the baking soda, which is high in sodium. Use cornstarch instead.

Stop the Water Shake

Don't you just hate it when your dog does that post-bath shake and water goes flying everywhere? The shake starts at the dog's nose. The second you see that happening, gently but quickly, grab hold of his nose and you'll quell his urge to shake.

FYI: Heads or Tails?

Dogs generally shake only if their heads get wet. When bathing your pet, wash his body in the tub first and try to clean his head and neck separately.

Dry Shampoo

Massage baking soda into your pet's fur and then brush it out. The baking soda rubdown and brush-out will clean his coat and get rid of any unpleasant pet odor.

CAUTION: Do not use this remedy if your pet is on a low-sodium diet. He/she might ingest or absorb the baking soda, which is high in sodium. Use cornstarch instead.

De-Skunking

*Oh, nooooo…*Fido just got sprayed by a skunk and he smells *terrible.* First, check the dog's eyes. If his face was sprayed, his eyes will probably be red and watering. Although the spray isn't blinding, it can be very painful—contact your veterinarian for help.

But if the dog's eyes seem to be OK, then you can proceed with the de-skunking. *Here's what you'll need…*

> 1 pair rubber gloves
>
> 1 bucket of lukewarm water
>
> 1 teaspoon mild liquid soap or dish detergent
>
> 1 quart 3% hydrogen peroxide (it's important that the bottle is fresh, not yet opened)
>
> ¼ cup baking soda

Put on the gloves. Mix the soap in the bucket of water, and wash the dog with it. The soap will break up the oils in the skunk spray. Then combine the hydrogen peroxide and the baking soda in a wide, open container.

While the mixture gurgles, it should be worked into the dog's fur—be sure to focus on the areas where he was sprayed.

CAUTION: Be sure to keep the skunk-wash solution away from the dog's face and eyes. And if you'll be rinsing his head, put a washcloth over his eyes to protect them.

Wait 5 to 10 minutes, and then rinse off the dog using lukewarm water. The oxygen-producing chemical reaction between the hydrogen peroxide and baking soda should get rid of the skunk smell.

CAUTION: Do not use this remedy if your pet is on a low-sodium diet. He/she might ingest or absorb the baking soda, which is high in sodium.

Skunk-Solution Alternative

If you don't want to use baking soda to clean the skunk smell, try this—wear rubber gloves and rub your dog's coat with distilled white vinegar, tomato juice or cola. Then bathe and shampoo your dog thoroughly.

Shedding

There are cleansing wipes made especially for dogs and cats—they're available at Petco and other pet stores. Rub them on your pet to pick up loose hair and get rid of any unpleasant pet smell. You can also use a baby wipe to clean your shedding pet.

Suction Up the Hair

With the small upholstery-brush attachment in place, carefully vacuum the just-shed loose hair that's still on your pet and will be all over everything if you don't vacuum it up right away.

Nonstop Shedding

If your pet's shedding seems to be year-round rather than seasonal, work a little lanolin or olive oil into his coat every day. Within a few weeks, there should be a noticeable difference for the better.

Removing Burrs, Tree Sap, Gum

You'll want to wear rubber gloves for this...work vegetable oil or baby oil into the sticky tangled areas of your pet's coat to break up the gunk. This will make it easier to extricate without causing yelps or whimpers.

Cornstarch can also be used to de-gunk your pet. Pour a little on the problem area and patiently work it in, de-gunking the mess.

Nail Care

Here are a few natural and inexpensive answers to the dreaded pet nail-clipping job...

- **Dogs**—Walk your dog twice daily on a paved surface. City streets and sidewalks are perfect.

    If you're not in a city, then you might have a paved driveway. Get out the Frisbee or a ball and play fetch on it.

- **Cats**—Get a big piece of corrugated cardboard and provide a toy—even if it's just a

piece of aluminum foil sculpted into a ball —and let him play on the corrugated cardboard every day.

The idea is that the rough surfaces of the pavement or corrugated cardboard will file down your pet's nails as they romp across them. How's that for a *peticure!*

> **NOTE:** Although these ideas might work for some dogs and cats, many others still require their nails to be trimmed regularly.

CALMING INFLUENCES

 Chances are, the calmer you are...the calmer your pet will be. The problem is, the more your pet acts up...the faster you turn into a nervous wreck. So both of you—calm down! *These suggestions should also help...*

Respect Your Pet's Hangouts

Take note of the places your pet likes to hang out. Cats tend to be territorial animals that want their place in the sun, while most dogs enjoy looking out of windows.

Do not place a plant, a lamp or anything similar in your pet's favorite spots that could block the sun or obscure the view.

Nervous Reaction to Strangers

If you're into alternative treatments, then this suggestion is a "gem"—place a jade charm on your pet's collar. It will lie in the vicinity of his/her heart *chakra*, which is the energy center that influences your pet's ability to feel love.

Jumping on Furniture— Foiled!

If your pet insists on getting on furniture that's off limits, put a big piece of aluminum foil on the taboo couch, chair or table. Next time he jumps up—SURPRISE!—the noise and glitter will scare him off. Keep the aluminum foil on the furniture until your pet is no longer interested in it.

It is believed that the vibrations emanating from the jade will make your pet more affectionate and generally calmer. If it works, it should help to take the trauma out of meeting new people.

When Company Comes

If your pet acts up—barks, runs around wildly, jumps up on your guests—when company comes, circumvent that behavior by calming him right before your guests are due to arrive.

Acupressure will get him into a relaxed state—just press the tips of both of his ears between your thumbs and index fingers, then pulse the spots for 45 seconds. There's no guarantee that this remedy will work, but it's certainly worth a try.

If your pet is calm, but your *company* acts up, try the pressing and pulsing on *them*.

Petting the Pet

Animals prefer to be petted the way their fur lies. So always "go with the flow" and don't rub him the wrong way.

FOR DOGS ONLY

American humorist Franklin P. Jones once remarked, "Scratch a dog and you'll find a permanent job." True…but considering the unconditional love you receive in return, we're sure you'll agree that it's worth it. *Here are some ideas that will help you do the permanent job more effectively and with ease…*

Stop the Barking

◆ If your dog barks for no apparent reason, spritz a little lemon juice (or plain water) in

his/her mouth and say, "Quiet!" Just be careful not to get any lemon juice in his eyes.

◆ Fill a small jar or tin with pennies or marbles. When your dog barks when he shouldn't, shake the noisy jar in his direction and firmly say, "No!"

Stop Hole Digging

Our friend's dog kept digging holes in their yard. The vet recommended that she fill in the holes with some of the dog's own feces, then cover the poop with dirt. As disgusting as it sounds, it worked. Once she did that, the dog stopped digging holes in the yard.

We've also heard that pine cones can be an effective deterrent.

 Mr. Clean Paws

When your dog comes inside after playing in the yard, catch him at the door, before he can track in dirt, and use a baby wipe or doggy wipe to swipe his paws clean.

While you're at it, clean in between his toes to get any caked-on mud.

Stop Furniture and Paw Chewing

◆ Boredom may cause your pet to chew on wooden furniture legs—or on his own paws. To prevent this type of destructive behavior, interact with him more, or get him some good chew toys or a companion.

◆ Dogs don't like the taste or the scent of hot chili sauce or strong-smelling soap, so rub some on the furniture that he likes to munch on so much.

◆ To get him to stop gnawing on his paws, wipe them with a little oil of cloves (available at health-food stores).

Leaving Dogs Home Alone

◆ If you go out during the day and your dog is home alone, put on the radio or television for him. Let an easy-listening station or the newscasters on CNN keep him company—and possibly keep burglars away.

◆ Make your pet feel safe and protected by providing a sheltered space for him—something with walls or sides, like a crate, is ideal. Place it in a spot where you spend lots of time and put something of yours inside. An old, worn T-shirt is perfect.

A pet that feels supported physically will be happier and more emotionally stable.

 FYI: Crate Training Advice

A lot of information is available about crate training. We found 2 good Web sites that provide details on the different kinds of crates, how to buy a crate, proper furnishings, good locations, guidelines for introducing the crate to your dog, when *not* to use a crate…and more.

Visit the American Dog Trainers Network at *www.tonypassera.com/thedogsite/www/new* …and Dumb Friends League at *www.ddfl. org/behavior/crate-train.pdf.*

◆ If your pet goes into a panic when you leave him alone, and he starts chewing and clawing the furniture—Bach Rescue Remedy to the rescue! It's a safe, flower-essence solution, and it's available at health-food stores.

About 30 minutes before you plan to leave your dog alone, add 4 drops of Rescue Remedy to his water dish or a treat that he loves. By the time you leave, he should be calm and no longer hell-bent on chomping on your couch. (We just hope you don't have

to leave your pet alone to go to the health-food store to get it.)

 CAUTION: If your dog consistently shows anxious, insecure and/or destructive behavior (such as urinating, chewing, excessive barking, etc.) when you leave him alone, this suggests separation anxiety or a more serious problem. Consult your veterinarian or a professional trainer for advice.

Doghouse Wood

The best wood for an outdoor doghouse is cedar. It stands up well to weather, keeps dogs cool in warmer months and repels fleas and ticks.

There are some treated woods that contain arsenic compounds, pesticides and other potentially harmful chemicals. If a dog chews on the treated wood, he can develop skin sores or even be poisoned.

 In the Doghouse

Foam rubber is soft as well as comfortable and makes excellent bedding in a doghouse or crate. Be sure to cover the foam with a zippered pillowcase or some other kind of fabric cover (which will make it easier to clean).

The covering should be securely sewn or zipped closed, so that it cannot be chewed open by your pet. If the foam is ingested by the dog, it can be very harmful to his health.

Giving Away Puppies

If your dog has a litter and you plan to give the puppies away, put pieces of cloth in the Mama-dog's bed—1 piece of cloth for each puppy.

Give 1 of those pieces to each adoptive family to use in their new puppy's bed. The cloth should help prevent the puppy from crying for its birth mother.

 NOTE: In general, puppies should not be weaned from their mothers any earlier than 6 weeks of age.

Adopting a Puppy

◆ Ask for something that smells of the puppy's birth mother. If it's not possible, you can help your frightened little charge make it through the night by keeping a ticking clock near him to simulate his mother's heartbeat.

◆ Let the puppy cuddle up to a warm hot-water bottle that's wrapped in a soft blanket. Or place something large you've just taken off—an old T-shirt or sweat pants (nothing small that could be chewed and/or ingested)—in his bed. Your scent nearby will help him feel more secure.

 NOTE: Don't give puppies anything you don't want destroyed! Puppies love to chew, especially if they're stressed or bored.

FOR CATS ONLY

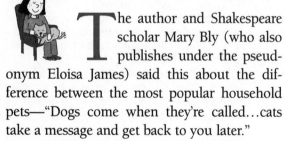 The author and Shakespeare scholar Mary Bly (who also publishes under the pseudonym Eloisa James) said this about the difference between the most popular household pets—"Dogs come when they're called…cats take a message and get back to you later."

And author Ellen Perry Berkeley summed it up perfectly when she said, "As every cat owner knows, nobody owns a cat." Cats may appear to be very independent, but they do need tending to. *Here are some helpful hints…*

Pick-Me-Up

Would you like to be picked up by the scruff of your neck? Neither would a cat. Do it right with 1 hand on his/her chest, under the ribcage, while the other hand gives him support under the rump and hind feet.

Cat Litter

Cats are like people in that they like their toilet privacy. So put your cat's litter box in an area that doesn't have lots of traffic. *Here are some more suggestions regarding cat litter…*

Clean Kitty's Litter Safely

Toxoplasmosis is a parasitic disease that can be transmitted to humans through contact with a cat's feces.

To protect yourself, always put on disposable rubber gloves to clean the litter box.

 CAUTION: People who have compromised immune systems and pregnant women should *never* clean a cat's litter box. Contracting toxoplasmosis is extremely dangerous and can damage a developing fetus.

Kitty Litter—Cheaper Is Better

Expensive cat litter that clumps when it gets wet, making it more scoopable, can actually be harmful to the cat—and to the person who does the scooping.

If a cat licks himself after using the litter box, he can ingest the litter dust, and the person who scoops the litter can inhale the dust. *Sodium bentonite* is the chemical that causes the clumping. A buildup of this chemical can be poisonous and result in respiratory and digestive problems for both humans and cats.

Opt for cat litter that contains no chemicals and no additives. There is a big selection. Visit a pet shop or supermarket, or let your fingers do the walking on the Internet.

Litter Box Deodorant

Layer the bottom of the litter box with baking soda, then add the litter.

Swimming-Pool Style

Cats prefer to have their litter at different levels for the different things they need to do. Arrange the litter like the water in a swimming pool—ranging from deep at 1 end to shallow at the other end.

CAT-ALOG

This section includes unique suggestions that we couldn't *cat*-egorize. But we hope that these ideas make you and your feline friend happier housemates.

Marking *Your* Territory

Whenever your cat goes to an off-limits area of the house, use a plant mister or water gun to spray water on him. After a few gentle sprays, he'll get the hint.

Bringing in a New Cat

To make a new addition welcome by your cat-in-residence, rub the new kitty with a cloth or towel and put it next to your current cat's food bowl (and if you can do this *before* the new cat arrives, so much the better).

Let Cat #1 get used to the scent of Cat #2 while associating it with something good (his meals). It should help the cats to become fast friends.

Fur-Ball Prevention

A hair mass that forms in a cat's stomach is better known as a hair ball or fur ball. Fur balls are the result of the cat swallowing hair as he grooms himself. But if the cat's digestive system is kept lubricated, the swallowed hair will pass through and out before a fur ball is formed.

Here's what to do—feed your cat sardines in oil once a week. If that doesn't totally stop the fur balls, then mix ½ to 1 teaspoon of vegetable oil or olive oil into his food every day.

You can also put ¼ to ½ teaspoon of petroleum jelly on the cat's paws once a day, and let him lick it off.

Repel with Cat's Sense Of Smell

As soon as your cat jumps up on an off-limits piece of furniture, wet a cotton ball with distilled white vinegar and dab it on his mouth. Then put the cotton ball on a piece of plastic wrap or a plastic bag and leave it on the furniture as a reminder.

You can also spritz the cat with a spray bottle filled with equal amounts of distilled white vinegar and water. We just hope *you* don't mind the smell of vinegar.

Stop Furniture Scratching

◆ Wipe Tabasco or chili sauce on the furniture's woodwork, let it dry, then buff it with a soft cloth. Cats are repelled by the spicy smell.

◆ If you don't want to put hot sauce on the furniture, sprinkle cayenne pepper on strips of tape and carefully attach the tape to any woodwork the cat likes to scratch.

◆ Use lemon polish on furniture—cats hate the citrus smell. If the cat scratches the furniture's upholstery, rub it with lemon-scented soap.

◆ If the soap might harm the fabric, place small plastic bags that contain lemon peel on the upholstery. Anyone who wants to sit on the chair or couch simply has to move the bags…not remove the cat.

◆ A scratching post will keep your cat's claws in good shape, and may divert his attention away from scratching valuable furniture.

To keep reviving your pet's interest in the scratching post, sprinkle some (if possible, freshly harvested) catnip on it every other week. Trimming the cat's nails weekly may also help.

PUPPY & KITTEN OVERPOPULATION

And now for a public service announcement...every day, more than 50,000 puppies and kittens are born in the United States. Only 1 out of 5 of these animals is properly cared for in a happy home...the other 4 are homeless, neglected or abused.

These tragic statistics (from veterinarian Holly Frisby at *www.dogsonly.org*) mean that millions of animals wind up in rescue shelters, and 4 million to 6 million of those animals are destroyed each year—simply because nobody wants to adopt them.

Fact: In 6 years, 1 female dog and her offspring can be the source of 67,000 puppies.

The solution to the problem starts with you and your pet. Please read the following information so that you can be a well-informed and responsible pet owner.

Benefits of Spaying Female Pets

◆ Eliminates "heat" cycles

◆ Prevents accidental pregnancies

◆ Prevents unwanted offspring

◆ Reduces risk of breast tumors or cancer

◆ Significantly reduces undesirable behavior

◆ Prevents uterine infections, which are common in older pets

Benefits of Neutering Male Pets

◆ Significantly reduces prostate and testicular disease or cancer

◆ Reduces undesirable behavior

◆ Eliminates urine odor of male cats

When to Spay or Neuter

Check with your veterinarian for his/her specific recommendations. But in general, the best time to spay or neuter your pet is when he/she is about 6 months old—sometimes earlier.

Spaying your female pet *before* her first heat cycle greatly reduces the risk that she will develop breast tumors and cancer. Neutering your male pet *before* he develops undesirable behavior patterns is better than trying to undo those anti-social, embarrassing behaviors after they happen.

Low-Cost Programs

There are many low-cost and free spay-and-neuter programs that can help animal lovers do their part in controlling the pet overpopulation.

Bob Barker, host of television's long-running game show *The Price Is Right* and an animal-rights advocate, established a foundation that funds qualified clinics and organizations so that they may provide low-cost or free spay-and-neuter services.

For a list of spay-and-neuter services in your state, visit *www.petsandanimals.org*. Or call Friends of Animals in Darien, Connecticut, for a directory of participating veterinarians nation-wide—800-321-7387.

SPAY/USA, a program of the North Shore Animal League America, provides the names, numbers and prices for low-cost spay-and-neuter programs in your local area.

For more information, visit *www.spayusa.org* or call 800-248-SPAY (7729). ■

■ Products ■

Travel Water Dish for Dogs

A perfect take-along during hot summer months, this pet canteen is cleverly designed and is a neat way of hydrating your dog. The squeeze-bottle snaps on to the water pan and is ready in seconds. No spills. No leaks.

No-Bark Collar

Do you have a neighbor with a noisy dog? This simple-to-use collar helps the dog break the barking habit, painlessly. Fits any size dog. Requires a 9-volt battery (not included).

Source: Miles Kimball, 800-546-2255, *www.mileskimball.com.*

UPCO has a great catalog with more than 200 detailed, illustrated pages with a huge selection of products for dogs, cats, birds and other pets.

We're listing some of our favorites here, but we encourage pet owners to explore the catalog for themselves.

Freeze-Dried Ice Cream for Dogs

We haven't sampled this ourselves, but our friend's Fido did—and he begged for more. This is a *real* treat made out of *real* ice cream, and it's rich in calcium and vitamin A. It's freeze-dried, so it will keep for years without refrigeration (but we're sure your dog will gobble it up before its expiration date). It comes in 2 canine favorite flavors—vanilla and peanut butter.

Car Harness

If you buckle up for safety, shouldn't your dog be safe, too? The harness (comprised of chest and shoulder straps) is safe and easy to use. The adjustable security strap, which is connected to the harness above your pet's shoulders, fits into any standard seat belt clip. Comes in 5 sizes.

Homeopet—Nature's Natural Medicine

Homeopet medicines are all naturally grown and scientifically formulated in a 100% organic solution, free of all chemicals. They have been clinically used on dogs, cats, fish, birds, rabbits, hamsters, ferrets and pot-bellied pigs. They're deemed safe for puppies, kittens, pregnant and nursing animals—*but be sure to check with your pet's veterinarian before trying them.* There are no known side effects from these fast-acting liquids. There are many formulas for specific ailments, including Anxiety, Joint Relief, and Skin and Itch Relief.

We have heard plenty of recommendations for this brand. Our neighbor's dog takes the Anxiety Formula, and she can attest to its effectiveness during a thunderstorm, at the vet's office or whenever she leaves her pet home alone. The drops give the pet—and the owner—a sense of calm. Also, our cousin volunteers at a dog shelter where they use the Homeopet line successfully.

Pee Post

The Pee Post is a pheromone-treated yard stake that encourages pets to do their "business" in a specific area of the yard. This simple and clever training device will help you maintain your lawn and garden, and makes cleanups easier.

Source: UPCO, 800-254-UPCO (8726), *www.upco.com.*

Gel-Pedic Pet Bed

This bed is available in 5 sizes, ranging from "toy" to "large," and is designed in a natural nesting shape for your pet's security and comfort. The bed is made of soft yet supportive GelFoam, which can be especially beneficial for dogs with arthritis—the GelFoam shapes to the contour of the pet's hips and joints, relieving any pressure that might be causing pain.

The GelFoam also provides insulation to keep your pet cool in the summer and warm in the winter. The embedded aroma of natural eucalyptus helps to repel fleas and mites, and keeps the bed smelling fresh.

Source: Gel-Pedic/Splintek, 888-PET-PADS (738-7237), *www.gelpedic.com.*

Index

A

Acupressure massage to calm animals, 186
African violets, 128
Air conditioners, care of, 94–95
Air quality, improving with houseplants, 139
Air travel. *See* Travel, general
Allergies
    to fabric softeners, 49
    pets', to brewer's yeast, 181
    sensitivity to wool, 44
Aluminum, cleaning, 33
Antifreeze and toxicity to pets, 175–176
Ants. *See* Pest control
Apple trees, 136–137
Aquasana Shower Systems, 84
Asthma attacks
    from commercial air fresheners, 83
    from fabric softeners, 49
Audio cassette recorder, cleaning, 93–94
Automobiles. *See* Cars
Azaleas, 128

B

Barbecue grill tips, 109–110
Bathroom
    chrome fixtures, cleaning, 81
    clogged toilet, 76
    drains, 81–82
    faucet drip, 78
    guests, having, 83
    mold and mildew, 79, 80–81, 163

nonslip tub appliqués, removing, 77
    odors, eliminating, 83
    overflow prevention, 76
    shower, cleaning, 78–79
    shower curtain, cleaning, 79–80
    soap tips, 82
    tile and grout, 80–81
    toilet, cleaning, 74–75
    tub, cleaning, 76–77, 78
Batteries, care of, 92
    camera, 94
Beans, 131
Birds. *See* Pest control
Bleach. *See* Laundry
Blinds, Venetian, cleaning, 96
Blister prevention when gardening, 117
Blue jeans, care of. *See* Laundry
Bluefish Bath Alarm and Temperature Sensor, 84
Bone, cleaning, 35
Books, care of, 89–90
Boots. *See* Shoes/boots
Brass. *See* Metal objects, cleaning
Bronze. *See* Metal objects, cleaning
Bugs, eliminating. *See* Pest control
Bulbs, 128

C

Cabbage, 129
Cabinet magnets, 98–99
Cacti and other succulents, 129
Cameras, cleaning, 94
Candle wax, removing, 53–54
    from candlesticks, 32
    from carpets and rugs, 6
    from pewter, 35

from upholstered furniture, 27
Cane furniture, care of, 28
Car Harness, 191
Carpets and rugs, maintenance of
    candle wax, removing, 6
    chewing gum, removing, 6–7
    cleaning, 4–5
    loose threads, removing, 8
    nap, raising, 8
    stain removal, 5–8
    static electricity, 9
    throw rugs, anchoring, 9
    urine, pet, removing, 6
    vacuuming, 9–11
Carrots, 129
Cars. *See also* Car travel
    battery maintenance, 150–151
    car-seat safety, 146–147
    cleaning, 152–154
    cold-weather maintenance, 147–149
    comfort tips, 151–152
    door locks, frozen, 149
    emergency-items list, 157
    fan-belt maintenance, 151
    fog, driving in, 147
    fuel-economy tips, 149–150
    garage floor/driveway stains, 155
    garage-parking tips, 155–156
    gasoline, pumping, safely, 147
    nicks and scratches, fixing, 153
    oil or grease stains, 155
    safety in, 146–147
    seatbelts, 147
    smells, eliminating, 156
    snow, traction in, 148
    steering position, 147
    tires, 149–150

vehicle identification number (VIN), 151
windshield frost, 148–149
Car travel, 157–158.
See also Travel, general
games, 158–160
racing school, 157–158
Cassette recorder, cleaning, 93–94
Cats. *See* Pets
CDs, care of, 93
Ceiling fans, care of, 96–97
Chewing gum, removing
from furniture/fabric, 6–7, 53–54
Chocolate and toxicity to pets, 178
Cholera, 170
Chrome, cleaning, 34
Citronella, 111
Cleanability codes for upholstered furniture, 26–27
Cleaning tips. *See also* Bathroom; Laundry
dusting, 28–29
vacuuming, 9–11
Climbing plants, trellis for, 129
Closets, organizing, 99–101
Coffee and tea stains, removing, 7
Computer maintenance, 91–92
Concrete
de-icing, 107–108
stains on, removing, 108
steps, traction on, 108
Contact lenses, care of, while traveling, 170
Copper. *See* Metal objects, cleaning
Cork, to clean metal, 29
Corn, 129
Correction fluid extender, 86
Crayon
marks, removing, 4, 7, 12, 16, 54–55
for scratches in floors, 2–3
Cucumbers, 129
Currants, toxicity of, to pets, 179

D
Deck
de-icing, 107–108
painting, 23
patio furniture, cleaning, 109
Deer. *See* Pest control
De-icing steps and pavement, 107–108
Denims, care of. *See* Laundry
Detergent. *See* Laundry
Diapers, cloth. *See* Laundry
Dogs. *See* Pets
Do-it-yourself tips

door, sticky, 104
drawer runners, 104
drywall, 103
hammering, painless, 103
hinges, fixing squeaky, 103–104
ladder safety, 109
nuts, bolts and screws, 102–103
screwdriver, using, 103
tools, 101–102
Doors
locks, unlocking, 108
sticky, fixing, 104
storm, removing, 108
Door STOP Alarm, 171
Down-filled items, fluffing, 48
Drains, unclogging, 81–82
clogged toilet, 76
Drawer glides, 104
Dry cleaning fabrics. *See* Laundry
Dry-erase board cleaner, 86
Dryers and drying. *See* Laundry
Drywall, 103
Dungarees, care of. *See* Laundry
Dusting, 28–29
ceiling fans, 97
Dust mites, removing, 51
DVDs, care of, 93
Dye Grabber, 73

E
Ear Planes, 171
E. coli, 170
Eggplant, 130
Electrical-cord chewing by pets, 173
Electrical tips
batteries, caring for, 92, 150–151
electrical cords, 92
Electronics, home, 90–94
Emergency-items list for car, 157
ENERGY STAR label, 47

F
Fabrics, washing instructions.
See Laundry
Fabric softeners. *See* Laundry
Ferns, 130
Fertilizing. *See* Gardening
Fingerprints, removing, 12
Fireplace maintenance, 97–98
Fire prevention and pets, 175
Fish tanks, care of, 37
Fleas and ticks, eliminating, 8, 11, 181–183
Floors, cleaning and maintenance of
creaky/squeaky, repair of, 3
hardwood, 1–3
linoleum and vinyl, 3–4

protecting, when moving furniture, 3
tile, 4
waxed, 2, 3
Flowers. *See also* Gardening; *individual plant names*
arranging, 145
artificial and dried, cleaning, 51
cut, 143–145
Footwear. *See* Shoes/boots
Forsythia, 130
Freeze-Dried Ice Cream for Dogs, 191
Fruit
stains, removing, 7
toxicity of, to pets, 179
trees, 136–137
Fuel economy. *See* Cars
Furniture
cane, 28
leather, 27
moving, 3, 9
patio furniture, 109
upholstered, 26–27
vinyl, 27
wicker, 28
wood, 24–26
wrought-iron, 23, 26

G
Games, travel, 158–160
Garbage can, cleaning, 110
Gardening. *See also* Lawn care; Perennials; Pest control; *individual plant listings*
fertilizing, 120
gloveless, 116–117
hoses, 116
knee pads, 117
seeds, planting and storing, 118–119
soil, testing and supplementing, 117–118
sun- and shade-loving produce, 133
tools, care of, 114–116
watering, 119
weeds, 121–123
Garden Kneeler/Sitter, 145
Gasoline economy. *See* Cars
Gel-Pedic Pet Bed, 191
Geraniums, 130
Grapes, toxicity of, to pets, 179
Grass. *See* Lawn care
Grease and oil stains, removing
from car finish, 154
on carpets, 7

on clothing, 55–56, 57
on floors, 2
on garage floor or driveway, 155
on shoes, 66
from upholstered furniture, 27
on walls, 12
Grill tips, 109–110
Guarantees and warranties, organizing, 88–89
Guests, treatment of, 83
Gum, chewing, removing from furniture/fabric, 6–7, 53–54

H

Hair, paint, removing from, 22
Halogen bulbs, 88
Hammering, painless, 103
Hand care after gloveless gardening, 117
HANDy Paint Pail, 23
Hardwood floors, caring for, 1–3
Hats, care of, 69–70
Herbs, 130
pennyroyal, uses and cautions, 182
Hinges, fixing squeaky, 103–104
Hollyhocks, 130
Home office tips, 86–87
Homeopet, 191
Hotels. *See* Travel, general
Houseplants, 137–142
first aid for, 142
poisonous to pets, 174
while you're away, 142–143
Humidifier, unclogging, 94–95
Hydrangea, 131

I

Ice, on steps and pavement, 107–108
Infection, preventing while gardening, 117
Insects, beneficial, 123, 127–128
Insects, eliminating. *See* Pest control
Ironing tips, 60–62
avoiding ironing, 62–64
Ivory, care of, 35

J

Jeans, care of. *See* Laundry
Jewelry, silver, care of, 32

K

Kale, 131
Keyboards, cleaning, 35
Knee pads for gardening, 117

L

Label on borrowed items, 99
Ladder safety, 109

Laundry. *See also* Stain removal
bleach substitute, 42
blue jeans, 45
colored clothing, 45
colorfast test, 40–41
denims, 45
detergent, 41–42
diapers, cloth, 46
down-filled items, 48
dry-clean-only fabrics, 42
dryer maintenance, 47
drying tips, 47–48
dungarees, 45
fabric softeners, 49–50
hard water, 41
ironing, avoiding, 62–64
ironing tips, 60–62
jeans, 45
laundromat, going to, 40
mothballs, 51
odors, removing, 50–51
permanent-press clothes, 42–43
pills on sweaters, 43–44
plastic items, 46, 51
sheets, 46, 48
silk and other fine washables, 43
slipcovers, 48
sorting and prepping, 39–41
starch, 49–50
washing instructions, 42–46
washing machine maintenance, 38–39
whites, 44–45
woolens, care of, 43–44, 48
Lawn care. *See also* Gardening
aerating, 121
fertilizing, 120
mowing, 120–121
watering, 119
weeds, 121–123
Leather
accessories, care of, 69
oil spill on, 57
shoes/boots, care of, 65, 66, 67
upholstered furniture, cleaning, 27
Legumes (beans and peas), 131
Lettuce, 131
Level, substitute for, 99
Lighting, 87–88
outdoor, unsticking, 108–109
Lilac, 131
Lime neutralizer, 117
Linoleum floors, cleaning and maintenance of, 3–4

M

MAAS Polishing Crème for All Metals, 37
Magnets, cabinet, 98–99
Magnifying Finger Attachment, 73
Marble, care of, 35–36
Marker stains on walls, removing, 12
Melons, 131
Menus, take-out, organizing, 89
Metal objects
aluminum, 33
cleaning, 29
mixed metals, 32–33, 34–35
painting, 23
silver, 29–32
stainless steel, 33–34
Mice. *See* Pest control
Mildew
in bathroom, 79, 80–81, 163
in books, 90
on clothing, 57
on shoes, 64
Mirrors, care of, 36–37
Mold. *See* Mildew
Mosquitoes. *See* Pest Control
Moss, removing, 108
Mothballs
as animal repellent, 125
smell of, removing from clothes, 51
Moth repellent, 101
Mud, removing from carpet, 8
Musty odors, removing. *See* Mildew

N

Nail care
when gardening, 116–117
for pets, 185
Nicotine stains. *See* Smoke; Stain removal
No-Bark Collar, 191
No-Jet-Lag, 171
Nuts, bolts and screws, 102–103
screwdriver, using, 103

O

Odors, eliminating. *See also* Smell
in bathroom, 83, 163
books, musty smell in, 90
in cars, 156
chemical or dye smell in new clothes, 50
closets, musty smell in, 100
in clothing, 50–51
furniture, musty smell on, 27
gym bag, 50
hamper, 83

home, preventing while away, 163
mothballs, 51
mustiness, 27, 90, 100
paint, 19, 21
perspiration, 50
plastics, 51
in shoes, 67
skunk smell on dogs, 184
smoke, in clothing, 50
smoke, on furniture, 27
soot in fireplace, 98
Oil and grease stains. *See* Grease and
   oil stains, removing
Oliso Steam Iron, 73
Onions, 131
   frost on windshield, preventing
      with, 148
   toxicity of, to pets, 179
Organizing
   gardening tools, 115
   menus, take-out, 89
   owner's manuals, guarantees,
      warranties, 88–89
   posters, 89
Organ/piano keyboards, cleaning, 35
Owner's manuals, organizing, 88–89

P
Pacific cloth/silvercloth, 30, 31
Packing and shipping tips, 87
Paint, latex, removing from carpet,
   7–8. *See also* Painting indoors
Painting indoors
   amount of paint, calculating, 19
   baseboards, 20
   cleanup, 22
   closets, 20
   doors, 20
   drip catchers, 20–21
   leftover, saving, 21–22
   odors, minimizing, 19, 21
   preparation, 16–19
   problems, 21
   radiators, 20
   stairs, 20
   yellowing, 20
Painting outdoors, 22–23
Pantyhose, 63–64
Paper shredder, sharpening, 86
Patio furniture, cleaning, 109
Peas, 131
Pee Post, 191
Pens and pencils, 86
   marks of, removing, 12
Perennials, 131–132. *See also*
   individual plant names
Pest control. *See also* Pets

ants, 106, 110, 123
aphids, 126
bees, yellow jackets, and wasps,
   110–111, 112, 123–124
beneficial insects, 123, 127–128
birds, 124
carpenter ants, 106
in carpets, 8
deer and other animals, 125
fleas and ticks, 8, 181–183
flies, 110, 111, 112
flying insects, 104–105
fruit flies, 105
gnats, 112
gophers, 127
humane rodent trap, 112
meal worms, 105–106
mice, 110, 112
moles, 126–127
mosquitoes, 111–112
moths, 101
pigeons, 110, 112
rabbits, 127
raccoons, 127
red spiders, 126
roaches, 106–107
rodents, 110, 112
silverfish, 90, 105
slugs and snails, 127
spider mites, 126
squash bugs, 127
squirrels, 110, 127
ticks, 8, 181–183
weevils, 105–106
whiteflies, 126
woodchucks, 127
Pets
acupressure to calm, 186
barking, 186
calming influences, 185–186, 187
cat deterrents, 124–125
chewing on furniture and paws
   (dogs), 186–187, 187
chocolate toxicity, 178
cleaning and grooming, 183–185
cold weather and, 177–178
crate training, 187
digging holes (dogs), 186
doghouse wood, 187
dog urine on lawn, 126
electrical-cord chewing, 173
fleas, 11, 181–183
food and water, 178–180
frightened animals, acupressure
   for, 186
fur balls, 189–190

furniture scratching by cats,
   189–190
in garbage can, 110
hair on furniture, 27
hair on rugs, 6
hot weather and, 178
introducing a new cat, 189
leaving dogs home alone, 187
litter, cat, 188–189
medications, giving, 176–177
microchip implants, 173
nail care, 185
naming, 172
poisonous plants, 174
problem behavior when home
   alone (dogs), 187
puppies, 187–188
safety, 173–176
sandbox as litter box, 111
shedding, 184–185
skunk smell, eliminating, 184
spaying and neutering, 190–191
tattoos for identification, 173
toxic foods, 178–179
traveling with, 158
urine, on lawn, 126
urine, removing from carpets, 6
weather and, 177–178
weed killer, pet-safe, 122
Petunias, 132
Pewter, cleaning, 34–35
Photos, care of, 94
Piano/organ keyboards, cleaning, 35
Pills on sweaters, 43–44
Plants. See Flowers; Gardening;
   Houseplants; Perennials;
   individual plants
Plaster walls, cleaning, 12
Plastic items
   artificial flowers, cleaning, 51
   patio furniture, cleaning, 109
   smells from, 51
   tablecloths, curtains, bath mats,
      cleaning, 46
   toys, cleaning, 51–52
Poinsettias, 132
Poison ivy, safe handling of, 135
Poisonous plants, 137–138
Pollutants, clearing with
   houseplants, 139
Pools. *See* Swimming pools
Popcorn, harvesting, 130
Posters, storing, 89
Potatoes, 132
Products
   Aquasana Pure Shower System, 84

Car Harness, 191
Door STOP Alarm, 171
Dye Grabber, 73
Ear Planes, 171
Freeze-Dried Ice Cream for Dogs, 191
Garden Kneeler/Sitter, 145
Gel-Pedic Pet Bed, 191
Gorilla Glue, 113
Gorilla Tape, 113
Gripping Stuff! 113
HANDy Paint Pail, 23
Homeopet, 191
MAAS Polishing Crème for All Metals, 37
Magnifying Finger Attachment, 73
No-Bark Collar, 191
No-Jet-Lag, 171
Pee Post, 191
Self-Watering Spheres, 145
Starfish Bath Alarm and Temperature Sensor, 84
SteriPEN, 171
Touch&Glide Iron, 73
Travel Water Dish for Dogs, 191
Ultra Soles, 171
Pumpkin, 132

R
Racing school, 157–158
Radishes, 132
Raisins, toxicity of, to pets, 179
Raspberries, 132–133
Restaurant tipping, 165
Rodents. *See* Pest control
Roses, 133
Rubber mats, laundering, 46
Rugs, caring for. *See* Carpets and rugs, maintenance of

S
Safety of pets, 173–176
Salmonella, 170
Scouring powder substitute, 76
Scratches, removing
    in hardwood floors, 2–3
    on wood furniture, 26
Screwdriver, using, 103
Scuff marks, removing. *See* Floors, cleaning and maintenance of; Leather; Shoes/boots
Seeds. *See* Gardening
Self-Watering Spheres, 145
Sewing
    buttons, 72

hems, 71
needle and thread tips, 70
patching, 73
sewing machine maintenance, 71–72
zippers, 73
Sheets
    drying, 48
    folding fitted, 63
    ironing, avoiding, 63
Shipping tips, 87
Shoes/boots
    boots, storing, 67
    cleaning, 68
    deodorizing, 67
    extending life of, 65
    high heels on floors, 4
    leather, care of, 65, 66, 67
    mold and mildew on, 64
    safety of, 67
    salt and grease on, 66
    scuff marks, removing, 65, 66, 69
    shining, 64
    shoe polish, reviving, 67
    shoelace maintenance, 68–69
    shopping for, 68
    squeaky, fixing, 67
    suede, 66
    tight, 68
    waterproofing, 66
    wet, 66
    white shoes, cleaning, 65
Silly Putty recipe, 91
Silver, care of, 29–32
Silvercloth/Pacific cloth, 30, 31
Sinks, 78
    stainless steel, 33–34
    unclogging drains, 81–82
Skin care. *See* Hand care
Skunk smell, eliminating from pets, 184
Smell. *See* Odors, eliminating
Smoke
    cleaning from walls, 12
    odor, removing from furniture, 27
    odor in car, eliminating, 156
    odor in clothing, removing, 50
Smoking
    and pet health, 175
    and tobacco mosaic virus, 134
Snow
    shoveling, 108
    tire traction in, 148
Soap tips, 82
Socks. *See* Laundry
Soil. *See* Gardening

Stainless steel, care of, 33–34
Stain removal. *See also* Candle wax, removing; Chewing gum, removing; Crayon
    baby formula/milk, 53
    ballpoint pen, 12, 56
    basic formula, 52
    bathtub and sink, 76–77
    beer, 53
    blood, 53
    canvas, cleaning, 53
    carpets and rugs, 5–8
    chocolate, 54
    coffee or tea, 7, 54
    cola, 54
    concrete, 108
    crayon marks, 4, 7, 12, 16, 54–55
    deodorant stick, 55
    fruit/juice, 7, 55
    furniture, upholstered, 26–27
    glue, 55
    grape juice, 55
    grass, 55
    gravy, 55
    grease/oil, 2, 7, 12, 15–16, 55–56, 57, 108, 155
    ink, 56
    kitchen curtains, preventing stains on, 56
    leather, 27, 57, 65, 66, 67, 69
    lipstick/makeup, 57
    marble, 35–36
    marker stains on walls, 12
    mildew, 57, 64, 79, 80–81, 90, 163
    milk, 57
    mud, 8, 57
    oil. *See* grease/oil above
    perspiration, 57
    pillowcases, 58
    plastic, 60
    "ring around the collar," 58
    rust, 58
    salt (road), 66
    scorches, 59
    shower curtain liner, 59
    smoke on walls, 12
    suntan oil or lotion, 59
    tape residue on walls, 12–13
    tea, 54
    ties, 59
    tobacco, 59
    toilet, 75
    tomato-based sauces, 59
    urine, 6, 60

vinyl/plastic tablecloth, 60
vomit, 60
wallpaper, 15–16
walls, 12–13
water marks, 25–26
wine, red, 7, 58
Starch, spray, 49–50
Static cling, eliminating, 48
Static electricity in carpets, 9
Steam-iron care, 62
Steps and pavement, de-icing, 107–108
SteriPEN, 171
Sweaters, care of. *See* Laundry
Swimming pools
    cleaning, 109
    controlling flies, 111
    and pet safety, 174–175

T

Tape residue on walls, removing, 12–13
Tea for wood floors, 2
Telephone, cleaning, 91
Ticks and fleas, eliminating, 8, 181–183
Tile floors, care of, 4
    paint, removing from, 22
Tipping ranges, 164–165
Tobacco. *See* Smoke; Smoking
Tobacco mosaic virus, 134
Toilet, cleaning. *See* Bathroom
Tomatoes, 133–134
Tools
    for do-it-yourself projects, 101–102
    for gardening, 114–116
Touch&Glide Iron, 73
Toxic foods for pets, 178–179
Toxic pollutants, clearing with houseplants, 139
Toys, cleaning, 51–52
Traction on concrete steps, 107–108
Travel, general. *See also* Car travel
    air travel, 160, 162, 166–168
    children, traveling with, 168
    contact lenses, care of, 170
    credit card expenditures, 164
    documents, copies of, 162
    home tips for while you're away, 163

hotels, 160, 165, 165–166
international travel, 168–170
luggage, shipping ahead, 163
mailing tips, 162
medications, 162, 164
packing tips, 160–162, 167
power outage tip, 162–163
safety tips, 165–166
tipping, 164–165
water, safety of, 166, 168, 170
Travel Water Dish for Dogs, 191
Trees, planting, 136
Trisodium phosphate (TSP), 12
Tulips, 135

U

Ultra Soles, 171
Unclogging drains, 81–82
    clogged toilet, 76
Upholstered furniture, 26–27
Upholstery, car, 154
Urine
    dog, on lawn, 126
    stain, removing, 6

V

Vacuuming, 9–11
    finding lost items, 10
    fleas, 11
    pet hair, 184
Vegetables, tips for growing, 136. *Also see individual plant names*
Vehicles. *See* Cars
Venetian blinds, cleaning, 96
Vinyl
    floor or bath mats, laundering, 46, 77
    floors, cleaning and maintenance of, 3–4
    toys, cleaning, 52
Vinyl upholstery
    car, cleaning, 154
    furniture, cleaning, 27
Volatile organic compounds (VOCs) in paint, 19

W

Wallpaper
    cleaning, 15, 16
    leftover, using, 15

paste, applying, 14
patching, 14–15
preparation, 13–14
removing, 13
stains on, 15–16
Walls
    cleaning, 11–12
    stain removal, 12–13
Warranties and guarantees, organizing, 88–89
Washing machines, maintenance of, 38–39
Water
    drinking, safety of, 166, 168, 170
    hard, remedy for, 41
    and pets, 180
Watering lawn and garden. *See* Gardening; Lawn care
Water marks on furniture, removing, 25–26
Wax, candle, removing. *See* Candle wax, removing
Weather, cold and hot, and pets, 177–178
Weeds. *See* Gardening
White-out extender, 86
Wicker furniture, care of, 28
Windows
    care of, 95–96
    removing paint from, 22
    screens, cleaning, 96
    storm, removing, 108
Wine, red, removing from carpet, 8
Wood furniture
    cleaning, 24–26
    scratches, removing, 26
    water marks, removing, 25–26
Woolens
    care of, 43–44
    preventing itchiness, 44
    reviving stored, 48
Wrinkles, removing without ironing, 62–64
Wrought-iron furniture
    painting, 23
    scratches, removing, 26

Y

Yogurt for gas prevention in pets, 179